Selective Service
and a Changing America

Merrill Political Science Series
Under the Editorship of
John C. Wahlke
Department of Political Science
The University of Iowa

Selective Service and a Changing America

A Study of Organizational-Environmental Relationships

Gary L. Wamsley
Vanderbilt University

Andrew S. Thomas Memorial Library
MORRIS HARVEY COLLEGE, CHARLESTON, W. VA.

CHARLES E. MERRILL PUBLISHING COMPANY
A Bell & Howell Company
Columbus, Ohio

355.2
W 181s

Copyright © 1969 by CHARLES E. MERRILL PUBLISHING COMPANY, Columbus, Ohio. All rights reserved. No part of this book may be reproduced in any form, electronic or mechanical, including photocopy, recording, or any information storage and retrieval system without permission in writing from the publisher.

Standard Book Number 675-09505-0

Library of Congress Catalog Card Number: 76-75390

1 2 3 4 5 6 7 8 9 10 —
73 72 71 70 69

Printed in the United States of America

Preface

If one compares some of the news media's coverage of the operations of Selective Service today with the coverage of 10, 30, or 50 years ago, some sharp contrasts are found. Coverage 10 years ago was often slim or non-existent; there was little newsworthy about the Service's activities. When it made the news 30 or 50 years ago there were pictures of blindfolded officials drawing names from fishbowls amid great ceremony, or lines of youths, smiling nervously as they lined up outside board offices. Today, however, headlines herald stories of sit-ins in board offices, bomb threats and building evacuations, and of protesters bursting in to pour blood over board files. Surely something has happened to Selective Service and its relations with the American public to bring about such dramatic changes.

The immediate reaction of some, including many Selective Service officials, would be to say that the Vietnamese War has plunged the System into controversy. This study is an effort to show that the bitterly divisive war in Viet Nam is only a catalyst that has triggered far more extensive and complicated difficulties for the System.

This is not only a study of why an institution is in trouble today but also a study of how it previously achieved such a long period of tranquil stability. The draft system of the Civil War triggered some of the greatest civil disorders this country had ever seen until recent urban riots. The study seeks to explain how Selective Service achieved quiet acceptance in the face of such hostility to its task of conscription.

I have tried to say something of interest to students of public administration, organizational sociology, national security, civil-military relations, and public policy. In trying to speak to such a broad audience, depth may be sacrificed. I hope that pitfall has been avoided. If not, it may be that the frail reed of "exploratory study" can be used as an excuse. When this work began there was virtually no independent, academic study of Selective Service. The situation has begun to change but only a start has been made.

This study is based largely upon interviews and observations of Selective Service operations between March and September of 1966. During these six months research was conducted at National Headquarters, the headquarters of the state herein referred to as Agdustria and among seventeen local boards of a metropolitan area which has been called Hill City.

Hill City is an historic city usually considered to be eastern but with many of the characteristics of the Midwest. It is internationally known as a center for heavy industry and transportation. Hill City's population as a center for heavy industry and transportation. Hill City's population is a little over one-half million and the population of the metropolitan area numbers two and one-half million.

Access was a major problem throughout the study. Initial negative contacts with Selective Service gave way to permissive access when my status as a Captain in the Air Force Reserve was made known. Persons at all levels seemed acutely aware of my military status and the impression was unavoidable that it greatly facilitated interviews.

Permission to conduct any interviews, observe any proceedings, and see any materials except the confidential files of registrants, was extremely circumscribed. One has to know something about Selective Service to appreciate the nature of the constraints upon the researcher. Permission was informal and oral and was not always sufficient to legitimate the researcher's presence at lower levels of the System.

All clerks were interviewed at least once. My constant presence soon took interaction beyond the level of interviews and I was largely accepted as a normal part of the clerks' environment. Nonetheless, this acceptance and access as a whole hinged upon circumspection and the avoidance of a threatening approach. It was in

Preface vii

part because of the need to be non-threatening that boards were observed non-selectively, simply on the basis of which one was scheduled. Of the seventeen boards, meetings of nine were observed, some of them more than once.

Limitation of time eventually forced a decision whether or not to observe all the boards at least once. It was felt that a point had been reached where no new understanding of board decisions was being gained and that only tabulation was being accomplished. Since the research at local board level was only part of a larger analysis and since full coverage of the boards would not alter inherent limitations of method and sample, it was decided to expend research effort at other levels which not only improved understanding of the System as a whole but placed board decisions in a clearer perspective.

Work was begun in March 1966. In August 1966 when the bulk of the field research was completed I received word that James W. Davis and Kenneth Dolbeare were conducting a study of Selective Service within the state of Wisconsin. In correspondence we informed one another of the rough aims of our respective projects. It was not until June of 1967, however, that we were able to exchange manuscripts for our respective chapters on local boards due to appear in a volume edited by Morris Janowitz. Davis and Dolbeare also kindly provided another of their papers, "Who Gets Drafted." In the same month I was able to obtain a copy of the Report of the Presidential Commission on Selective Service.

These two sources, which in some respects had fuller and more legitimatized access, confirmed the observations of the smaller Hill City study and provide larger sample data in many places where tenuous access had precluded collecting it. It is interesting to note that while Davis and Dolbeare were permitted to administer questionnaires to System participants they were not allowed to observe meetings of the boards. The study of the Presidential Commission apparently made few first hand observations but concentrated on collecting data at a broad general level. Consequently the findings of this study and the data from Wisconsin and national sources are highly complementary. As this study was prepared for publication in August 1968, Davis and Dolbeare provided a copy of their book titled *Little Groups of Neighbors*. Some data from this study has been inserted where possible.

I have tried not to inject my values and policy preferences into the analysis, something that requires considerable restraint in the case of Selective Service. In order that the reader will not have to wonder about these preferences, I can state that I agreed in most essentials with the recommendations of the National Commission on Selective Service and am attracted to the concept of universal national service though I doubt that it is politically feasible in the immediate future. Though I have no particular hesitancy in advocating these preferences, I do not feel this study is the proper place to do so.

Without pretending to have done justice to all those who have contributed to this effort and with apologies to any whom I have overlooked, I would like to express my gratitude to the following: Morris Janowitz and Roger Little for their suggestion that Selective Service was a great uncharted area within the field of civil-military relations and for their criticism and encouragement in the early stages of the work; those Selective Service officials, board clerks and board members who extended their time and cooperation in the spirit of objective inquiry though they had little reason to expect anything laudatory in the outcome; James Davis and Kenneth Dolbeare for sharing their findings with me and permitting the use of valuable graphs and charts; Joseph Pois, Daniel Cheever, John Wahlke, Charles Perrow, James Heaphey, Mayer Zald, and James Gerhardt for the valuable criticism they provided; Alex Dragnich for encouraging this work in the variety of ways available to a good departmental chairman; and Betty McKee and Susan Gauthier for enduring endless secretarial crises with good humor. If faults exist in the work, it is not for want of valiant efforts at eradication on the part of the aforementioned; the responsibility lies with the author.

The contribution of some is so extensive and invaluable that it deserves special mention. Such is the contribution (sacrifice is a more fitting word) of my wife Diane and my children, Christina, Carrie, Maria, and Alissa. It literally could not have been written without the former and it was written largely in spite of the innocent efforts at sabotage by the latter.

Contents

1 Introduction 1
2 The Institution in Historical Perspective 13
3 Institutional Adaptations to American Political Culture 51
4 Local Boards: Mainstay or Weak Link? 103
5 Other Institutional Defenses 165
6 The Strain on Institutional Equilibrium 195
7 The Draft War of 1967: Strategic Victory or Delaying Action? 225
Bibliography 246

Selective Service
and a Changing America

1

Introduction

A step can be taken toward understanding why Selective Service has come under attack after years of anonymity if one examines the public's reaction to the policy of drafting men for military service and its reaction to the way the policy is administered. Historical contrasts are revealing. In May 1941, the Gallup Poll asked its respondents to assess the administration of the Selective Service System which had at that point completed nine months of peacetime operation. The Poll asked the question: "Do you think the draft has been handled fairly?" The replies were 93 per cent *yes*, 7 per cent *no*. As George Gallup remarked, "Virtually no one interviewed thought the draft boards were not trying to do an honest and conscientious job."[1]

Despite this overwhelming demonstration of confidence in the administration of the System, conscription itself enjoyed somewhat less than widespread acceptance. Three months after the poll the draft law was barely renewed. The bill passed the Senate by only one vote and the debate was bitter. This hair-breadth passage was not a result of the public's ignorance about the tense international situation. Crisis had followed upon crisis in international affairs and the National Guard had just been activated. The picture was thus one of widespread acceptance of the administration of a public policy despite deep and passionate divisions over that policy.

Almost three decades have passed since then and today's observer finds the picture totally reversed. Opinion polls have for years indicated that the public accepts conscription for military service. As Louis Harris and Associates point out: "The vast majority of Americans favor drafting young men for military service. This support is expressed almost equally by those who have relatives in the Armed Forces, those who say they have a family member eligible to be drafted, and those who are not involved in the Viet Nam War."[2] Thus support for conscription as a public policy is amazingly solid despite the influence of one of this nation's most divisive wars. But in stark contrast to 1941, public attitudes towards the administration of the System have become decidedly unfavorable, only 43 per cent of the Public in December, 1966, feeling that "the way it works is fair."[3]

This study will attempt to explain why this reversal in attitudes has come to pass. The answer lies in the politics of administration. The orientation of political scientists would often lead one to believe that politics is a phenomenon or process that terminates when the ballots are counted or a bill signed into law. If confronted with this charge the profession would deny it to a man and many have devoted their careers to work that runs counter to the charge. Nonetheless, this truncated version of politics remains the general impression conveyed.

Public administration as a sub-field bears a responsibility to offset this impression conveyed by its parent discipline. Its record is not impressive on this score. The sub-field has spent decades trying to "separate policy from administration" with some persons casting the argument in new terms and others dropping it from exhaustion and boredom. Others working in public administration have busied themselves with applied concerns — training for the public service, prescription, and description—but all of this has been short of capturing the politics of administration. True, most textbooks on the subject make assertions like "public administration works in a highly political environment, and that even routine decisions include a normative element."[4] But despite such assertions public administration has not really offset the "truncated version of politics." It is hoped that the attempt to explain why the policy of conscription is solidly accepted but its administration is increasingly rejected will contribute to an appreciation of the political aspects of administration that seems to have been slighted over the years.

This study will seek to shed light on two other questions. The first, a corollary of the contrasting public attitudes of 1941 and today, is: How did Selective Service achieve such a long record of acceptance and stability? The second asks why there were no significant changes made in the law or the System in 1967 despite the greatest wave of criticism it has ever encountered in its long history.

The System is an institution that has seldom been the subject of scholarly attention.[5] This inattention to an institution of such importance to so many Americans testifies to two characteristics of the System that will be explored in detail. One of these is the institution's ability to achieve acceptance by relating its structure and processes to American political values. The other is the defensiveness and hostility of rank and file members to examination by outsiders and an institutional myth of decentralized power which has constrained the leadership of the System to respect these feelings.

The defensiveness of the System and the constraints upon the researcher required that this study be an exploratory one. Among the purposes of such a study are to gather data about basic aspects or variables of the Selective Service System and its relationship with the American society of political system; to do some preliminary testing of some basic hypotheses about how the variables interrelate; and to do some hypothesizing as to which aspects and which relationships among them are most significant and suggestive for further research.[6]

The only practicable strategy in an exploratory study would seem to be to pursue a broad and simple theme that emerges clearly from the phenomena confronted. The theme is as follows:

Throughout American history, military conscription has run counter to certain key values of American political culture — voluntarism, civilian control of the military, local decisions are better decisions, sovereignty of the states, etc. Selective Service, by identifying its structure and processes with these values, was designed to ease the constraints posed by them. It has thus sought to meet the functional demands arising from defense needs without violating those values. Due to changes in American society and to institutional rigidities developed within the system, it is becoming increasingly more difficult for it to maintain an equilibrium that satisfies both defense needs and societal values.

It will be useful to the reader if he views this theme in light of three interests of the author which had to remain implicit due to the limitations of an exploratory study. The utility of setting forth these interests in the introduction is that the reader is thus informed of the factors that played a part in the selection of aspects and relationships to be analyzed. It may also be that with these interests in mind the reader can develop questions and hypotheses of his own. The interests alluded to are:

(1) national security policy;
(2) civil-military relations;
(3) administrative and organization theory.

The Theme Viewed in Light of National Security Policy

Structural-functional analysis, now fashionable in political science, begins by addressing the phenomenon one confronts with this question: "What function does this structure (process, role, institution) perform for the larger political or societal system?" Or more basically: "What functions must be performed if a political system is to exist?"[7] Such an analysis does more than simply demonstrate the analyst's attunement to fads of his discipline. It provides more powerful insights into the interrelationships among phenomena than he might otherwise have achieved.

If we address the basic functional question to a political system, i.e. what functions must be performed in order for it to exist, it seems logical that a functional requisite in today's world would be the capability for defense. For most political systems this means that manpower must be mobilized. If foreign policy issues involving defense were clearly understandable; if defense always meant the actual preservation of life and limb, hearth and home; if there were no need for large standing military forces in "peacetime"; the manpower needs of a nation might be met in voluntary enlistments. During some of this country's earlier years these conditions existed to an extent that made reliance on voluntary enlistments possible, though such a reliance often seemed to verge on disaster.

Though some persons have recently expressed hope that a growing supply of manpower and increased national affluence might make feasible an all-volunteer military establishment, this has not as yet been accepted as a direction for national policy. Compared to earlier periods in our history the need for conscription may have intensified rather than diminished. National interests become increasingly complex and less amenable to understanding; threats to security become increasingly remote and abstract; and a "large standing army" so often inveighed against throughout our history has become a permanent necessity. The Vietnamese war and the controversy over Selective Service which is related to it are prime examples of these changed conditions.

American foreign policy for better or for worse has followed the conceptual outline of containment laid down by George F. Kennan in 1947.[8] There have been many criticisms (including some by Kennan himself) and attempts to find other guides, but containment remains at the center of our foreign policy. Presently America is in the throes of trying to apply this outline in the rimlands of Asia. Though the difficulties encountered in its application in Viet Nam may result in more selective use of the doctrine in the future, it seems likely that America will face more limited wars in which the morality and the national interests of intervention are increasingly problematic for citizens and as a consequence the military costs seem inordinately high.

Under such circumstances a functioning, accepted, conscription system would seem to be at least as essential as ever and possibly a dire necessity. This study finds, however, that because of changes in American society and changes in the original purposes of Selective Service's structure and processes, America is in danger of losing public acceptance of a system that is vital to foreign and defense policy purposes.

The Theme Viewed in Light of Civil-Military Relations

In his excellent bibliographic essay on Military Sociology, Kurt Lang points out that World War II focused attention on how military organization functioned at the operational level but left two important sociological gaps. One was the lack of attention paid to the process by which military policies are normally formulated. The other was the place of the military within society. A host of writers have devoted their efforts to filling these gaps as Lang's essay testifies.[9]

Interestingly enough Lang's essay, which by all odds must be the most thorough ever done on the subject, does not take up the subject of conscription agencies or mechanisms. In Lang's examination of research on the functional integration of the military system and in the area of civil-military relations there is no mention of the subject.[10] The omission is curious particularly with reference to the American scene because of the historical antipathy towards militarism and conscription.

Studies of the place of the military in society have so far concentrated on analysis of the military subculture, its values and norms and how they compare to those of the civil society. The implicit concern has been with the preservation of democratic values in the face of the need to maintain a hierarchical and authoritarian subculture within a democratic society. The outstanding examples are Morris Janowitz's sociologically oriented work, *The Professional Soldier;* and Samuel Huntington's political-historical approach in *The Soldier and the State.*

Virtually nothing has been done with the junctures or points where the civil and military societies are linked. There have been some studies of military academies as assimilating institutions.[11] These are valuable studies, but the academies are different types of civil-military junctures than Selective Service. The entrant into the academies has voluntarily committed himself to the subculture world of the military. He is free to leave at any time. To be sure he will probably pay a high psychic price but his submission to assimilation is a voluntary exercise of his will. A conscription system is of a different order, and the most crucial difference is its compulsory nature. Society demands sacrifice by the individual and expresses its needs through the authority of the state. Failure to obey can result in arrest, fines and imprisonment.

Aside from the study of academies there has been no attempt to study the input or output junctures between the civil and military societies. On the output side might be the retired cadre, the Veterans Administration, veteran organizations and perhaps the Reserves.[12]

What can studies of such junctures tell us about civil-military relations? This study suggests the following points that might serve as foci for further studies:

(1) more data concerning attitudes of the civil society toward the military subculture;

(2) the nature and composition of such juncture agencies, personnel that staff them, their motivations and attitudes, and how they function as a bridge between civil culture and military subculture;

(3) key symbols and values of American political culture, especially those that relate to the application of a compulsory sacrificial statute, how they may act as constraints in mobilization and how they clash with claims for civilian manpower.

The Theme Viewed in the Light of Administrative and Organization Theory

One of the burgeoning fields of study in social science is organization theory, based for the most part in the disciplines of sociology and business administration. The strengths of the approach lie in its rigor, its contemporary behavioralism, its ability to handle complex organizations, and its relative lack of prescription or normative proclivities. Organization theory is strong in precisely some of the areas where administrative theory, which has grown out of political science and public administration, is weak. One of the chief concerns here is the tendency of organization theorists (admitted and lamented by some) to slight the importance of organizations' environments.

Among theorists, Mayer Zald has been one of those most aware of the tendency to neglect environments. As he notes: "Organization theory has focused on internal aspects of organizations on adaptations of groups to each other. Aware of the outside world and the larger organizational structure, they take as their object for analysis the microsystem of parts of the organization."[13]

This reductionistic tendency results in their considering internal structure or some aspect thereof "without studying the organization-qua-organization."[14] Zald expresses well the concept of organizations upon which this study of Selective Service rests—

> Organizations have collective identities and systemic properties; they can and should be considered as whole systems insofar as their components are integrated into collectivities.[15]

Since writers in the field of organization theory and analysis have tended to draw heavily upon the private sector for their examples and theorizing, their tendency to slight environments is a natural one. Political scientists have less of an excuse.

An emphasis on the importance of organization and environment comes easily from the perspective of a political scientist who possesses a trained awareness of the permeation by politics of administrative and organizational relationships in the public sector. And yet, studies of organizations by political scientists have been few in number and devoid of fruitful theorizing. They have been largely programmatic in their remarks, suggesting the desirability and efficacy of transferring polity-level concepts and analytical techniques to the study of organizations or vice versa.[16]

A few political scientists like Herbert Simon, James March and Richard Cyert have engaged in studying large-scale organizations but they have been as severely reductionist as organizational sociologists and have relied heavily on psychology for their concepts. They have not seen the study of organizations as a means of analyzing larger questions of political relevance. Their works have been more widely read in business schools than in departments of political science.[17]

Orion White is one of the few political scientists who has made an attempt to sharpen the distinction between systems for which environment is critical and those for which it is of negligible significance.[18] White distinguishes between administrative systems that are political and those that are apolitical. He also notes that the distinction cuts across traditional private-public categories. To White the most significant dimension that differentiates between political and apolitical administrative systems is the degree of self-containment which can be attained by each. Given an apolitical environment, "a system can establish a fairly definite boundary around itself" and can "restrict negotiations with the environmental system to solely what it offers at the boundary as its product or 'goal.' "[19] The apolitical administrative system thus achieves a certain environmental detachment. It interacts with, and is sensitive to, that environment "on its own terms," or in terms of the goal or product it wishes to produce and offer to the environment.[20]

White feels that the apolitical administrative system offers concrete and specific goals that are easily discernible by the apolitical environment. But the goals of the political administrative system suffer from vagueness and the lack of consensual unity. These conditions encourage the political environment to violate the system's boundary—to penetrate it. As White says,

> The consequences of this one fact for a system's structure and the mode of administration which it can employ cannot be overestimated. For in fact this aspect of environmental relations can determine the whole orientation of a system toward itself.[21]

It is hoped that this study may contribute to offsetting the reductionism of organizational theorists and the "truncated version of politics" offered by political science and public administration. It will be shown that the mode of operation, formal and informal structure, processes, and goals (formal and informal) of Selective Service are overwhelmingly influenced by what it perceives to be a threatening environment.

Introduction

While the administrative system with an apolitical environment can follow a natural bureaucratic inclination to focus on internal rationality, the system confronted with a political environment must be forever concerned with boundary maintenance and environmental interchange. Because the apolitical administrative system defines its role as specific and narrow, its environment is predictable, "constant, certain and benign."[22] It may be problematic but it is malleable—not threatening.

The efforts of Selective Service to severely limit its goals and product involvement, and to create for itself a neutral instrumental role should be noted. It is striving to cope with what it sees as a hostile political environment — seeking to make it constant and benign. It has sought to develop a specific and narrow role for itself, expanding that role cautiously and usually by lip service only.

Selective Service's failure to adjust itself to its present environment may in part be explained by the nature of the exchange process involved in a political environment. The system in a threatening political environment is often unable to take part in rational reevaluation and restructuring of a system. In devoting considerable institutional energy and attention to securing and sustaining legitimation of its product the political administrative system develops rigidities that make reevaluation and restructuring difficult if not impossible.

To the extent that any single case can contribute to theorizing, it is hoped that this one might point up areas where organization theorists could profitably direct attention to the elimination of the spurious distinction between administrative theory and organization theory.

Notes

[1] *Backgrounds of Selective Service,* Special Monograph No. 1, Vol. II, Pt. 1 (Washington, D.C.: Government Printing Office, 1947), 123.

[2] Quoted in June A. Willenz, ed., *Dialogue on the Draft* (Washington, D.C.: American Veterans Committee, 1966), p. 64.

[3] Reported in *Life,* December 9, 1966.

[4] John Pfiffner and Robert Presthus, *Public Administration,* (5th ed.; New York: Ronald Publishing Co., 1967), p. 3.

[5] This study began in February of 1966. Over the next two years repeated attempts were made to obtain the only scholarly study of the System. The study is on the natural pressures operating in a bureaucracy to narrow the authority of an unpredictable volunteer component. In explicating this process it touches upon several points uncovered by this study but the thrust of the earlier one is markedly different. See Donald Stewart, "Local Boards, A Study of the Place of Volunteer Participation in a Bureaucratic Organization" (unpublished Ph.D. dissertation, Columbia University, 1950).

[6] For a discussion of exploratory studies see Eugene Jacobson, "Memorandum on Study Design," mimeo, University of Michigan, Summer, 1964.

[7] See Don Martindale, ed., *Functionalism in the Social Sciences,* Monogr. 5, The Annals of the American Academy of Political and Social Science, Philadelphia, Pa. (February 1965). See especially the article by Robert T. Holt and one by William Flanigan and Edwin Fogelman. See also chapter 3 of Eugene J. Meehan's book, *Contemporary Political Thought* (Homewood, Ill.: Dorsey Press, 1967).

[8] See his famous Mr. X article in Foreign Affairs, "The Sources of Soviet Conduct", XXV, No. 4 (July 1947), 566-82.

[9] Kurt Lang, *Military Sociology: A Trend Report and Bibliography,* (London: Basil Blackwell and Mott, Ltd., 1965), pp. 3-4.

[10] *Ibid.,* pp. 13-22.

[11] John P. Lovell, "The Professional Socialization of the West Point Cadet," Morris Janowitz, in *The New Military,* (N. Y.: Russell Sage Foundation, 1964), pp. 119-58. Sanford M. Dornbush, "The Military Academy as an Assimilating Institution," *Social Forces,* XXXIII (1955), 319.

[12] Martha Derthick's excellent study of the National Guard conceptualizes it as an interest group rather than a civil-military juncture. See Martha Derthick, *The National Guard in Politics* (Cambridge, Mass.: Harvard University Press, 1965). On the output side see Timothy Alden Williams, "The Warrior Unhorsed: Politics of Large-Scale Officer Retirement" (paper delivered at Western Political Science Association, Tucson, Arizona, March 1967).

Introduction 11

[13]Mayer Zald, "The Political Economy of the Y.M.C.A.: Structure and Change" (unpublished manuscript, Vanderbilt University, 1967), pp. 1-6. The earlier works of Charles Perrow also manifest this awareness. See, "Organizational Prestige: Some Functions and Dysfunctions," *American Journal of Sociology*, LXVI (1961), 335-41, and "The Analysis of Goals in Complex Organizations," *American Sociological Review*, XXVI (1961), 854-66. In more recent works Perrow has emphasized other variables of organizations for purposes of analytical strategy. See "A Framework for the Comparative Analysis of Organizations," *American Sociological Review*, XXII (1967), 194.

[14]Zald, *op. cit.*, pp. 1-10. As he notes, the major exception to this tendency, as well as the slighting of environment is the "Selznick school." See Philip Selznick, *TVA and the Grass Roots* (Berkeley: University of California Press, 1949); also his "Foundations of the Theory of Organizations," *American Sociological Review*, XIII (1948), 25-35; and his *Leadership in Administration* (Evanston, Ill.: Row, Peterson, 1957). Students of Selznick that have taken a similar approach are Charles Perrow, *op. cit.*, and Burton Clark, *Open-door College* (New York: McGraw-Hill, Inc., 1960), and Clark, "Organizational Adaptation and Precarious Values: A Case Study," *American Sociological Review*, XXI (1956), 327-36.

[15]Zald, *ibid.*, pp. 1-10.

[16]See Richard S.F. Eels, *The Government of Corporations*. (N.Y.: Free Press of Glencoe, 1962); Earl Latham, "The Body Politic of the Corporation" in Edward S. Mason, ed., *The Corporation in Modern Society* (Cambridge, Mass.: Harvard University Press, 1959); also Robert A. Dahl, "Business and Politics: A Critical Appraisal of Political Science," *American Political Science Review*, LIII (1959), 1-34.

[17]See Herbert Simon, *Administrative Behavior* (2nd ed.; N.Y.: The Macmillan Company, 1957); James G. March and Herbert A. Simon, *Organizations* (N.Y.: John Wiley & Sons, Inc., 1958); Richard M. Cyert and James G. March, *A Behavioral Theory of the Firm* (Englewood Cliffs, N.J.: Prentice-Hall, Inc., 1963). For a discussion of why Simon's writings have been given less attention by political science, see Dwight Waldo, "Comparative Public Administration: Prologue, Problems, and Promise," Comparative Administration Group of the American Society for Public Administration, Special Series No. 2 (Bloomington, Indiana, 1966), pp. 8-10.

[18]Orion F. White, Jr., "Notes for a Model of Political Administration" (unpublished manuscript, University of Texas, 1966). White's distinction between administrative systems with products of high consensual unity and those of low is a valuable one. It is possible however to quarrel with him over labeling these systems as apolitical and political. To do so is to narrow politics solely to matters of controversy and conflict. As Aristotle, Max Weber, and Harold Lasswell (to name but a few) would insist, politics is a set of relationships involving rule, authority or power. Those subject to authority may submit to it without conflict or controversy and the relationship would be no less political in nature. White's apolitical administrative system may function unconcerned about its malleable environment but it still functions on a political basis.

[19]*Ibid.*, p. 36.

[20]*Ibid.*, p. 37.

[21]*Ibid.*, pp. 37-38.

[22]*Ibid.*, p. 39.

2

The Institution in Historical Perspective

A component of the reductionism syndrome in organization theory is the failure to view institutions in historical perspective.[1] Because theorists have not viewed institutions as collectives with systemic properties and collective identities, histories have seemed inconsequential. To understand organizations or institutions in such terms, to analyze them or to predict directions of change, it is necessary to look at their history. The history of conscription in America and the history of Selective Service is one of the most revealing things about the institution.

The leadership of Selective Service is itself acutely aware of history. They have authorized several written historical monographs and part of the System's public relations program has been to ceremonially observe the anniversaries of major events in its history and the history of conscription.[2]

Each of these historical monographs tries to show that Selective Service and conscription have deep roots in American history. This purpose was specified in a System manual which advised state directors of ways to observe the 140th birthday of General James Oakes, who is often cited as the source of ideas for designing Selective Service.

A chance is also presented for Selective Service to give better perspective for its consistent contributions to the Nation's survival by the procurement methods used in war emergencies, especially since the Civil War. In brief, commemorative activity with respect to General Oakes could center with the fact that today's Selective Service is a logical successor. It has grown from earlier techniques of selection and the fundamental and long-standing responsibility and obligation of the citizen to defend his country.[3]

Sometimes the monographs present American military history in ways that differ markedly from other historical interpretations. For example many historical accounts indicate that the compulsory service aspects of the early militia seldom, if ever, came into play; but Selective Service monographs dwell pointedly upon these conscription features and cite them as proof that America has always accepted conscription.

This attention to history by an institution is itself interesting evidence of sensitivity to environment. To be sure it is hard to imagine an institution producing an unbiased account of its history but the point is that few administrative systems outside the military concern themselves with history to such an extent. History has deep significance for Selective Service, lying at the center of its institutional ideology. The Service sees itself as the logical successor of past attempts to furnish manpower necessary for national defense, and sees local boards and decentralization as the key elements which made it a success as contrasted with past failures at conscription. The importance of history in its perceptions is seen in a statement made during the 1966 hearings:

> It would be essential to avoid in any way interfering with the present decentralized approach of the System which proved so successful in contrast with the centralized ones of both the Federal and Confederate governments during the Civil War. The decentralized, or local board, or grass-roots operation of Selective Service began with the First World War and demonstrated that the Nation would much more willingly support compulsory military service operated by their neighbors at home, than they would a program operated by a remote, impersonal organization.[4]

A review of history is important primarily because it reveals the pressure upon an institution performing a conscription function, and the ways in which it seeks to equilibrate these pressures. Samuel Huntington speaks of the balance a military institution such as Selective Service must maintain.

> The military institutions of any society are shaped by two forces: a functional imperative stemming from the threats to society's

security and societal imperative deriving from the social forces, ideologies, and institutions dominant within society. Military institutions which reflect only social values may be incapable of performing effectively their military functions. On the other hand, it may be impossible to contain within society military institutions shaped purely by functional imperatives. The interaction of these two forces is the nub of civil-military relations.[5]

It is suggested that societal imperatives can be more clearly understood if characterized as political culture. Therefore, a conscription system must always seek an equilibrium between efficiently procuring manpower to defend the society and society's demands that the procurement be done in accordance with norms and values of political culture.

The demand that a conscription system procure men efficiently can be thought of as a functional demand — a function assigned to it by society. The demands of political culture are a little more complex and involve at least two identifiable clusters of values. (Political culture denotes beliefs, values and myths with which a society surrounds power relationships between men and the state.)

The two clusters of values of particular relevance for conscription are (1) that which demands that conscription decisions be made in a way that is fair and equitable and (2) that which demands that the war be a just war. National security crises have created tensions between functional efficiency and societal values and between the different demands found within political culture. For example, if Americans cannot see a war as just, issues of equity in administering conscription assume greater importance; if perceived of as just, the issues recede and the focus is upon efficient manpower procurement. Agencies of conscription throughout American history have been forced to satisfy the demands of efficiency and political culture as well as different demands within political culture. Another reason for focusing on the history of conscription arises from the fact that it reveals the fundamental hostility of American political culture towards it. To be sure efforts to develop conscription in some form did appear early in American history but more important were the strong anti-militarism and anti-conscription sentiments that were revealed by these efforts. Both were basic values of American political culture. An appreciation of the depth and extent of this anti-militarism, anti-conscription (and a pro-militia) sentiment will more clearly reveal Selective Service as an institution designed to deflect and mute hostility to its function. It will also make clearer why Selective Service is so acutely sensitive to its political environment and yet paradoxically unable to develop within itself responses that satisfy demands for changes coming from that environment.

Much of Selective Service's environment is encompassed in political culture, a term used often, though it bears some handicaps. To the lay reader it sounds unnecessarily pretentious and academic; to some political scientists it either seems a rather amorphous term — a sort of conceptual waste basket used to cover anything that could not be explained by some empirical referent — or it reminds them of impressionistic national character studies. It is tempting to succumb to these handicaps and to substitute in its stead terms like "societal values and attitudes" or to use political culture as a "short hand" term to cover these but the utility of the concept, particularly in a broad exploratory study, outweighs its admitted handicaps.

These beliefs, symbols, and values define: the way people perceive and interpret the nature of a political relationship; the way they feel toward political institutions, leaders, and administrative processes, (including such things as loyalty, identification, and commitment); and the standards used to evaluate political demands, processes, and products.[6]

So far attempts to define American political culture have been highly impressionistic or sweepingly global. An example of the latter is Almond and Verba who characterize American political culture as allegiant, participant and civic.[7] It would obviously take some time to explain what they mean by these terms and it would be ludicrous to attempt to elaborate on the totality of American political culture. The purpose of briefly reviewing the history of conscription here is to point up what seem to be elements of American political culture that are relevant for the present condition and future direction of Selective Service. There is every reason not to refer to these off-handedly as societal values or public attitudes, because something more specific is intended — i.e. beliefs, symbols, and values by means of which a society relates to its governing elites, structure, and processes. Because those aspects of earlier American political culture which shaped Selective Service have changed, but the System has not, its structure and processes are out of harmony.

Americans have been able to indulge themselves in anti-militarism and anti-conscription sentiment to a far greater degree than almost any modern nation. This has been due primarily to a relatively isolated period of national development and to the long unchallenged belief that the nation had an alternative to conscription in the militia or "minute man" system.

The English colonists brought anti-militarism with them to these shores.[8] Some historians attribute it to general English culture, others trace it to the Cromwell dictatorship, but all seem agreed that anti-militarism is a feature of English and American culture.[9] Anti-militarism did not mean that the new Americans were pacifists. Coates and Pellegrin point out that Americans have participated in every major global conflict since 1689 and have initiated several that were less than global.[10]

The militia system was the Englishman's antidote to the power of the monarch or to militarism of the sovereign state. It limited the need for the use of mercenaries or a large standing army for several centuries prior to the founding of the North American colonies. Composed of all the free men of a county between 16 and 60 years of age and under the command of a County Lord General, the militia was essentially untrained, undisciplined, exempt from foreign service, and self-provisioned. The compulsion involved in mustering it was unlikely to stir much resentment in citizens who perceived of its purpose as defense of their land and homes.

It was this transplanted militia system with negligible or acceptable compulsion which formed the basis of the cherished "minute man" concept for defense. This concept held that a democracy could best defend itself and avoid militarism by mobilizing the citizenry rather than by maintaining a standing army. The concept contributed to the ability of Americans to participate in so much warfare and still think of themselves as anti-militarists.

The reliance on the militia system or "minute man" myth had the effect of postponing the problem of finding an institutional structure that balanced both functional and societal demands. Debates over conscription have been over "whether" it should be effected, seldom over "how."

Colonial Period

The colonial militias were active during King William's, King George's and the French and Indian Wars, but the conscription involved was largely theoretical. Colonial life was frontier life, and attendance at an occasional muster day was the only prudent thing to do in such perilous environs. The entire militia of a colony was seldom called out for a campaign against the Indians. Usually it served as a base from which volunteers could be selected. Furthermore, after the French and Indian War, the "call-outs" declined to an annual Muster Day. This event became largely a festive social gathering or as one source puts it — "more a combination of barbecue roast and whiskey-guzzling than anything else."[11]

The Revolutionary Period

For some years prior to the Revolution the militias had been unworthy of description as military units, if in fact the description had ever been apt. A dismayed General Washington upon first seeing his militia "troops" in 1775 wrote:

> I found a mixed multitude of people here, under very little discipline, order or Government... confusion and disorder reigned in every Department. The men regarded their officers no more than broomsticks.[12]

After the Battles of Lexington, Concord, and Bunker Hill it was planned to convert the militia units gathered at Boston into a Continental Army by enlisting them until the end of 1776. The Continental Congress was to pay, supply, and administer them, but reenlistments were extremely slow. The so-called "Continental Line" never became sizeable and Washington was forced to rely mostly on militia units recruited (seldom conscripted) by the states.

In 1776 it was also decided to have the states raise forces to be placed in the Continental Line and to pay a generous continental bounty to each man; but again results were dismal. The nearest thing to real conscription were attempts made by states in 1780 to conscript men to their militias for one year's service, but this failed to produce the men needed due to lax organization and administration.

Washington was forced to rely on the voluntary militia. Most military historians credit him with military genius on the basis of his ability to hold together any semblance of an Army and achieve even limited successes under the conditions of service on which his forces were based. Of the militia men he wrote, "They come in, you cannot tell how; go you cannot tell when; act, you cannot tell where, consume your provisions, exhaust your stores, and leave you at last at a critical moment."[13]

There were continuing disorders in the Army stemming from lack of pay and poor provisioning. Most involved militia, and only one involved the regular officers at Newburg, New York, who were in alliance with large creditors in favoring establishment of a strong national government. But whether such problems originated with the militia or the regulars they did little to dampen feelings of anti-militarism or pave the way for conscription and a permanent Military Establishment.

With the British surrender at Yorktown in 1781 there remained no immediate threat and the militias and regulars of the Continental Line were both disbanded over the next three years. Conscription never became a meaningful issue in either the colonial or revolutionary periods. The success of the Revolution elevated the "minute man" myth to an unassailable position of primacy in American national security policy.

Consideration of Conscription During the Formation of the Republic

With the end of hostilities some cursory consideration was given to the problems of defense and military manpower. Despite the fact that some historians refer to this period as though conscription was seriously considered, there was never any real change in the pattern of avoiding a consideration of conscription and relying on the militia. Washington, in 1783, replied to a letter from a Congressional Military Committee seeking his views on a peacetime military establishment. His reply was titled "Sentiments on a Peace Establishment" and it has often been cited as proof that Washington favored conscription. The most frequently cited passage states,

> It may be laid down as a primary position, and the basis of our system, that every citizen who enjoys the protection of a free Government, owes not only a proportion of his property, but even of his personal services to the defense of it, and consequently that the Citizens of America [with a few legal and official exceptions] from 18 to 50 years of Age should be borne on the Militia Rolls, provided with uniform Arms, and [be] so far accustomed to the use of them, that the Total strength of the Country might be called forth at a Short Notice on any very interesting Emergency.[14]

A careful reading, however, reveals that Washington is urging a universal military obligation through the militia system, *not* national conscription.[15]

Washington's "sentiments" were ignored. The pattern of anti-militarism, anti-conscription and reliance on the militia that would dominate our history was plainly evident in a resolution by the Continental Congress in 1784.

> And whereas, standing armies in time of peace are inconsistent with the principle of republican governments, dangerous to the liberties of a free people and generally converted into destructive engines for establishing despotism;
> It is therefore resolved, That recommendations in lieu of requisitions shall be sent to the several States for raising the troops which may be immediately necessary for garrisoning the Western posts and guarding the magazines of the United States ... [and] that the commanding officer be, and he is hereby, directed to discharge the troops now in the service of the United States, except twenty-five privates to guard the stores at Fort Pitt and fifty-five to guard the stores at West Point and other magazines, with a proportionable number of officers, no officers to remain in service above the rank of captain.[16]

The Congress then called upon the states to provide volunteers from their militias for *enlisted* service on the frontier.

As the former colonies tried to operate under the Articles of Confederation, there was a resumption of the debate over the Military Establishment. Conscription was a submerged issue because it was obscured by the "militia vs. regular" feature of the debate. Moreover, the threats to the new nation and the need for manpower were so slight that it seemed inconceivable that conscription could be necessary.

In 1786, the Congress asked General Henry Knox to propose the form of the Military Establishment. He drafted a plan along the sweeping lines of Washington's. Some historians claim to see a more explicit reference to conscription in this plan than in Washington's.[17] In any event conscription was roundly ignored.

The government's weakness in the face of Shays's Rebellion in 1786 intensified debate over the Military Establishment. These and other problems were responsible for the calling of the Constitutional Convention in 1787.

Conscription and the Constitution

The Constitution for the new federal republic was, of course, a result of many compromises. For this reason and because of adherence to the doctrine of separation of powers, there is a bewildering diffusion of power and responsibilities and a vagueness throughout the document. The vagueness certainly extends to conscription for there is no specific provision for it.

The ambiguities are quite evident if one looks at the powers and responsibilities of Congress toward military matters.[18] It was the lack of clarity in this realm that left the conscription picture cloudy. Congress could declare war and issue letters of marque; *raise and support armies;* provide and maintain a Navy; *provide for the calling out of the militia* to execute the laws; suppress insurrections and repel invasions; provide for organizing, arming, and disciplining, the militia and for governing such part of them as may be employed in the service of the United States. Appropriations for the Army were to be for two years only. At the same time, however, the states were given the right to appoint militia officers, and "the authority of training the militia according to the discipline prescribed by Congress.[19]

Did the power to raise and support armies mean that the national government could directly recruit and conscript men? The references to calling out the militia spoke only of domestic use such as insurrections and repelling invasion. Did this language mean that the militia could not leave the country? And how could a national government provide for organizing, arming, and disciplining of the militia without wielding great influence, if not control, over the state militias? Were the militias a national or a state military force? To claim the former to the exclusion of the latter was impossible in view of the wording. If the militias were both national and state forces, which had priority and under what circumstances? Fortunately, the nation was not immediately called upon to resolve all these questions at one time.

Walter Millis views the ambiguities regarding a military establishment as calculated. He feels the Constitution attempted to provide for defense and a small regular army (subject to abolishment biennially) while placing primary reliance on the states. This left the states control over national military policy and avoided "rousing the universal fear and loathing of irresponsible standing armies."[20] Alexander Hamilton evidently interpreted the Constitution in the same way. Millis quotes him as saying that the arrangement

> will not only lessen the call for military establishments, but if circumstances should at any time oblige the government to form an army [that is, a national, regular army] of any magnitude, that army can never be formidable to the liberties of the people while there is a large body of citizens, little if at all inferior to them in discipline and the use of arms, who stand ready to defend their own rights.[21]

As Millis says, this curious intimation that the trained militia might find its function not in assisting in the national defense but in defending the people from the defenders whom the national government might have to raise, suggests how far the underlying dilemmas had been left unresolved.[22]

Finally it should be noted that the Constitution did not give the government the authority either expressly or implicitly to conscript. Leach puts it this way:

> The founders of the new federal system either did not understand or did not consider the problem of conscription. One can wade through the literature of pre-Constitution days the debates at Philadelphia and the state conventions *in extenso* without finding a discussion of the concept of a federal emergency conscription.[23]

Interpretation of the Constitution by the Supreme Court has given Congress that power.[24] In Arver vs. the U.S. the Court asserted that the constitutionality of conscription rested upon Article 1, section 8, which authorized Congress to "declare war, *to raise and support armies, and to make rules for the government and regulation of the land and naval forces,* and *to make all laws necessary for carrying the foregoing powers into execution.*"[25]

In delivering the opinion of the Court, Chief Justice Edward D. White made short shrift of the claim that the Constitution did not provide for conscription.

> As the mind cannot conceive of an Army without men to compose of it, on the face of the Constitution the objection that it does not give power to provide for such men would seem to be too frivolous for further notice.[26]

Not surprisingly, of course, the Court chose to ignore the historical evidence of which Leach speaks. Since "raising Armies" in the context of the writing of the Constitution meant raising them by means of the largely voluntary militia system, it would seem correct to say that interpretation of the Supreme Court has given Congress the power to conscript.[27]

Conscription in the New Federal System

Shortly after adoption of the federal Constitution, the small army, largely recruited from militia, suffered severe defeats at the hands of the Indians. This caused a flurry of congressional investigations and concern. Several efforts were made to make militia training and equipping uniform enough to increase effectiveness. General Henry Knox, who had become Secretary of War under the President rather than the Continental Congress, reintroduced his earlier proposal but it engendered bitter opposition and died in committee. A bill incorporating Washington's earlier ideas suffered a similar fate. Had these bills passed, they might have been sufficient in their impact (training, drills, etc.) to have made an issue of conscription into state militias.

In 1792 Congress, under considerable pressure, produced the Militia Act, making every citizen of a certain age liable to military service.[28] The act stated that "every free and able-bodied white male citizen of the respective states" between the ages of 18 and 45 would be enrolled in the local militia organizations but its conscription aspects apparently had no impact. Military historians seem to agree this act was merely a means of passing the problems along to the states.[29] Even ardent backers of Selective Service like Fitzpatrick who would like to read conscription into it are unable to do so. He says of the 1792 act that "the legislation for organization of these militiamen had been left to the states. In many states the militiamen had not even enrolled or had at one time, and then enrolling lapsed."[30]

Conscription and the War of 1812—The Issue Emerges

Federal conscription first emerged as a controversial issue as a result of the inadequacies of the militia system during the War of 1812. By 1814 the future of the United States was bleak; American fortunes of war had gone from bad to worse. President Madison asked a special session of Congress to modify the militia system "in order that the most capable elements of the nation's manhood could be made ready for immediate service in the field; this could be done by 'classing and disciplining' them."[31]

As a result of this vague and desperate proposal, Secretary of War James Monroe developed what Leach refers to as "the first reasoned statement of the theory of national conscription."[32] There can be no doubt that he was requesting a national, federal, conscription into the regular army, *not* merely a conscription into state militia units which then would serve the nation.

Monroe had four different plans but the heart of his first and favorite carried a clause that clearly provided for national conscription. *It provided that should a district prove unable or unwilling to supply its quota within a month after classification, the required number of men would be called to the national service by 'draught.'* "[33]

The bill the Senate Military Affairs Committee produced from Monroe's proposals was called the Giles Bill. Though couched in terms of "calling up the militia" it went far beyond that. In the bill the word militia was used synonymously with citizenry, something opponents of the bill were quick to point out. The bill would have empowered the President to draft men into the Regular Army and to issue orders directly to militia officers, thus enabling him to circumvent reluctant governors.

The Republican press and leaders responded with somewhat strained support but the Federalists opposed the bill with bitter denunciation. Editorials threatened resistance by force and dubbed it a death blow to freedom. Anti-militarism and the unresolved issues of federalism were brought to a quick rolling boil. The most serious opposition came from the secession-minded New England states where the war was quite unpopular. Federalists in the area sponsored the Hartford Convention which had conscription as one of its major rallying points. The war situation, however, was desperate enough to result in the narrow passage of the bill by both houses with most of Monroe's conscription proposals intact.[34] It then went to the conference committee.[35]

The War of 1812 thus stimulated the first open debate over conscription. The negative reaction was strong. It is important to note the extent of the controversy and opposition at a time when the very survival of the nation was in serious doubt. If Britain had wished to continue the war, it is not at all clear how the United States could have survived without the means of raising a larger and stable military force.[36]

The Mexican War

The Mexican War (1846-1848) did not raise the issue of conscription. President Polk's announcement that Mexican soldiers had invaded United States territory and shed American blood undoubtedly contributed to the voluntary response. The Regular Army, which was of course volunteer, was augmented with one year enlistees, while the militia enlistments were lengthened. Little else was done with the militia since it was restricted from use outside the United States. The President's apparently unjustified belief that the war could be won in six or twelve months was another factor in keeping conscription a dormant issue. As it turned out the war was prolonged by the inability of the U.S. to sustain troops in the field.[37] The Mexican army, which probably could not have provided a serious field exercise for the army of another nation, was repeatedly able to regroup itself and stave off defeat while American forces awaited replacements for volunteers who left as their commitments expired.

The Civil War and the Conscription Trauma

The questions and controversies associated with conscription in America begin to take familiar forms with the Civil War. The serious disorders touched off by Civil War conscription shaped the Selective Service System that came into being 54 years later in 1917. Conscription was not considered necessary in the early stages of the war. Lincoln issued several calls for volunteers to serve the militia for a few months. As the situation worsened for the Union he asked for militia volunteers to serve as long as three years. All of these calls for volunteers were oversubscribed to such an extent that recruiting offices were closed. In contrast, the calls of the Regular Army for volunteers were never fulfilled.

At the same time the Union was optimistically closing its recruiting offices the Confederacy was resolutely enacting a conscription law. Within two months the Union forces had been so depleted by sickness, losses and desertion that recruiting was hastily resumed.

The war that had started as a glorious crusade rapidly lost its appeal. Dissension grew and the "Peace Democrats" became bolder in expressing opposition to the war. By 1862 contention had developed among the Union states over the equitableness of the war burden and calls for volunteers thereafter had to be apportioned on the basis of population.

The dwindling response to the calls for volunteers was extremely alarming. Congress in desperation passed the Militia Act of 1862. This, according to one student of the Constitution, was a conscription law without a conscription clause; a transitional step toward more complete national conscription.[38] The act was designed to force the states to conscript men to fill quotas. It granted the President the power to enroll men and to issue such rules and regulations as were necessary to execute the act should the states fail to do so.

Lincoln immediately issued new calls for volunteers and ordered those states who could not meet their quotas by volunteers to make up discrepancies by special drafts to be paid for by the United States. These efforts by the states generally failed. Attempts at evasion were so widespread that borders had to be sealed and travel within the nation restricted. Violence broke out in five states and Lincoln suspended the writ of habeas corpus, tried resisters by court martial, and permitted as many as 13,000 persons to be arrested by the Provost Marshal General's office.

Two calls were issued under the Militia Act. The first was filled a month late; the second produced a mere fraction of the men needed. Just as military disasters signaled the failure of the militia system to provide capable fighting forces, so did resistance, corruption, substitution brokers, and professional deserters, mark the collapse of militia voluntarism (and conscription) in providing manpower in anything but short, crusading wars.

At last the desperate Union government, its survival at stake, turned to conscription by the federal government. The bill that emerged from Congress was hotly debated, though not as extensively as its 1814 predecessor. The extent of the debate was nonetheless remarkable in light of the desperateness of the situation.[39] One historian who did an intensive study of the passage of the bill describes the debate as "one of the most acrimonious in its (the House's) history," claiming that the apparent ease with which it passed the Senate was deceptive.[40]

Dissonance with Political Culture

Due to the rising unpopularity of the war it is not surprising that the demands of equity assumed primacy. It is interesting to note that the desperateness of the situation and the threat to national survival seemed to matter less than demands that a policy and its administration be carried out in a way that satisfied equity values of political culture. Unfortunately, the administrative system designed for conscription in 1863 was not at all in accord with the norms and values surrounding the exercises of political power and, rather than legitimating the policy, the administrative system virtually discredited it.

The draft of 1863 used Congressional districts, and the territories of states that lacked districts were divided similarly. The draft was under the general responsibility of the Secretary of War. The President appointed a Provost Marshal General as national head and acting Assistant Provost Marshals General for each state and territory, a Provost Marshal for each district and two other members who made up an enrollment board. One of the latter was a physician or surgeon and the third was commonly referred to as a commissioner of enrollment. The district Provost Marshals held the rank, pay and emoluments of Captains of Cavalry. Some were appointed to such ranks by the President, some were regular officers assigned by him to such duty.[41]

The board in turn appointed two or more enrollment officers. They were to enroll all men in their areas between the ages of 20 and 44 years, other than those exempted by law, and report their names to the district board. The district board made the final determination of whom should be inducted, though it is difficult to see how they were left much discretion. Quotas were assigned and exemptions set forth in the law. Enrollment officers decided who would or would not be enrolled upon the basis of exemptions and exceptions permitted by the law.[42]

The impact on the average citizen came in the form of the uniformed federal enrolling officers searching out men to enroll them. If there existed any knowledge or awareness of the district board it is likely that the perception was of a board headed by a military officer. The general administrative structure could scarcely have been conceived of as anything but a military organization — a bureau of the war department.

The Acting Assistant Provost Marshals General were federal officers who had some political relationship with the President or state and local politicians. The state Governors were formally excluded from the system and in fact were placed in a position of negativism and opposition to the Provost Marshal General's draft system. Governors were called upon by the President to provide quotas of volunteer militia. If such were not forthcoming the Provost Marshal General was given quotas to fill for each of the districts within a state by draft. There was never effective and publicized reconciliation of the two potentially conflicting quotas. Bitterness and controversy resulted from suspicions that a state was being forced to contribute more than its fair share.

Thus the draft appeared as a threat, a sanction, a symbol of states' lack of patriotism. The role of the Governors in the System during the twentieth century has been largely titular but to exclude them and juxtapose them to the federal military in 1863 at a time when "states rights" was such a significant element of our political culture was an invitation to disaster. The war was, among other things, primarily a struggle over differing concepts of federalism and where the preponderance of power lay within our federal structure. It was scarcely a propitious time to exacerbate such issues with the sensitive matter of conscription.

Also compounding the problems of the draft was the fact that the district provost marshal was responsible for the apprehension of deserters, evaders, those urging opposition to the draft; and for detecting, seizing, and confining spies.[43] Any registrant who was notified that he was drafted but became delinquent was labeled a deserter, arrested by the Provost Marshal and court martialed. The intermingling of these duties exaggerated the image of the provost marshal as a military policeman and linked the conscript with evaders, deserters and spies. Finally there was the considerable capacity for socio-economic injustice that lay in the fact that in addition to a federal bounty, states and localities could offer additional amounts, and if quotas were filled, conscription could be avoided.

The extent of the dissonance with American political culture is noteworthy and the startling details serve to point up the trauma that resulted. By the end of the war 38 officers of the Provost Marshal General had been assassinated, 60 wounded and 12 others suffered heavy property losses from rioters.[44] The Provost Marshal General reported that "there was no district in which the boards were free from the annoyance of persons hostile to the government, who were willing to embarrass its operation by stimulating resistance to the draft or discouraging enlistments."[45] Riots and armed resistance broke out in several small towns in Ohio; Boston; Portsmouth, New Hampshire; Troy, New York; and other cities. The Secretary of War was faced with requests for troops from 200 cities, towns and counties.[46]

The most famous outbreak of violence was in New York City, where, until eclipsed by recent urban disorders, the riots probably ranked as the greatest civil disturbances in American history.[47] Mobs controlled much of the city for three days. Union forces were ordered not to pursue Lee south from Gettysburg and a total of 10 regiments of New York militia were detached from the Army of the Potomac and sent to restore order in the city, followed by another 10,000 infantrymen and 3 batteries of artillery.

The first effort at federal conscription produced but a fraction of the men needed, though it did stimulate enlistments. The gravity of the political dissension it created was clear in Lincoln's refusal to establish a commission to investigate the cause of the riots. To do so he said would

> have simply touched a match to a barrel of gunpowder. You have heard of sitting on a volcano. We are sitting upon two; one is blazing away already, and the other will blaze away the moment we scrape a little loose dirt from the top of the crater. Better let the dirt alone — at least for the present. One rebellion at a time is about as much as we can conveniently handle.[48]

Introspective Aftermath

Provost Marshal General James Frye composed his final report after the war came to a close. Both Lincoln and Frye had been past political associates of the Acting Assistant Provost Marshal General for Illinois, General James Oakes, whose report makes up most of the second volume of the Provost Marshal General's report. Volume I of the report was written by Frye and he used a politically "prudent" tone that minimized the difficulties his office and the nation had encountered in their first conscription effort. It is not hard to imagine that Frye wanted any admission of error or criticism to come from a source somewhat removed from the national administration and that he therefore had Oakes' report serve the purpose of admitting the less pleasant details and recommending changes. Oakes recommended the following:

(1) In future wars all men legally liable to conscription should be obligated to report themselves for enrollment instead of having to be hunted down by enrolling officers in house-to-house canvasses. "If the government has a right to the military service of its citizens in times of public peril, rebellion, and war, it has the right to secure such services in the simplest, cheapest, and most direct manner."

(2) National conscription, he felt, was a new and untried experiment in the United States and one against which public opinion had "conceived a most violent prejudice." Therefore, an educational policy by the government should be used to bring the people to a more rational view of the nature and necessity of the draft.

(3) Simultaneously with an educational program, the government should demonstrate its inflexible determination to execute the law in spite of threats of opposition.

(4) Every man should be drafted from and credited to the quota of the district in which he had actual residence and not to that of another district where he might have been enrolled.

(5) Each state and not each congressional district should be made responsible for a quota by national authorities.

(6) No man should be allowed to hire a substitute.

(7) The law should forbid the payment of bounties as an inducement for volunteering.

(8) The term of service should be the duration of the war.

(9) There should be a supervising medical aide and legal advisers at each state headquarters.[49]

The report was to lie dormant in War Department files until World War I approached. Conscription was never seriously considered for the Spanish-American War, since Americans entered the war with such a blend of imperialism and righteousness that a supply of manpower was never problematic.

Judge Advocate General Enoch H. Crowder was appointed to the position of Provost Marshal General in 1916. Crowder was a lawyer as well as a soldier and had studied the Oakes and Frye reports as early as 1890 while stationed as a Lieutenant in the Eighth Calvary at Fort Yates, Dakota territory. He later studied military manpower mobilization as a member of the General Staff and as a military observer stationed in Japan.[50]

Crowder was told by Secretary of War Baker that the President wanted a draft bill that would mobilize manpower, but was given no particulars.[51] Working with assistants he literally produced a draft bill overnight that incorporated virtually all the features of the Oakes Report.[52] What is not clear is the point at which it was decided that all-civilian, local boards would be used. Apparently they evolved naturally without any special consideration. Since the Office of the Provost Marshal General no longer was concerned with deserters, spies, etc. and since it was specifically planned to avoid enrollment by officers, its size was insufficient to consider placing military men on boards. Crowder was also quite concerned that "before and after the enactment of the law the democratic and civilian features of the draft were emphasized so that public confidence would be won."[53] Finally there was the tacit assumption in development of the bill and the System that state officials would be carefully "co-opted," which tended to preclude anything but local citizens on the staff of local boards.[54] The "local board" feature of the law which apparently developed so casually was to become one of the most important of all in the future.

The day after Congress declared war the Senate Military Affairs Committee began hearings on Crowder's draft bill even though it had not yet been formally introduced. In approximately six weeks a bill emerged and became law. If the passage of the law was easier and swifter than the near catastrophic delays of 1814, it was still bitterly contested. Anti-militarism and anti-conscription were still extremely strong. The Congressional Record from April 17 to May 18 of 1917 is filled with denunciations of conscription as a "plot of the militarists."[55] Regardless of how the passage should be characterized, it is clear that only unusual circumstances made passage of the bill possible.

The acceptance of conscription seems to have been a universal surprise. Edward Fitzpatrick, the State Director for Wisconsin, remarked "a really surprising thing about conscription in the World War was its quiet acceptance, practically without incident, its amazing success, and its expansion."[57]

How is it that a public policy which caused some of this country's greatest civil upheaval 54 years earlier was so calmly accepted in 1917? Clearly not because anti-militarism and anti-conscription had vanished.

The tempering of the debate can be traced to several subtle factors. First there were changed outlooks on the legitimacy of conscription by the federal government. Emmette Redford and David Truman assert that

> Between 1861 and 1913, American federalism underwent significant changes. While identification with state and locality did not vanish, the post-Civil War generations came increasingly to think of themselves fundamentally as Americans, and this flood of nationalistic sentiment marked the end of any taint of illegitimacy or secondary status for the national government.[58]

Second, the symbolic potency of the militia system had declined. Evidence of this can be seen in the changing legal status of the militia which up until 1903 was under state control in peacetime and dual control during war. In 1903 the Dick Act brought federal support and supervision of the militia, and made it into National Guard units. State control gave way to dual control in peacetime and national control in wartime.[59]

The third and most important element dampening debate was the preparedness campaign of 1915-16. This remarkable campaign began as a Republican attack upon President Wilson but caught on to become widespread among all ages and types of citizens. It had as its intellectual well-spring a group of men of renown and intellect that Huntington calls the Neo-Hamiltonians, men like General Leonard Wood, Theodore Roosevelt, Captain Mahan, Henry Cabot Lodge, etc. These men viewed international politics as a struggle for power for which America had to be strong and prepared.[60] Military historian Walter Millis claims that "preparedness laid the whole groundwork of ideas and conditioned the attitudes which were to make possible the American intervention upon those terrible fields (Verdun and the Somme)."[61]

The preparedness campaign received its final impetus from the Mexican Mobilization in 1916.[62] The National Guards of Arizona, Texas and New Mexico were called out to pursue Pancho Villa. Millis feels that the sluggishness of recruiting for the mobilization left the "attentive public" inclined to feel that volunteering had ceased to be a practical way of alloting the burdens of modern war.[63] Viewed in the light of the above factors, acceptance of conscription does not run counter to anti-militarism and anti-conscription sentiments.

A Structure and Processes in Harmony With American Political Culture

The broad features of General Oakes' recommendations are clearly evident in the bill signed in 1917. The basic features of the System developed then have remained much the same down to the present, as can be seen in **Figure 1**.

The President was designated the pro-forma head of the System and was to appoint members of local boards and district boards. Then, as now, this was turned over in all but form to the governors with the only requirements for appointment being civilian status and residence in their jurisdiction. At the base of the organizational pyramid were the statutorily required local boards (4,647 at the time) and affiliated agencies like the Government Appeal Agents, Medical Advisory Boards, Legal Advisory Boards, and Boards of Instruction.

According to the Provost Marshal General, local board members were chosen for "environment" rather than professions, since their classifying function was principally to decide questions of dependency.[64] The range of occupations he reports is all the more interesting because it is difficult to see how it could have been very "environmental" in a truly representative sense if one notes a few of the occupations and the degree to which they were represented, as shown in Table 1.

The heavy representation of the medical profession can be explained by the fact that each board had to handle its own medical examination. The large numbers of public office holders is attributed to the inclusion of the sheriff and county clerk on so many boards after they had been placed on the original registration boards, more for reasons of convenience than legitimation. But the strong representation of law, commerce and banking is only understandable in political-sociological, not in "environmental" terms.

Jurisdictional lines for boards seem to have evolved without any particular purpose except convenience and there was not continuous registration by date of birth as found in the System today. There were three registrations carried out by special boards in electoral

The Institution in Historical Perspective 33

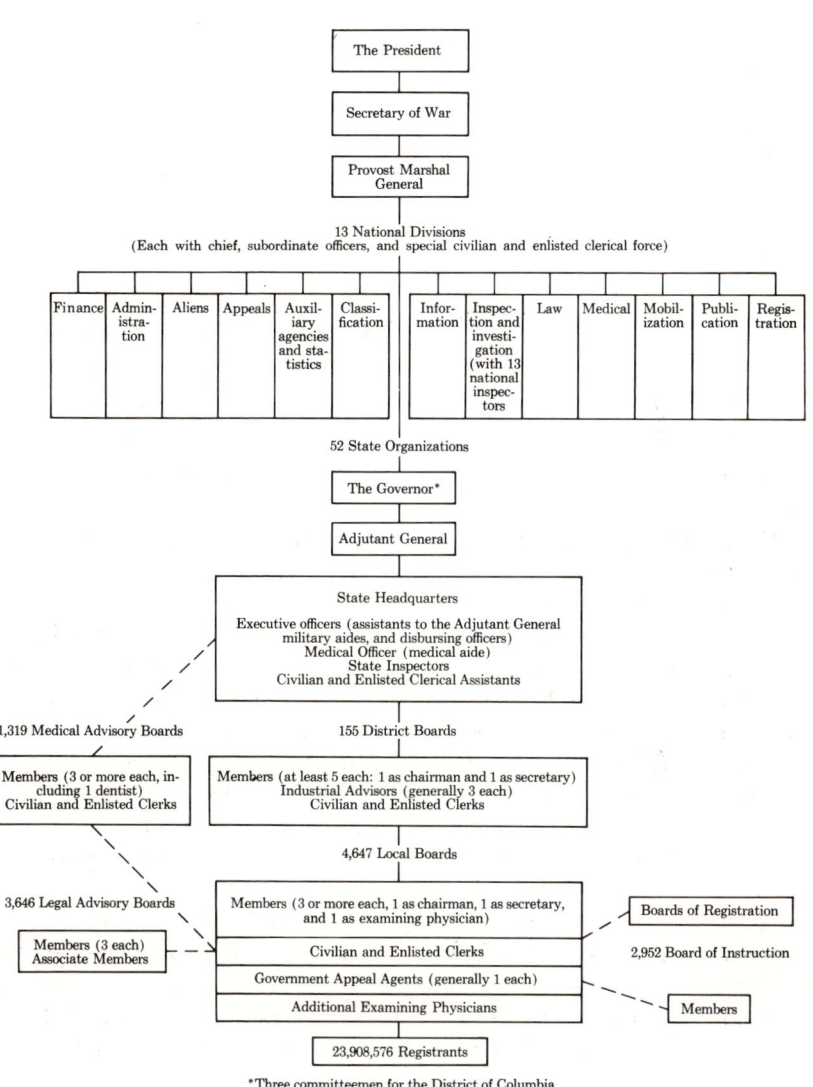

Figure 1. *The Selective Service System, 1917-18*

TABLE 1. Occupations of Local Board Members of the Selective Service System, World War I

Total personnel reporting as to occupations	13,564
Medicine	4,246
Public Office	2,841
Law	1,517
Agriculture	982
Commerce	975
Banking	379
Manufacturing	313
Education	142
Labor	121
Transportation	102
Clergy	74
Other occupations	1,872

Source: Provost Marshal General, Second Report (1918), *op. cit.* p. 11.

precincts prior to the establishment of the local draft boards. The jurisdiction of draft boards were usually an amalgamation of electoral precincts which may have reflected "neighborhoods," though this is not certain.

The next layer of the organization required by statute was composed of the district boards. There were 155 of these (at least one for each federal judicial district) with one board covering 30 local boards. While the powers of local boards were just as sweepingly ambiguous then as they are today, the district boards had more far-ranging powers than their modern counterparts, the appeal boards. The district boards had both original and appellate jurisdiction. Original jurisdiction operated in "all questions of agricultural or industrial necessity or of other occupations found to be necessary to the maintenance of national interest during the emergency."[65] The district boards also had more explicit occupational representation than today's appeal boards. The five members were drawn from agriculture, industry, labor, medicine, and law.[66] The district boards had attached to them three non-compensated industrial advisers — one nominated by the Department of Labor, one by the Department of Agriculture and one by the district board itself. These advisers were to inform themselves of the requirements of individual establishments in industry, of priorities of the War Industries Board—and of the labor situation in industries and locales.[67]

There was also a headquarters for each state which was responsible "for coordinating the activities of district and local boards," seeing that calls were met by the local boards, and "performing liaison between the district and local units and National Headquarters."[68] The descriptions of National Headquarters refer vaguely to its function as "coordination," apparently operating much as it does today. Both national and state levels were staffed with military personnel "commissioned from the National Army or the Reserve Corps—and paid by the Federal Government to give full-time to the work of the draft."[69] Though they represented a minority of the staff at all levels, the military officers held virtually all executive positions then as now.

The assignment of the Provost Marshal General to direct the System was a holdover from the Civil War, and indicative of original American attitudes toward conscription. The Provost Marshal General was originally the director of the military police force and in 1863 was charged with hunting down deserters and evaders and court martialing them. But in 1917 the office was relieved of all responsibility for spies and deserters though the System still carried out automatic induction of delinquents.

There were some other minor differences between the 1917 System and today's.

(1) Board members were compensated, a feature dropped in 1940.

(2) Enlistees or inductees found fit only for non-combatant service were used as board clerks.

(3) The government appeal agent, who was theoretically supposed to protect the interests of both the government and the registrant, was much more active than has been the case in the years since World War II.

(4) Medical advisory boards who took cases appealed from the local board were active in ways that are no longer true, largely because the System rather than the Armed Forces was responsible for medical decisions.

(5) For a brief period there existed Boards of Instruction designed to help the soldier "define the principles of American democracy, personal character, conduct, personal habits, patriotic abstemiousness and soldierly ideals and obligations."[70]

The 1917 System was viewed as temporary for the purpose of meeting a military emergency. The boards were more active than they have been in the post-World War II era. Nonetheless, their induction-deferment decisions were simpler and focused largely on dependency. They carried the added burden of medical decisions but these probably fell to medical men on the boards.

The System developed has been described by Selective Service as "supervised decentralization" or a "combination of centralized-decentralized organization and administration."[71] Both observers and participants felt its consonance with American political culture was a key factor in securing acceptance of such a contentious public policy.

Dupuy described it this way:

> The inductee came before a board of residents of his local community, who could be expected to know him and his necessities. The enforcement of the law was a duty of the Justice Department. It was all fair, honest and democratic. There was no saber-rattling, no vestige of impressment. It was the American way. And it worked.[72]

In an official monograph Selective Service says this:

> Predicated on the concepts that selection should be made within local communities rather than by the Federal Government, and that the responsibility for registering should be with the individual rather than some agent of the Government, a System was evolved that tended to surpass the hopes of the people responsible for its administration.[73]

The relationship of the structure and processes of Selective Service to American political culture were well described by General Crowder who stated that "such a stupendous undertaking could not have been accomplished through a system not in harmony with the National Spirit."[74]

System Survival in the Interim Years

An interesting part of the System's history is its survival after World War I. Though the 1917 law did not lapse until March 1921, dismantlement of the System began with the end of the War. However, the success of the System in procuring military manpower assured that it would not be ignored or dropped from mobilization planning. A number of the officers who had been with the System throughout the War were convinced that Selective Service should be an integral part of mobilization planning and that the nation should be prepared to adopt it again. These men were Regular Army Officers in the War Department's Personnel Division, and National Guard and Reserve Officers of the Provost Marshal General's Headquarters staff, whose motives can only be a matter of speculation. Perhaps some who were in the War Department saw an opportunity for task expansion or empire building; perhaps some who had been with the Provost Marshal General's office were reluctant to give up the excitement, status and activity of the recent emergency and retire to more mundane pursuits; and perhaps many of them were Neo-Hamiltonians who were convinced that the national interest dictated preservation of the System and preparation for future use.

In any case, they began meeting informally "probably from Armistice Day in 1918."[75] General Hershey's recollection is that a Colonel Harry C. Kramer who had been on the national staff was the source of initiative in bringing together those concerned with keeping Selective Service viable.[76]

The first official initiative came from the Personnel Division in the General Staff of the War Department (G-1), which had statutory authority to engage in manpower mobilization planning.[77] Between 1920 and 1926, G-1 (apparently in conjunction with Kramer and the unofficial group interested in the problem) met in the offices of the War Department to draft a basic law and regulations.[78]

By 1924 the War Department had contacted the State Adjutant General for comments on the proposed law and regulations. National Guardsmen and Reservists seeking active duty assignments or reserve positions as a result of organizational consolidations in the Guard, began to take interest in Selective Service. In 1925 the Personnel Division formally recommended formation of a Selective Service Committee formed of officers from all the Services and designated the Joint Army and Navy Selective Service Committee.

The committee's proposal that a Selective Service Reserve cadre be formed was accepted and the first national conference was held in 1929. The organization and operation of the 1917 System was reviewed, modifications were suggested, detailed plans were drawn up and contacts were established in all of the states — all on a confidential basis. It was not until 1938 that the international crisis was sufficient to make the committee feel it could make its activities public.[79]

The growing range of the committee's activities had called for some executive coordination and the role had fallen to the executive secretary. In 1936 Major Lewis Hershey, a regular army officer who had entered service through the National Guard, had been assigned to the Personnel Division of the War Department. Within a few months he was assigned to the committee because of his background and contacts in the Guard and his ability to get along with the difficult Colonel Kramer.[80]

The Burke-Wadsworth Bill of 1940

The passage of a conscription bill prior to the outbreak of war was not a result of the disappearance of anti-militarism and anti-conscription from the American scene. The passage was bitterly fought and narrowly successful. The tenacity of anti-conscription is evident if one realizes that the passage was so close despite the fact that the United States had been developing its military establishment in a state of "limited national emergency" since September 1939, and that both France and the Low Countries had fallen to Hitler.[81]

Its passage can be generally attributed to the severity of the international crisis and the fact that Americans could easily cast themselves in a righteous role when faced with Nazi Germany.[82] Huntington feels that passage of the conscription bill can also be credited in part to the revival of Neo-Hamiltonianism. He asserts that men like Grenville Clark, Stimson, Robert P. Patterson, and Elihu Root "played a major role in stimulating American rearmament and in securing the passage of the Selective Service Act of 1940."[83]

It would be natural to assume that the above factors made passage of the law possible and that the "sneak attack" upon Pearl Harbor clinched acceptance for conscription, and this is partly true. But there is evidence that the attunement of Selective Service to American political culture was a major factor in acceptance. As mentioned earlier the draft began in September 1940, and the law came up for renewal in the summer of 1941. Though the renewal was as close as it possibly could be, the Gallup Poll a few months earlier had shown that 93 per cent of those polled felt the draft was being handled fairly. It is not unreasonable to assume that the congruence of the System with political culture made the difference between renewal and defeat.

Selective Service in 1940-41 and World War II

World War II was the longest period of the System's operation under conditions of high mobilization. Considering their magnitude, duration, and complexity, the operations were relatively smooth and achieved wide acceptance. For this reason and because the structure and processes were so similar to those of World War I there is little need to dwell on this period of its history despite the abundance of literature on the era.

The System went into operation smoothly: Major Hershey was authorized by Executive Order to assume administrative direction of the System and rose from Major to Brigadier General and Director in a series of rapid promotions; Selective Service Reservists were called to active duty; plans went into effect; concern over acceptance prompted the President to appoint a National Advisory Commission on Selective Service and a noted educator, Clarence Dykstra, was appointed the first director, though both the Commission and Dykstra soon left the System.

A few of the changes made in the System should be noted. District boards covering congressional districts were replaced by at least one appeal board per state or 1 per 70,000 registrants. The appeal boards lost their adjunct advisory panels and their original jurisdiction over agricultural and industrial cases. In formal terms this meant that the powers of local boards were broadened, but the change meant considerably less in actuality. Because there were increased reasons for deferment, local boards were less able to focus on dependency cases. At the same time, however, the boards received far more "advice and guidance" from state and national headquarters.

After six registrations, the registrations were placed on a daily basis for all those individuals turning 18. After 3 of the much publicized "fish bowl lotteries" the order of call up was based on date of birth rather than lottery.[84]

Further changes included the end of compensation for board members; civilian use in the position of board clerk; the take-over by the Armed Forces in 1942 of medical and dental examinations though clerks or board members continued to screen out those with obvious defects (crippled persons or amputees); the end of automatic induction and courts-martial and the Federal Bureau of Investigation's handling of delinquencies.[85]

Postwar Continuation and Evolving Acceptance

The Selective Service Act of 1940 expired on March 31, 1947, after two successive renewals, each more controversial than the last. But in the post war era the controversy was changing and subsiding. The changes in American attitudes and the mounting tension of the Cold War assured that the 1947 demise would be more statutory than real.

The first postwar renewal came in May of 1945, and was accepted as a means of maintaining the strength of the Army for the apparently formidable invasion of Japan. The second renewal came in 1946 on the pleas of concerned administration officials who found that they had almost no military power with which they could counter Soviet aggressiveness.

Evidence of slowly evolving changes in attitudes and the nature of the controversy can be found in the debates over Universal Military Training (UMT). Proponents of UMT claimed it was a descendant of the militia concept and not conscription and that its plans for a citizenry trained in arms would eliminate the need for conscription and reduce the size of the standing army.[86]

It is not clear whether UMT was seen as a substitute for conscription as its backers claimed or whether its apparent popularity contained spillover support for conscription among an undiscerning public. The debate over UMT continued into the 1950's without the program's ever being implemented. The UMT debates do, however, indicate that Americans were becoming aware of military necessities in a tension-ridden world and perhaps that antimilitarism and anti-conscription attitudes were abating.

Many of the backers of UMT felt that as long as Selective Service existed it stood in the way of UMT's passage. Partly for this reason President Truman recommended that the Selective Service Act be allowed to expire and urged passage of UMT. He made it plain that if UMT were not passed and if voluntary enlistments lagged, he would recommend reenactment of Selective Service.

To say that the Act expired is not to say the institution of Selective Service came to an end. Many treatments of the subject imply such to be the case. The nucleus of the System was maintained intact as the Office of Selective Service Records. It was formally charged with the completion of liquidation of the System, with maintaining, preserving and servicing records, and with planning for future operations. The shift to an Office of Selective Service Records was a brilliant means of preserving the institution from extinction.

Despite the fact that the Cold War was rapidly reaching a crescendo of intensity, enlistments lagged seriously. The Navy and Air Force managed to maintain their assigned strengths but the Army found that it could only obtain between 12,000 and 24,000 enlistments per month despite intensive campaigns. To hold to a strength of 669,000 it needed at least 30,000 enlistments per month.

With UMT unlikely to obtain passage and enlistments sagging, President Truman in 1948 came before Congress with a special message urging reenactment of Selective Service. The congressional debates over reenactment were heated but the elements of American political culture that related to compulsory service were clearly changing under the pressure of world events.

In 1814 it appeared that the nation would have perished rather than accept conscription; in 1863 with national survival again at stake a conscription law was passed but bitterly and violently resisted; in 1917 and 1940 conscription was grudgingly instituted as a temporary measure and won wide acceptance because its administration conformed to political culture. In the post-World War II era the temporary necessity began to assume inexorably an air of permanency. To be sure such momentous changes did not come easily. Few were willing to regard Selective Service as permanent and its temporariness was constantly reiterated.[87] It was finally passed with a life span of two years.

Some 30,000 men were inducted under the 1948 Act but as enlistment rates stabilized they were released after 12 months of their 21 month obligation. Two years later, despite the continuing increase in Cold War tension, the bill for its renewal, providing only the power to register and classify, was predictably stalled in conference committee on June 25, 1950, when South Korea was invaded. On the following day the committee approved the bill and it went on to passage.[88]

Because it is difficult to separate attitudes toward conscription from those toward UMT, it is not possible to say definitively when Americans ceased to question whether or not there should be conscription. If one can assume support for UMT reflected support for conscription, opinion polls would indicate that conscription was accepted after World War II. Between December 1945 and January 1956, there were nine public opinion surveys on the question of UMT. Only once did the majority supporting it drop below a remarkable 65 per cent, in March 1952, when it was 60 per cent.[89]

Noted military historian Walter Millis ties acceptance of conscription to the advent of the Korean War.[90] Whatever date one chooses is less important than recognition that the American people in a period of five or six years had to confront the realities of world politics and this entailed acceptance rather than temporary toleration of a large standing Army maintained by conscription.

The institution used for conscription achieved a state of equilibrium that held for over two decades. In this instance it rested on the popular acceptance of a Cold War rather than a "hot" one. If the Cold War lacked some of the immediacy and urgency that popular hot wars provided in the past to dampen demands of political culture, the harmony of Selective Service with political values served the same purpose. Equilibrium became stability and stability moved toward rigidity while both the popularity of the Cold War and American political culture underwent extensive changes.

The Universal Military Training and Service Act of 1951 was renewed quadrennially in 1955, 1959, and 1963 after lengthy but stylized hearings with final passage never in doubt. Though this pattern changed abruptly after 1966, support for the general policy of conscription seems undiminished. The Louis Harris survey of March and December 1965 showed 64 and 90 per cent of those questioned were in favor of "having all young men who are able-bodied and eligible drafted for military service."[91] Even among students, who are often presumed to be most opposed to the draft, a 1966 poll by the National Student Association showed a remarkable 90 per cent of those polled felt a nation was justified in using a military draft.

Conclusion

This chapter has attempted to view the historical development of Selective Service from 1917 to the present. It has pointed up the following:

(1) The long-standing antipathy for militarism and conscription in American political culture was complemented by faith in the militia system.[92]

(2) The 1917 System was patterned directly upon recommendations made in 1866, as a consequence of the traumatic difficulties that beset Civil War conscription. Those who directed the Civil War system felt that its principal features were not in harmony with American values. Those who drew upon their experience accepted this analysis as fact and tried to design the 1917 system accordingly.

(3) The Selective Service System was extremely successful and its structure and processes were at least partly responsible for winning and sustaining acceptance of conscription.

(4) The System has undergone only minor changes since 1917. Most have been efforts to perfect the "fit" of the institution to its political culture. The changes between World War I and World War II seem largely to have been the elimination of structures and processes that no longer seemed necessary for acceptance.

(5) The System has survived between wars through the efforts of the Armed Forces which recognize their need for it; and through

the efforts of individuals and groups motivated by self-interest, Neo-Hamiltonian outlooks, and a desire to remain actively involved in military affairs in some way.

(6) The fluctuating and contradictory attitudes toward conscription after World War II reflected the shifting American outlook toward the realities of world politics. The "off again-on again" fate of Selective Service and the constant claim by political leaders that it was temporary, fostered the insecurity of the institution and the "temporariness" of its posture.

(7) Contentiousness over conscription, while still present, subsided as there came to be acceptance of it along with concurrent acceptance of the responsibilities of a world power. The historic question — whether or not there should be conscription — was resolved to the extent of becoming of secondary importance.

Notes

[1] The term "institution" will be used frequently in place of organization and particularly with reference to Selective Service. The meaning implied is adapted from Philip Selznick who describes an institution as "a natural product of social needs and pressures... a responsive adaptive organism"... an organization "infused with value." See Selznick's *Leadership in Administration* (Evanston, Ill.: Row, Peterson, 1957).

[2] See *Backgrounds of Selective Service*, Monograph 1, Part II, (Washington, D.C.: Government Printing Office, 1946); *An Outline of the History of Selective Service*, (Washington, D.C.: Government Printing Office, 1951); "The 50th Anniversary of the 1917 Selective Service Law," 1917-1967; *Observance Manual* (mimeo, National Headquarters, Selective Service System, Washington, D.C., February 22, 1967); Lieutenant Colonel Arthur Vollmer, *A Compilation of Conscription Laws*, Vols. 1-14 (U.S. Government Printing Office: Washington, D.C., 1947).

[3] "Manual of Observance, A Tribute to General James Oakes," (mimeo, National Headquarters, Selective Service System, Washington, D.C., March 17, 1966), p. 6.

[4] *Review of the Administration and Operation of the Selective Service System,* Hearings before the Committee on Armed Services, House of Representatives, 89th Cong. 2nd Sess. (Washington, D.C.: Government Printing Office, 1966).

[5] Samuel Huntington, *The Soldier and The State* (New York: Vintage Books Inc., 1964), p. 2.

[6] This definition is combined from two sources: Samuel H. Beer and Adam B. Ulam, *Patterns of Government* (2nd ed. N.Y. Random House, 1965) p. 34; and Lucian W. Pye's essay "Comparative Political Culture" in Lucian W. Pye and Sidney Verba (eds.) *Political Culture and Political Development* (Princeton, N.J.: Princeton University Press, 1965) pp. 512-60. If the term political culture has not won enthusiastic acceptance among political scientists, the author is at least in esteemed company. Some of the leading names in the discipline continue to grapple with the concept and find it useful. The most extensive effort to operationalize the concept and utilize it for research is Gabriel Almond and Sidney Verba's *Civic Culture,* (Boston: Little, Brown and Company, 1965). Some critics feel that this massive cross-national effort stretched both the concept and data too far but it remains a land-mark work.

[7] Almond and Verba, *op cit.,* pp. 440-50.

[8] Anti-militarism can be assumed to be the opposite of militarism, which has been defined as a doctrine or system that values war and accords primacy in state and society to the armed forces. It exalts a function — the application of violence — and an institutional structure — the military establishment. It implies both a policy orientation and a power relationship. See Kurt Lang, "Militarism," *Encyclopedia of the Social Sciences,* Vol. 10 (New York: The Macmillan Co., and The Free Press, 1968) 300.

The Institution in Historical Perspective

[9] Joseph C. Bernardo and Eugene H. Bacon, *American Military Policy: Its Development Since 1775* (Harrisburg, Pennsylvania: Military Service Publishing Company, 1955), Ch. 1; Arthur A. Ekrich, Jr., *The Civil and Military: A History of the Anti-Militarist Tradition* (New York: Oxford University Press, 1956), Ch. 1; and Walter Millis, *Arms and Men: A Study in American Military History* (New York: New American Library of World Literature, Inc., 1958).

[10] Charles H. Coates and Roland J. Pellegrin, *Military Sociology* (University Park, Md.: Social Science Press, 1965), p. 22. For a thorough dissection of the many facets of militarism and anti-militarism in the U.S., see also their discussion on pp. 40-42.

[11] For a discussion of the colonial militia see *Background of the Military Policy of the U.S.* (H.Q. AFROTC, Air University 1958). Above quote from R. Ernest Dupuy, *The Compact History of the U.S. Army* (Rev. ed.; New York: Hawthorn Books, Inc., 1961), p. 27.

[12] *Ibid.*

[13] Quoted in M.R.D. Foot, *Men in Uniform*, (London: Weidenfeld and Nicolson, 1961), p. 91.

[14] Quoted in Walter Millis, *Arms and Men, op. cit.*, pp. 38-39. It might also be noted that he pays obeisance to anti-militarism with the remark that large standing armies "hath ever been considered dangerous to the liberties of a country." See also Bernardo and Bacon, *op. cit.*, p. 49.

[15] This interpretation has been confirmed by Jack Leach who has made the most exhaustive study of the origins of conscription in America. He concludes that Washington differentiated between "enlisted" and "drafted" and that "Washington did not here argue for national conscription." See his *Conscription in the United States: Historical Background* (Rutland, Vt.: Charles E. Tuttle Co., Inc., 1952), p. 3.

[16] Quoted in Dupuy, *op. cit.*, p. 38.

[17] See Millis, *op. cit.*, p. 44, and Bernardo and Bacon, *op. cit.*, p. 64.

[18] Such a lack of clarity is of course found throughout the Constitution. It has been described as a deplorable weakness but more often as a brilliant means of providing for growth under a basic law without restrictive details that might foreclose the future.

[19] See U.S. Constitution Article 1, Section 8, Item 15.

[20] Millis, *op. cit.*, p. 42.

[21] *Ibid.*, p. 43.

[22] *Ibid.*

[23] Leach, *op. cit.*, p. 3.

[24] *Arver v. United States*, 245 U.S. 366.

[25] Author's italics.

[26] *Supreme Court Reporter* 245-247 U.S. Vol. 38, 1917 (St. Paul: West Publishing Co., 1918).

[27] In the same case the Supreme Court dealt with three other issues. It attacked the claim that conscription of individual citizens by the federal government was contrary to the original intent of the Constitution that state citizenship take primacy. The Court simply asserted that because the power to raise armies was delegated to Congress its power over the citizen

was supreme in that regard. To the claim that the power to raise armies referred to raising volunteers, the Court said such a claim "challenges the existence of all power, for a governmental power which has no sanction to it and which therefore can only be exercised provided the citizen consents to its exertion is in no substantial sense a power." As for involuntary servitude, the Court simply was "unable to conceive upon what theory the exaction by government from the citizen of the performance of his supreme and noble duty" could be said to be involuntary servitude.

[28] Fitzpatrick, Edward A., *Conscription and America* (Milwaukee, Wisc.: The Richards Publishing Co., Inc., 1940) p. 20.

[29] See for example Bernardo and Bacon, *op. cit.*, p. 81.

[30] Fitzpatrick, *op. cit.*, p. 20.

[31] Leach, *op. cit.*, p. 33. This section draws heavily upon Leach's extensive analysis, which is apparently the only one of its kind.

[32] *Ibid*, p. 35.

[33] Leach, p. 37, citing *Annals*, 13th Cong., 3rd. Sess., p. 405.

[34] The Senate vote was 19-12 and an amended version was passed by ten votes (83-73) in the House.

[35] Leach, *op. cit.*, describes public reaction in detail. See chs. 4 and 5 and especially ch. 6 and pp. 67 and 97.

[36] *Ibid*, p. 124.

[37] At the height of his campaign General Scott lost 40 per cent of his enlisted personnel whose terms expired. See Emory Upton, *The Military Policy of the United States*, War document no. 290 (Washington, D.C., 1917), p. 203.

[38] Randall, James G., *Constitutional Problems Under Lincoln*, (New York: Appleton and Company, 1926), pp. 244-47.

[39] One day in the Senate, four days in the House.

[40] Duggan, J.C., "The Legislative and Statutory Development of the Federal Concept of Conscription for Military Service," (Washington, D.C.: unpublished Ph.D. dissertation, The Catholic University of America, 1946), pp. 42-44.

[41] *Organization and Administration of the System*, Special Monograph No. 3, Vol. 1 (Washington, D.C.: Government Printing Office, 1951), 185-186. Citing, *An Act for Enrolling and Calling Out the National Forces, and for Other Purposes*, March 3, 1863, sec. 8.

[42] The original act of 1863 exempted: those rejected as physically or mentally unfit for service; the Vice-President of the U.S.; federal judges; federal department heads; state governors; and men in situations of family dependency or with conflicting religious principles. *Backgrounds of Selective Service*, Special Monograph No. 1, vol. II, part 1 (Washington, D.C.: Government Printing Office, 1947) 15, 17, 21, 34-37.

[43] *Organization and Administration of the System*, p. 11.

[44] U.S. Provost-Marshall-General's Bureau. *Final Report Made to the Secretary of War by the Provost Marshall General of the Operations of the Bureau of the Provost Marshall General of the United States, from the Commencement of the Business of the Bureau, March 17, 1863 to March 17, 1866.* (Washington, D.C.: Government Printing Office, 1866), I, 143.

The Institution in Historical Perspective

[45] *Ibid*, p. 14.

[46] Leach, *op. cit.*, p. 321.

[47] An interesting account of the New York riots is "New York's Bloodiest Week" by Lawrence Lader in *American Heritage*, Vol. X, No. 4 (June 1959), 44.

[48] Leach, *op. cit.*, p. 296-97.

[49] Provost Marshal General, *Final Report*, II, 1-50 is the Oakes Report.

[50] David A. Lockmiller, "Enoch H. Crowder: Soldier, Lawyer, Statesman 1859-1932," The University of Missouri Studies, Vol. 27 (1955), pp. 54 and 153.

[51] *Ibid.*, p. 153.

[52] Major General Enoch H. Crowder, *The Spirit of Selective Service* (New York: Century, 1920), pp. 115-25.

[53] Lockmiller, *op. cit.*, p. 164.

[54] *Ibid.*, p. 160. During congressional debates on the bill Crowder carried on confidential correspondence with all governors and many mayors in order to smooth passage and implementation of the act.

[55] See the *Congressional Record* for the above period or the list of references under "conscription" on p. 53 of Index to the Record, *Congressional Record*, Vol. 55, Part 8, Appendix and Index Parts 1-8, 65th Cong. 1st sess., Oct. 2-6, 1917 (Washington, D.C., 1917).

[56] Crowder, *op. cit.*, p. 62.

[57] Fitzpatrick, *op. cit.*, p. 34.

[58] Emmette S. Redford, David B. Truman, *et al.*, *Politics and Government in the United States*, (Harcourt, Brace & World, Inc., 1965), p. 119.

[59] Samuel P. Huntington, *The Soldier and the State*, pp. 70-171.

[60] Samuel P. Huntington, *Ibid.*, pp. 271-72.

[61] Millis, *Arms and Men, op. cit.*, p. 198.

[62] The National Guards of Arizona, Texas and New Mexico were called out to pursue Pancho Villa.

[63] Millis, *op. cit.*, pp. 230-31.

[64] Provost Marshal General, *Second Report to December 22, 1918*, (Washington, D.C.: Government Printing Office, 1918), p. 11. The word environment is Crowder's and evidently means that board members were to reflect the socio-economic patterns of their communities rather than dominant interests, or high status occupations, etc.).

[65] *Organizational and Administration of the System, op. cit.*, p. 22.

[66] Provost Marshal General, *Second Report* (1918), *op. cit.*, p. 13.

[67] *Organizational and Administration of the System, op. cit.*, p. 22.

[68] *Ibid.*, p. 19.

[69] *Ibid.*, p. 20.

[70] *Ibid.*, p. 28.

[71] *Ibid.*, pp. 31-32.

[72] Dupuy, *op. cit.*, p. 223.

[73]*Organization and Administration of the System, op. cit.,* p. 32.

[74]Provost Marshal General, *Second Report,* (1918), *op. cit.,* pp. 41-42.

[75]"The 50th Anniversary of the 1917 Selective Service Law," *op. cit.,* p. 10.

[76]Interview No. 41. Kramer was later Adjutant General of the New Jersey National Guard.

[77]See 29 Stat. 167 (June 3, 1916), sec. 5; 41 Stat. 762 (June 4, 1920), sec. 5, and other successive statutes down to 1940. "The duties of the War Department General Staff shall be to prepare plans for national defense and the use of military forces for that purpose both separately and in conjunction with the naval forces, and for the mobilization of the manhood of the Nation and its material resources in an emergency, to investigate and report upon all questions affecting the efficiency of the Army of the United States, and its state of preparation for military operations; and to render professional aid and assistance to the Secretary of War and the Chief of Staff."

[78]Interview No. 41, *op. cit.*

[79]*Organization and Administration of the System, op. cit.,* p. 40.

[80]Interview No. 41, *op. cit.*

[81]Military historians like professional soldiers emphasize the lack of U.S. preparation for war. Diplomatic historians however are generally agreed that President Roosevelt had a substantial majority of opinion behind him in each of his preparedness steps and some argue that he trailed behind public opinion. See Thomas A. Bailey, *A Diplomatic History of the American People* (6th ed.; New York: Appleton-Century-Crofts, 1958), pp. 711-23.

[82]America's needs to moralize war has been the subject of many books. See Gabriel Almond, *The American People and Foreign Policy* (New York: Frederick A. Praeger, Inc., 1966), p. 60; or George E. Kennan, *American Diplomacy: 1900-1950* (New York: New American Library of World Literature, Inc., 1951).

[83]Huntington, *op. cit.,* p. 271. See also Samuel Reid Spencer, Jr., *A History of the Selective Training and Service Act of 1940, from Inception to Enactment* (unpublished senior honors thesis, Harvard University, 1951). See also Clark's obituary in the *New York Times,* January 14, 1967, p. 31.

[84]The last lottery was held on December 11, 1942.

[85]From 1943 to 1945 the System used Medical Field Agents to gather medical, social, and educational information needed by the Armed Forces in handling mental and personality disorders. From 1943 to 1947 the System used Veterans' Assistance Units to assure veterans employment or reinstatement.

[86]Most plans called for short military training for all but the unfit at age 18 or 19 and release to the Reserves thereafter. For an example of the attempt to distinguish UMT from conscription see President Truman's speech to Congress. U.S. *Congressional Record,* 79th Cong., 1st sess., part 6, p. 8370.

[87]The renewal bill cleared the House by a vote of 249 to 136 with floor leaders constantly emphasizing its temporary nature. See U.S. *Congressional Record,* 80th Cong., 2nd sess., part 3, pp. 2997-98. Also see Denis Sinclair Philipps, "American People and Compulsory Military Service" (unpublished Ph.D. dissertation, New York University, 1955).

[88]The fight over UMT continued. In 1951 the Universal Military Training and Service Act was passed, which was the statute under which the System

operated until 1967. The law extended Selective Service for 4 years and called for implementation of UMT at a later date subject to further consideration and approval by Congress. The House took up the subject in 1952 but rejected it.

[89]Samuel Huntington, *The Common Defense* (New York: Columbia University Press, 1961), p. 240.

[90]Walter Millis, *Individual Freedom and the Common Defense* (New York: The Fund for the Republic, 1957).

[91]*Washington Post,* December 2, 1965. See also Minnesota poll of the Minneapolis *Star and Tribune,* in which 82 per cent favored continuing the draft and 71 per cent favored two years of civil or military service for everyone.

[92]Denis S. Philipps, *op. cit.,* after reviewing the history of conscription in America comes to a somewhat opposite conclusion. It is based, however, on the assumption that finding compulsory clauses in militia statutes constitutes an accepted and operative conscription system. I feel this assumption is clearly unwarranted.

3

Institutional Adaptations to American Political Culture

The traumatic draft riots of the Civil War probably would have occurred regardless of what administrative system had been developed. Negativism was directed toward the policy more than its administration. But the men who designed Selective Service had nothing to say about whether or not there should be conscription. They started with the assumption that there would be conscription and that their task was to devise an administrative system that would make it palatable. In drawing upon the experiences of the Civil War, Crowder and his associates seemed most sensitive to issues of local and civilian control. In the aftermath of World War I they felt in retrospect that their main purpose and principal success had been in developing a System in harmony with these two values.

General Hugh Johnson, who was once an assistant to Crowder, stated that

> It was only by taking a firm stand and having local people appointed on local draft boards that we got by with it. We tried to get away from the military aspect at the time of the draft.[1]

The responsibility of local boards for "impressment" and the handling of complaints was to Johnson "the saving of the whole draft system."[2]

Whether Johnson and all Selective Service officials that have followed him are correct in perceiving local and civilian control as the crucial factors in acceptance matters little. In point of fact, General Oakes in 1866 had declared that the most crucial factor in future acceptance would be replacement of door-to-door enrollment by officers with the requirement that citizens report for enrollment. One might reasonably wonder if one of Selective Service's central myths was ever well founded in reality. What matters is the designers' perception of American attitudes and their resultant behavior in structuring and operating Selective Service. The institution from 1917 to the present has seen favorable attitudes toward localism as the most important value to which it must respond. Concern with playing down the military aspects of the System have been important but have gradually faded as antimilitarism has ebbed. Identification with localism, however, has remained to this day at the core of Selective Service's institutional character.

The Myth of Decentralization: The Appeal to Localism

The basic institutional myth of the System is that it is decentralized.[3] It makes this claim in all representations to its environment.[4] The members of the institution feel that a claim of decentralization is essential to maintaining legitimacy and acceptance for its conscription function. As Felix Nigro remarks:

> In the American environment, centralization is generally condemned and decentralization praised; political forms are decentralized and the virtues of local initiative and responsibility emphasized.[5]

But as the current trend of cities seeking direct federal aid indicates, Americans are more likely to honor decentralization in the abstract than as a basis for action.

To attempt to affirm or deny that the System is decentralized is an exercise in futility, since the term is too vague and formless.[6] Let it merely be said that decentralization usually means that decision-making is dispersed to field units, and seldom means that final political responsibility for those decisions is also dispersed. Politically elected or appointed executives perform a particular role—to make or carry out authoritative, legitimate, and binding decisions. The President and the Director of Selective Service must therefore see that the deferment-induction decisions, which are statutorily the sole and final province of the local boards (subject to appeals), are considered legitimate, authoritative and binding. This means that local board decisions must be controlled within certain limits, and though the statutes make deferment-induction decisions the responsibility of the local boards, they simultaneously say that the boards shall hear and determine cases under rules and regulations prescribed by the President.

Decentralization is thus a very delicate matter of balancing demands by means of delegation and control. Political culture demands that decision-making be delegated to local boards (at least those controlling the destinies of the System feel this is so). But at the same time the decisions made must satisfy the function assigned to Selective Service as its part in the total political system — the withdrawal of necessary military manpower from the civil population with minimal disruption of the economy and a minimum of political dissent. The demands of function and political culture are not always compatible. The functional demand of the overall system (procurement of manpower) may demand efficiency while the perceived demands of political culture may result in slowness and inefficiency. Inefficiency may be the cost of acceptance but that cost can never be allowed to become too high, for manpower needs must be met on demand. It is cross pressures such as these that make decentralization a delicate balance between delegation and control of decision-making.

The problems of balance inherent in decentralization have yet another facet and that is the sometimes contradictory demands of different values of political culture. The values of political culture are not necessarily a logically consistent and compatible set of values and attitudes. It is more likely that there is a constant "dialectic" among competing values.[7] For example, the positive value of localism has led to the institutionalization of "decentralization" or supposedly "local decisions." But it appears that other values, such as legal-rationalism, which demand equity, uniformity and consistency in decisions are now beginning to impinge upon localism. Local decisions do not always have the characteristics demanded by legal-rationalism and increasingly large segments of society are becoming aware of this fact. Thus decentralization must not only balance political culture against assigned function but also competing demands of political culture.

The myth of decentralization has one other function that is related to its identification with localism, that is the vital role it plays in sustaining the allegiance of thousands of local volunteer members. It is unlikely that the remarkable allegiance of these volunteers could be held without their believing that they played the crucial role in decision-making. Upper levels of the administration need to pay constant attention to sustaining board members' belief in their efficacy.

Decentralization and Control Mechanisms

In order to satisfy this complicated set of demands the System has developed a variety of control mechanisms to offset the local board "autonomy" that the decentralization myth demands.

Control rather than decentralization takes primacy in conversations with System officials. An official at state headquarters put it this way: "Sometimes board members get pretty far afield and you have to bring them back." The same concern for control was expressed at the national level in somewhat blunter terms when an official said, "Well you *do* have to keep discipline. Sometimes they get sore and quit—resign or sometimes you have to take it out of their hands."[8]

Value Integration

Decentralization can rest upon two major bases. Those who are politically responsible for decisions can delegate decision-making to subordinates because they are relatively certain that the subordinates share the same values as they do and therefore can be relied upon to make roughly the same decisions. James Heaphey refers to this as "value-integrated" decentralization. The other form possible is "professionally determined" in which subordinates are permitted to make decisions on the basis of their professional skills and expertise recognized as legitimate by both superiors and surrounding society.[9]

In representations to its environment Selective Service claims that its decentralization is "professionally determined," i.e. that local boards make expert decisions on the basis of their special knowledge by the registrant as his "friends and neighbors." But in practice decentralization rests on value integration. From the director to the local board members there exists a common outlook on national defense, conscription, foreign policy, the value of certain education and occupations, etc.

This integration of values has been achieved primarily by "closed personnel systems" which allow the System to selectively recruit and institutionalize members with minimal interference from noninstitutional sources. Board clerks, local board members, and the staffs of state and national headquarters are all products of these closed personnel systems. Philip Selznick has noted the relationship of decentralization to social integration.

> The need for centralization declines as the homogeneity of personnel increases. A unified outlook, binding all levels of administration, will permit decentralization without damage to policy. When top leadership cannot depend on adherence to its viewpoint, formal controls are required, if only to take measures that will increase homogeneity. On the other hand, when the premises of official policy are well understood and widely accepted, centralization is more readily dispensable."[10]

The closed personnel systems provide homogeneity of viewpoint and uniform decision premises that make up the fundamental component of control so necessary for decentralization.[11]

A second means of securing value integration is General Hershey's personalistic style of leadership. Some might describe his leadership as charismatic. Through constant personal contact with all levels of the System he manages to give informal guidance and direction, and to establish and occasionally shift the general control parameters. Hershey meets with all state directors semiannually; he or trusted members of his staff attend regional conferences of state directors, state meetings of appeal board members and the personnel of state headquarters.[12] One of the national headquarters staff commented:

> I don't think there is anybody in government that makes as many speeches and travels as much as the "Old Man." Why he must make — I don't know how many a week — but an awful lot and each one is just as witty, interesting and informative as can be. He has a natural talent for it.[13]

Hershey reinforces these official contacts by easy accessibility. According to another official:

> The "Old Man's" door is always open. Board members and clerks from any corner of the country are made to feel like they're visiting a personal friend. He's never too busy to see anyone. Internal problems never really get too big because anyone can walk in there and get a hearing. He has a way of getting people to do what he wants and do their best without being high handed.[14]

A third means of integrating values is the "in-house organ" of the System which is titled *Selective Service*. It is a monthly publication featuring news of the System that has a folksy "family news" aura about it. Each issue features a monthly editorial by Hershey in which the outlines of a new general policy direction or rationalization for current policy can be ascertained. For example, in the midst of controversy over the deferment of college students and the induction of students who had led a sit-in in a local board office, an editorial appeared which emphasized that students were deferred on the basis of privilege not right, and that deferment was to be based upon preparation for a career which would contribute to the national interest. Even more interesting is the fact that this editorial appeared about the time local boards had received *formal* advice to consider inducting college drop-outs and school changers and *informal* (word-of-mouth) guidance to "get tough" in general with students.[15] *Selective Service* is thus supportive of and supplementary to other channels for policy guidance.

As soon as a man is recruited as a reserve board member or joins Selective Service as a reserve officer he begins to receive the monthly publication. Board clerks as well as all others connected with the System also receive it. Board members commented on how "useful" it was and one remarked, "I always enjoy reading it. I think ol' General Hershey's got some good things to say in there. It keeps you 'up' on things."[16] One high ranking official in national headquarters admitted that "it gives a sort of informal policy" to the thousands of System participants.[17] And another remarked:

> *Selective Service* is a good way to let out policy. I quote it all the time in correspondence [to state field representatives]. You have to look for what *isn't* there with the old man. That's the way it is in this outfit. You get so you're pretty good at reading between the lines. Once you get to know the "Old Man" it's no trick. But I'll tell you this, when he says "It would be my guess that local boards will," you can bet that about 4,000 boards are going to do it.[18]

Regulations

Resting upon the foundation of value integration are other more explicit control mechanisms. Among the mechanisms that are the most comprehensive but least specific in terms of effecting the actual decisions are the Systems' regulations. They are derived from statutes and developed on the basis of executive orders signed by the President. Like most executive orders they are largely a product of the agencies' desires and initiatives subject to Presidential review.

The regulations tend to reflect only the broadest matters on which there is the widest possible consensus within the System, the executive branch and the government as a whole, and have the force and effect of law. An example of such a regulation would be a change in the order of call which dropped married men to a lower priority or assigned new priorities to different age groups.

Auditors[19]

Logically the next control mechanism that might be discussed would be the auditors sent out at least once a year by state headquarters to review the classification actions of local boards. However it is not at all clear that logic prevails in this matter.

General Hershey claims that the auditors "try to see that there is some basis in fact on each classification and try to see that there is some continuity throughout the state in the action." They may bring things "to the attention of the local board for reconsideration but they don't always go along with the auditor."[20] But as one clerk said: "There is no way they can really review board decisions for anything but the grossest violations of regulations and that just doesn't happen."[21] System participants at all levels dismissed the audits as inconsequential and few board clerks could remember when the last one was held. They obviously did not manifest any anxiety over them.

It is possible that the System may attempt to utilize this control mechanism more fully, though it is hard to see how board decisions can be meaningfully audited. Published reports in the spring of 1968 indicated that the System was augmenting its auditor staff.

Oral Communications and Field Representatives

One of the things that startles the observer of the System is the widespread use of oral communications. Clerks constantly receive policy guidance by phoning state headquarters and state headquarters is in constant touch with national. The purpose is to avoid written, blanket commitments on policy, and to keep policy decisions confined to individual cases on an *ad hoc* basis as far as possible.

Both General Hershey and the state director of this study were described by subordinates as men who use "word of mouth" for policy direction. The authorization given the author by the state director to study local boards was made by a phone call. When it was pointed out that this had resulted in one board's refusal to cooperate, an official expressed regret but said, "That's the way the General operates. He prefers word of mouth. It's safest and his written word doesn't come back to haunt him."[22] In fact the state director confirmed this when he described the use of his field representatives:

> They [field representatives] are some of our key people. They talk to the board clerks and see that policy is carried out. You see part of my job is to protect General Hershey and so you want to be careful what you put in writing. But I can tell the field representatives what policy is and they can go out and see that it is carried out.
>
> I draw many of the field representatives from among the board clerks. So they know the ins and outs of the System, the problems of the clerks and the boards and the regions in which they operate.
>
> I meet with them about once a month or perhaps more often when things are popping.[23]

It was also pointed out that the state director often initiated major policy and process changes by meeting with board members and clerks of a region and discussing the matter. An official in national headquarters was asked, "How do you get out the word on policy?" His reply was automatic and instead of referring to written communications he said, "Well, we are in touch with the state directors every day. There's also the Annual Conference of Directors. Take the matter of the Peace Corps. When the director decided, we had no trouble getting the word out."[24]

Local Board Clerks

It should also be noted that the clerks which represent the full-time, compensated and bureaucratic element of the System help maintain control. The volunteer board members would feel overwhelmed if confronted with all the written communications. As one put it:

> I know for a fact that it would take a man at least two hours a day to read the stuff that comes from Washington and Harrisburg. I didn't have time for that sort of thing. We hired a clerk we could trust and turned the whole thing over to her. She was a crackerjack.[25]

An official at national headquarters described the clerks in a way that made their control function clear:

> [Clerks are] one of the ways to keep all these different boards on the beaten path. The clerks after all are the ones who keep up on all the regulations and policy. Board members couldn't possibly do that so we rely pretty heavily on the clerks.[26]

Other Written Communications

In addition to the regulations there exists a wide variety of formal communications. (See Table 2) They include the following:

TABLE 2. Selective Service Formal Communications Channels

National Headquarters issues:
  Operations Bulletins to State Headquarters and Local Boards
  Local Board Memoranda to State Headquarters and Local Boards
  Local Board Bulletins to State Headquarters and Local Boards
  Memoranda to State Directors at State Headquarters

State Headquarters issues:
  Local Board Advices to Local Boards

---

(1) Operations Bulletins (From national to state headquarters and local boards). These interpret regulations under changing conditions. An example is Operations Bulletin #46, titled *Graduate and Professional School Students*. It defines a "full-time course of study" and "progress through his program at a normal rate" and contains the significantly vague sentence: "Graduate students making *satisfactory progress* should be given an opportunity to complete degree requirements."[27]

(2) *Local Board Advices* (From state headquarters to local boards). Their purpose is to interpret and adjust the Operation Bulletins in light of particular state conditions. An example is Agdustria Local Board Advice No. 496 titled, *Teachers*. The entire text reads: "It is the policy of the Selective Service System to consider favorably requests for deferment of qualified teachers at all levels of the educational system who are engaged full time in the practice of their profession." Quite often local board clerks make notes on the file copy which reflects word-of-mouth clarification from upper echelons. This one in Hill City files had on it the notation, "Have a degree."[28]

(3) *Memoranda to State Directors*, occasionally referred to by World War II designation, *State Director Advices* (From national headquarters to state directors). These are more likely to deal with narrower aspects of administration but may have important policy implications that must be filtered or altered by state directors to fit their circumstances. Sample topics range

from national Civil Service Career awards, to a Memorandum which quotes a presidential memorandum: "It is my desire that ... agencies help provide personnel for International Organizations."[29]

(4) *Local Board Memoranda* (From national headquarters through state headquarters to local boards). These are usually temporary changes in processes that are intended to be national in uniformity, often with policy significance. They do not set forth policy but require boards to take some action in carrying out Local Board Advices and such action may have policy implications. An example is a Memorandum directing local boards to begin processing June graduates for induction.

(5) *Local Board Bulletins* (From national headquarters through state headquarters to local boards). These deal with non-policy matters of a technical nature relating to the management of local board offices. An example is Local Board Bulletin No. 901 titled *Lease Contracts Covering Local Board Premises.*[30]

Local board members are not statutorily *required* to follow the policies (only regulations) set forth in the written communications, and often they do not. Most are probably ignorant of them; or if they have seen them, they have forgotten the bulk of these communications and are only aware of them when the clerks bring them to their attention. Value integration is the factor which assures general conformity and is supplemented by the desire of most boards for *any* information or guidance that will help them. This desire means that they turn to the communications, or more specifically to the custodians and interpreters of them—the clerks.[31]

"Appeals to the Directors" and "Appeals by the Directors"

The control mechanism with by far the most pervasive influence is the handling by National and State Manpower Divisions of registrant's or intercessors' informal "appeals to the directors"; the more formalized "appeals by the directors" to the appeal boards; and requests by directors to boards to reopen and reconsider cases.[32] In its usual understated fashion a System monograph says:

> Other coordinating activities of the Director included his power to take an appeal to an appeal board, of the local board determination regarding any registrant. He could similarly take an appeal to the President from an appeal board decision. The significance of this authority with reference to local and appeal board coordination should not be overlooked. Of further importance along the same

line was his power upon written request to cause a local board to reopen and consider anew the classification of a registrant.[33]

The official at national headquarters quoted earlier was less subtle:

> Well, you *do* have to keep discipline. Sometimes they get sore and quit — resign or sometimes you have to take it out of their hands. But the law gives State and National Directors power to review a case and they should have that power. They can take an appeal and that *ought* to be possible.[34]

Neither the regulations nor the law mention "appeals to the directors" but a large volume of work has grown up around this informal control mechanism, and it should be emphasized that it is not merely an appeal channel but a control mechanism as well. Because Selective Service takes an institutional stance designed to secure compliance without direct compulsion, it leaves itself open to a wide variety of efforts for special informal appeals and delays. All are tolerated in the apparent belief that eventually a cathartic effect will be achieved and the registrant will accept induction, satisfied that he has had a fair opportunity to appeal his case. Or barring that happy eventuality, he may fall into some deferrable category that will remove him as a problem for the System. "Appeals to the directors" grow out of such circumstances.

The volume of these informal appeals stems from three sources. First, the formal appeals channel is slow and crisis tends to clog it easily. Second, the myth of decentralization itself creates a need for such a procedure. If, as often happens, a registrant fails to avail himself of the many opportunities to appeal his case with the result that his hysterical parents or a powerful and influential intercessor descend upon the local board clerk, it is felt that the clerk should be afforded some protection by being able to deflect the situation to higher headquarters.[35] Or looked at from another angle, the clerks should not have in their hands the power to stay an induction in situations with such potential for damaging the institutional image.

But the most important reason for its use is the fact that it gives higher echelons a means of wielding flexible control over policy while sustaining the myth of decentralization. A description of World War II operations emphasized:

> The law of supply and demand was, throughout the life of Selective Service, a determining factor in developing classification policies, and regulations were rightly and justly written and revised to accommodate changing needs and conditions.[36]

The functional task of Selective Service — the efficient delivery of manpower on demand — requires great flexibility. On the one hand there are the ever fluctuating quotas which may vary from almost non-existent to a sizeable portion of a local board's available manpower. On the other hand there are the variations in the criteria for deferment which arise constantly from a variety of circumstances.

This requisite flexibility is difficult to maintain in the face of the means of legitimization, i.e. decentralization, indirect compulsion, and elaborate appeals procedures. If the System relies solely upon regulations or even on its other written communications it badly cuts its flexibility. There are factors today that demand even greater flexibility than regulations or other communications can provide.[37]

By supplementing formal appeals with informal channels, Selective Service can more readily respond to changing demands for military manpower and for deferments. The state directors have the power to stay induction, revise policy through Local Board Advices, ask a local board to reconsider a decision, refer the matter to the national director, or take a "director's appeal" to the state appeal board. Observations in this study point to a director's request to reopen a case and in the more or less explicit threat to take a case to the appeal board as the most common means of achieving compliance.

The national director can ask a board to reopen and reconsider a case. He may take an appeal to the National Appeals Board and he may classify a registrant IV-F himself if it is in the interest of national security. The latter action is taken to defer persons employed in C.I.A., the National Security Agency or some other classified activity vital to national security.[38]

The informal appeals to directors not only provide the flexibility needed in balancing the myth of decentralization against control but they also afford an opportunity to improve legitimacy of decisions by giving more uniformity to board decisions. If a flood of appeals come in from school boards on behalf of teachers facing induction, the System is alerted to the fact that certain influential segments of communities are unhappy about drafting teachers and they are unhappy enough to appeal through informal means rather than letting the registrant proceed through the cumbersome formal process. They are also alerted as to which boards are inducting teachers and thus out of step with the other boards. Corrective action can then be taken to see that legitimacy and acceptance of System decisions is not threatened by too much disuniformity or too many controversial inductions that stir influential and articulate groups to opposition.

The "appeals by the directors" provided for by the regulations are equally important as a control device. They may be initiated as a result of an "appeal to the director" that asked for intercession or as a result of state headquarters having reviewed reports of local board actions. An "appeal by the director" permits corrective uniformity. State and national headquarters can generally obtain the sort of decision they want from the state and national appeal boards. One official put it this way: "When we appeal something to the boards we don't have much doubt about how it's going to come out."[39] And Donald Stewart points out that

> appeal boards worked in close collaboration with the administrators of various state headquarters (some of the appeal boards had their offices in the state headquarters buildings) and aided the administrators of the state headquarters in the standardization of local board procedures and in the promulgation of policies determined by the headquarters.[40]

This is not to imply some sort of wrong-doing by headquarters, nor that some harm necessarily befalls the registrant. The situation is apparently much more simple and subtle than that.

State headquarters will take an appeal to the state board when they feel that a local board's decision was wrong, inequitable, or out of line with policy. Since this is the natural reason for taking an appeal it is also the natural reason for the appeal board to perceive this to be so and to issue a decision that conforms to the desires of state headquarters. This may or may not work to the advantage of the registrant. Similarly at the national level, it is readily apparent to the National Appeal Board what national headquarters wants in the way of a decision. The latter will likely be taking an appeal if it is in disagreement with the last decision made.[41]

Thus it is that the two channels of appeal are most important mechanisms of political control, maintaining within allowable limits an output that will satisfy system requirements, the requirements being "*adequate* but *accepted*" inductions.[42]

This lengthy discussion of control mechanisms should not leave the impression that power in the System is totally transitive or in other words that it is a system where upper echelons always prevail in any test of strength. Upper echelons must take care that in exercising control they do not damage the institutional image of local board autonomy. The myth of decentralization creates very real constraints upon upper echelons. They are not able to exercise control at will and in any manner they please.

A division head at national headquarters expressed the dilemma of the System:

> Well, you know, four of five guys like you might sit around a table and argue and discuss the facts of a case. And maybe you finally say "That son-of-a- —— is I-A." Not cause you have it in for him but just on the facts. *Then* someone comes along from National and says they want to review it! Well — you say to yourself — "What the ——?! I'm not getting any pay for this — grumble, grumble." Then you've got problems.[43]

Accordingly, headquarters personnel constantly make diplomatic missions to meet with boards over problematical cases in which it is hoped the boards will reconsider their decision. The headquarters representative wears his military uniform and his most tactful and friendly demeanor. His approach is usually to listen patiently to the board and the problems it faces in the case until a certain cathartic effect has been achieved and then to explain in a confiding manner the problems faced by headquarters in the case.

Sometimes, however, these efforts fail and a board remains intransigent. If the consequences of the board's decision seem unlikely to embarrass the System or create notoriety, headquarters will yield to the board. In such instances a wrong, inequitable or disuniform decision is viewed as the price of legitimacy. But if the price for permitting the board to have its way seems too great, headquarters turns to such things as "appeals by the director," or more likely the threat of them, while at the same time trying to avoid antagonizing the boards.

Decentralization thus represents an operational, subjective, reality for the System. It is a mode of operation, an institutional myth that is functional for the System but also creates problems for it. Local boards *are* the basic decision-making units but they make their decisions within control limits set by the upper echelons that are responsible for those decisions. Furthermore, the upper echelons can and do vary the control limits in order to maintain an equilibrium between the sometimes conflicting demands of political culture and the functional demands levied by the Department of Defense. The institution must use great discretion in exercising control and it is not always successful. The power relationship is non-transitive, like a card game in which jacks sometimes take kings. Decentralization is not only functional in the above sense

— as the heart of operations — but it is functional in several derivatory ways.

Other Functions of Decentralization

Decentralization has become functional to Selective Service in some ways not clearly related to variables of political culture. The first of these is the influence of decentralization on the patterned interaction of the interest groups.

Interest Groups

Most political bureaucracies operate in a milieu in which interest groups are extremely influential. As David Truman has indicated, every high level administrator is in politics vis-a-vis interest groups. He must deal with them, maintaining the strength of supporters and bargaining with his opposition, or resign. He must try to make the controversial policy routine by getting an equilibrium of interests.[44]

The pressure or potential pressure of interest groups is a major source of Selective Service's institutional posture and oral policy communication, emphasis upon the individual nature of a case, and avoidance of general policy direction unless necessary. The II-A occupational deferments were particularly important in this regard because the registrant seeking deferment on the basis of a critical occupation was most likely to be valuable to someone — that someone often constituting a powerful interest group.[45]

The busiest and largest branches of state and national headquarters are the Manpower Divisions. As the director of another division said, "Manpower is the main operational unit here. They generate all the action. Rest of us just support it."[46] This situation exists because the Manpower Division comes close to making the national manpower policy that no one openly admits exists.

While no one uses the term national manpower policy, it is hard to construe it as anything else. To be sure, it is largely unwritten, informal and made on an *ad hoc*, individual case basis. But by using "appeals to the directors," requests to boards to reopen a case, and "appeals by directors," the manpower divisions negotiate with interest groups — resolving conflict and reaching consensus as to which inductions and deferments are equitable and in the national health, safety, and interest. One official said philosophically:

All this balancing of interests, and appeals, and fighting over cases, when all is said and done is what democracy is all about. But you can't write national manpower policy. Too many [interest groups] involved in keeping Viet Nam and the Economy both going.[47]

Perhaps the American political system has avoided open and explicit manpower policy not only because it runs cou..ter to our political culture but also because of the extreme difficulty with interest groups that it would occasion. For manpower policy has the potential to affect more interest groups than virtually any other public policy. The more centralized the organization administering a manpower-related policy, the clearer a target it is for interest groups seeking to influence the administration of the policy. The more decisions are guided by specific, standardized, and detailed criteria (in other words the narrower the control limits), the more interest groups will strive to influence the development of such guiding criteria and their application.

One good example of the difficulty to be encountered in developing specific standards is the badly outdated Critical Skills List developed in 1955 through the joint efforts of several government agencies.[48] Observation of local boards revealed that it was scarcely, if ever, referred to. A national official pointed out that

> With Viet Nam coming on top of as nearly full employment as possible, everybody is screaming for men. Lot of people around here would have been happy if the President had given them something to hang deferments on — some written hook, so to speak. But he hasn't. Still have the Critical Skills List. It was such a big fight to get together. Many are howling for another. There's the ingredients for a new one over there [gesturing toward files]. But we can't hold to it — it's not binding — can't be.[49]

The perils of putting in writing a policy touching upon manpower and affecting interest groups were illustrated by a state director.

> There was a naval captain who was State Director over in Virginia — Captain B — and he sat down and wrote a memorandum to all boards saying, "Now, I want you to be pretty tough on agricultural deferments because the nation has all this surplus food." Well, it took only 24 hours for that memo to hit the floor of Congress — "Mr. President, what business has General Hershey got telling us how to run American agriculture?"[50]

Unintentionally, Selective Service was admirably structured to minimize these problems. Decentralization is invaluable in handling interest group pressure to which the System responds. The

Manpower Divisions of national and state headquarters have as their central concern relations with interest groups and negotiation over exceptions to policy. The System's greatest flexibility and cushion against pressures comes from its ability to point to 4,000 plus local boards as the "real" decision makers. If a few chemical engineers were facing induction or had been inducted, the System did not need to confront the question of whether or not chemical engineers were essential to the national health, safety, and interest with attendant lobbying for revision of the regulations or written policy. It could handle the matter through the appeal channels described above or by oral policy guidance and could always respond to pressures by saying that there had been no central decision made concerning the deferment-induction of chemical engineers. This, it could be said, was a matter for the local boards to decide. Those not satisfied with such a reply have usually had American political culture, specifically individualism and localism, thrown back at them.

> Mr. Stafford: General, I would like to pursue right along the line of questioning that you have just been discussing and ask you, should the Selective Service make an effort to assure that its regulations are interpreted identically throughout the country?
>
> General Hershey: Well, in the first place, I would like to see your maples this fall and the maple syrup next spring, so I want to be as generous as I can. But in the first place, I think you are dealing with human beings, and I think you are asking for somebody to create a machine that will defeat human beings, and I don't believe you have liberty and uniformity at the same time.
>
> Now, that is not a very good answer, but on the other hand, I have more confidence in those people who live up in Vermont, for them to decide who ought to go from up there than I have — and they have more compassion, even when they are a little granity — they have more compassion than any of these machines have.[51]

Also to be considered is the diversity of circumstances in a nation of this size and heterogeneity. The more detailed the policy or decision criteria, the more difficult becomes the problem of adjustments. General Hershey gave some indication of this in the 1966 draft hearings:

> Mr. Love: Are there any guidelines established?
> General Hershey: Sure.
> Mr. Love: In the matter of classification?
> General Hershey: They have more guidelines, generally, than they can read.

> In the first place — well, no, but it is true. For instance I am not overworked, but I suppose I have 25, 30 people a week that come in with the exact things I ought to put out. For instance, I had a college — I will not name it, because I am not advertising them — but they came in yesterday and all they want me to do is explain the trimester plan which they have, which is different from most everybody else's, and they want me to furnish each local board with that, so they will know they have a trimester plan, so when you are out in the wintertime you are in in the summertime, your vacation is at a different time.[52]

Selective Service finds it occasionally convenient or necessary to turn to interest groups for assistance in making decisions. This occurs with particularly powerful groups or in circumstances where expert or professional knowledge is needed for a decision. Examples are doctors, dentists, veterinarians, scientists, and technicians. Whenever it seeks such assistance, however, the System is careful to protect the integrity of the decentralization myth by insisting that such assistance constitutes "advice only" to local boards.

To assert that decentralization disperses the access points for interest groups is not to say that access is any more difficult for them. It would seem to be easier. But the process is less visible and therefore less dangerous to Selective Service. What takes place in fifty, small, obscure offices that are not quite federal but not quite state in nature, is far less visible than if this activity was all concentrated on the national headquarters of the System. Decentralization also eliminates questions of providing for or accommodating regional differences in national policy.

The state director in this study was described this way by a subordinate:

> He knows the right people — travels in the top circles. Now take the Scientific Advisory Committee he established. It's hand picked by him with presidents of U. S. Steel, General Electric, Westinghouse, the State University and so on. You know the General was a stock broker in Blank City — was in a big investment house before he joined Selective Service in 1943. Of course, his wife was well-to-do and knew "the right people" so to speak.[53]

Another official said of Agdustria's director:

> The General loves to lock horns with these groups that are always stomping in here. There's always someone representing unions, companies, farmers, wanting some consideration for their special problem. He had a bunch of dairy farmers in the other day. He let

them go on for half an hour of belly-achin' and then pointed out that dairy farmers in New York had drawn up the dairying part of the policies we use for agricultural deferments. He knows how to handle them.[54]

State directors and their Manpower Divisions were therefore in a position to wield the control mechanisms described previously so as to respond to pressures at the state level in a comparatively inconspicuous way. If a state had trouble recruiting state police officers the matter could be handled by appealing to a state director; if an industry which was the major employer for a town felt its operation would be in jeopardy if it lost a floor supervisor (he and the employer having neglected to seek occupational deferment), these and thousands of other situations could be handled by an informal appeal to the director.

The Manpower Division of the state headquarters studied operated in an atmosphere of sustained semi-crisis. Long distance phone calls and telegrams came from every part of the state and from Washington. Letters poured in from corporations, football coaches, implement dealers, congressmen, distraught parents, etc. The work was divided along functional lines with one officer handling students, another occupational deferments, etc. Many long distance calls would come directly to the director's office. If the party seemed important enough the director would take it while secretaries scurried to the files to see if "there is anything on this one."

The same situation prevailed in the Manpower Division at national headquarters. An official spoke of interaction with interest groups in this way:

> H——, everyone claims a critical occupation. How are you going to decide? Well, one way is to keep contact with the experts in different fields and we are in constant touch. On students Colonel —— is up on that. He knows all the college presidents and registrars, and meets with them often. We also have good liaison with the Department of Defense and with the Department of Labor. Industry is in here all the time.[55]

Public policy must inevitably make a myriad of adjustments and accommodations. A decentralized Selective Service is extremely functional when one thinks of the sacrificial nature of the law and its far reaching effects. To be sure, a price must be paid in a certain amount of "wrong" or inequitable decisions but this is considered tolerable if kept within control limits that protect the System's legitimacy.

Decentralization and Congress

Decentralization has been extremely valuable to the System in identifying with the localism bias of Congress. Every freshman who has taken Introduction to American Government has come away with an awareness of such a bias on the part of Congress. As William S. White says, if Thomas Jefferson could return to Washington tomorrow

> the only institution that would not seem surpassingly strange to him would be the House of Representatives. For the House yet remains an anachronistic embodiment of many things in which he believed so much — the due and proper dominance of agrarian life over city life; the deliberate separation and fragmentation of Federal power; the primacy of the small over the large, and of local government over central government. Take it as it is today, the House chamber does not, in terms of human occupants, appear vastly different from the House of a century and a half ago.[56]

Or we can look to Marion Irish's more general description: "the organization and electoral base of Congress makes it more responsive than the President to conservative and local interests."[57]

Selective Service describes itself as an independent executive agency reporting directly to the President. It is thus prepared to draw upon the resource of national prestige which the institution of the presidency provides. But simultaneously the System has worked to establish a semi-autonomous position in the "no man's land" between Congress and the presidency which separation of powers has created.

The System has successfully avoided incorporation into other departments. It was placed under the War Manpower Commission in the Office of War Mobilization for one year during World War II; and the First Hoover Commission recommended that it be placed in the Department of Labor in the postwar era. Selective Service officials readily admitted using congressional allies to thwart these efforts.[58]

An example of the System's use of Congress to protect it lies in the story behind the Annual Report of the Director. An official of national headquarters told it in this manner:

> We had decided this provision that would let a kid enlist in the Guards or Reserves when he got his notice was a good thing. We got up before committee and Uncle Carl [Carl Vinson, Chairman, House Armed Services Committee] said, "General Hershey, I understand you have some opinions on this." Well, later in the day the Old Man got a call from the White House. He got over there and

Institutional Adaptations to American Political Culture

General Marshall was there and complained that General Hershey wasn't following the "party line." Well, General Hershey said, "They asked me." Well, he came back pretty unhappy. So I went to Vinson next day and asked him not to question the Old Man about that matter 'cause he would answer and it would get him in trouble. Vinson was madder than h—— about that and he said, "What can we do?" Well, I had a suggestion and we got written into law the requirement that the Director present an annual report to Congress. And now when Pentagon crowds us we just say, "Look, boys, the law says we have to report to Congress."[59]

Its success in such efforts is largely attributable to the relationship between decentralization and the localistic bias of Congress. Congressmen can scarcely be oblivious to the fact that there are 42,991 plus members of Selective Service.[60] More importantly, these members are dispersed into every corner of the country. One can hardly conceive of a more thorough grass-roots coverage of the country than that represented by the System. Furthermore, these members, while they may not be community leaders, are at least informed and articulate men. The characteristics of congressmen are strikingly similar to those of board members. Irish and Prothro characterize congressmen this way:

Most men come to Congress as we would expect, from occupations of at least upper-middle class standing.... Lawyers account for more than half the membership of Congress, and businessmen and bankers fill almost a third of the seats. Congressmen are similarly unrepresentative in family background, race, ethnic origins, education and religion. The groups of high social status enjoy a disproportionately large share of offices in comparison with their proportion of the total population; groups of lower status tend to be virtually excluded from office.[61]

This description is similar to the social background of board members in this study.

Irish and Prothro point out that two crucial variables in the ability of an interest group to be influential are the geographic distribution of its members, and the similarities of its members' socio-economic backgrounds to the politicians they seek to influence.[62] Redford and Truman assert that the degree of involvement of group members and the relative conservatism of their goals are variables of interest group power.[63] Involvement of most Selective Service members is of course high and their main goal, if aroused, is conservative System maintenance. Therefore, on all the above counts the members of Selective Service have an unusual capability to influence Congress if they are moved to do so.

Few Congressmen have directly attacked Hershey or the local boards. If criticism has been leveled at any aspect of the System it is usually preceded by fulsome praise of Hershey and/or board members.[64] Every congressman or Senator must reckon with the fact that his constituency holds a considerable number of Selective Service members, some of them prominent and influential or at least politically articulate, and that there is a considerable overlapping of membership between Selective Service and powerful interest groups which support it like the American Legion, the Veterans of Foreign Wars, the National Guard Association, etc.

A typical manifestation of the hold of Selective Service on Congress is the following:

> Mr. Ellsworth: General Hershey, I want to join my colleagues in saying how nice it is for you to come down and testify this morning.
>
> I know that many of the things that you have said this morning about your fine system are true, because my wife's father serves on a selective service board out in Kansas. He lost two sons in World War II. He was put on the local board and has remained on the board up until now.
>
> I know, also that every time he has come to Washington to visit us he has gone to your office to say hello. I know of the high esteem in which he holds you. I know the problems that he has in that community out there in Ellsworth County, with the registrants and their families. I know how much he relies on the local clerks and office managers.[65]

In addition to this kind of grass roots contact between the System and Congress, there are System ties to influential politicians and National Guard leaders in state capitols. Through this linkage national headquarters can be on a first-name basis with influential political figures in a congressman's constituency. General Hershey is always capable of dropping a few important names from a congressman's state into any reply to a question during hearings.

This lengthy consideration of decentralization, its meaning and relation to control, its relationship to the localism component of political culture, and the power patterns that stem from such a relationship, seems justifiable in view of the centrality of the concept to Selective Service's structure and process and its compatibility with the American political system. Consideration shall now be given to the relation between the System's structure and processes and other variables of political culture.

Anti-Militarism and Selective Service as a Civilian Agency

It would be interesting to know whether the public perceives of Selective Service as a military or a civilian organization. It is probable that the majority of people do not think beyond the local board and that it is visualized as civilian. This was the intention behind the development of the System. It is also probable that they would be surprised to learn that military men staff the key positions in state and national headquarters. Alf Evers wrote a highly popular book on Selective Service which aimed at informing the high school student on the operation of the System and of his obligation. In it he spoke of his surprise at finding that the System was not a purely civilian agency.

> I knew before I began working on my report on the draft that the Selective Service System was classed officially as a civilian organization. But I soon found that as of 1956 the National Director and all but two of his principal assistants were military men — mostly colonels. Of the fifty-six State Directors, fifty-two were officers of the armed forces.[66]

While Selective Service makes no special effort to hide the fact that it is not exactly civilian in composition, neither does it do anything to alter the image the public seems to have of it as civilian. Evers notes:

> I did not find the Selective Service officials whom I interviewed on this point very eager to discuss it. One denied that the upper levels of the system were dominated by military men until I showed him the figures.[67]

In fact Selective Service has in the past gone to some effort to avoid the appearance of militarism. In a memorandum to all state directors in 1940, at a time when the System was particularly concerned about acceptance, the following directions were given:

> October 16, 1940
> National Headquarters has received a number of inquiries regarding the wearing of uniforms by officers connected with the Selective Service System. Since it is believed desirable the entire emphasis be placed on the civilian nature of Selective Service, National Headquarters has adopted the following ruling:
> National Guard officers, members of State Detachments, Navy, Marine, or Officers Reserve Corps assigned to the Selective Service

System will neither wear uniforms at the State Headquarters nor in the field.

With kindest personal regards, I am
Sincerely,
Lewis B. Hershey
Lt. Col., Field Artillery,
Executive[68]

A System monograph also was candid about the conscious effort on the part of the System to manipulate the symbols of political culture by appearing to be civilian.

> It appears at the outset that the Army and Navy were definitely committed to the assignment of officers in the formative period of Selective Service during the 1920's and 1930's because that was the only way an organization expressly designed to study and plan the System could function without legislation. When the program had reached the point where a law was required to activate it, the role of the armed forces was deemphasized to guard against criticism on the part of the general public. Civilian direction, on the other hand, was given considerable emphasis and the general understanding was that the operation would be carried out under such auspices.[69]

In correspondence with the author, Alf Evers discussed the "civilian impression" left by the System.

> Public acceptance of the Selective Service System is a remarkable phenomenon. I came to the conclusion that the acceptance stems from the outward appearance of being a civilian agency which the System gives to the public. Actually this civilian character is a shallow façade behind which a military organization makes policy and exercises complete control under the laws which set up the agency. The civilian members of local boards carry out policy and have little right to do anything but follow instructions.... I questioned a good many people about their attitudes toward board members and found that their subservience to the military was not realized nor indeed, when I brought it up — believed. A young man entering the office of his local board is likely to meet with a motherly lady or a mild, gray-haired man who answers his questions and seems as civilian as the clerk in the post office. There are no uniforms, there are no weapons to be seen, the whole first impact is that of a completely civilian agency. If a man objects to the way he is classified he finds local board clerks perfectly willing to have the man appeal—he is made to feel as far removed as possible from the military way of doing things.[70]

Institutional Adaptations to American Political Culture 75

Evers may overstate the control of upper echelons but it is likely that he captures with some accuracy the impression the System makes on the public.

Others have been surprised to learn that "military men" staff the upper echelons. One case taken to the federal courts rested on the defendant's challenge of the propriety of the presence of a uniformed member of the national headquarters staff at a local board meeting.[71]

Selective Service also encountered criticism during and after World War II for the use of military men. The criticism during the war grew out of a general effort on the part of the War Department to reduce the number of officer personnel assigned to the Washington area. Because of the widespread assumption both in and out of government that the System was civilian, it was most vulnerable in War Department efforts to reduce officer personnel in the area, and had to fight constantly to maintain and expand the officer personnel to meet the increased tempo of operations.[72] After the war, one of the major points at issue during Bureau of the Budget hearings over the 1948 Selective Service Act was the necessity and propriety of using military men.[73]

Of the 138 members of the national headquarters staff fifty-four are listed as military men. But as the roster of "Selective Service Officials, National Headquarters" shows, this means that all management positions are military with the exception of the Chief of the Division of Research and Statistics.[74] No accurate breakdown of the status of state headquarters personnel is available. Agdustria Headquarters had eight military men out of a staff of forty-nine, but this meant that all key positions save one were held by military men. Of the present fifty-six state directors all but nine carry military rank by their names. Many of them are serving concurrently as Adjutant Generals of the state National Guards. Martha Derthick points out that "a large majority of the state directors of Selective Service who are appointed by the governors, have been Guard officers, and many have been adjutants general, holding the two posts simultaneously."[75]

By many legal or formal definitions perhaps these men are not military. Most of them are National Guardsmen or Reservists from all branches of the service serving on extended active duty on a reimbursable basis. They are paid by the services which are reimbursed by the Selective Service System. If by some formal standard they are not "military," they nonetheless qualify in more important ways, i.e., in attitudes, values, and perceptions. General Hershey says of the Selective Service cadre, "If they're not National Guard, Reserves, or Military, they've served at one time or another. There's only one state director without a military background and he's a labor organizer. But he's sometimes more military than the military."[76] They are, in other words, functionally military regardless of formal definitions. For purposes of clarity the term paramilitary will be used in this study.

The original reasons for the use of paramilitary rest on several grounds. First there were the historic reasons. Conscription was first carried out by the Provost Marshal General's Bureau which was an integral part of the Military Establishment. This pattern was picked up in World War I, during which all important holders of office in the System were military, a natural outgrowth of the fact that it was an integral part of the War Department. In a war situation it is probable that the best source of military officers that could be found for such an important but secondary and non-command duty would be the older National Guardsmen who wanted to serve but in a less adventuresome and more sedate capacity. Earlier it was shown how some of these men kept the System alive during the interim years.

As the Joint Army Navy Selective Service Committee began to grow in influence and gather support, it turned for help to the military organization that reached into each state capitol, the National Guard. Most of the committee members were in fact a part of the Guard. They found in it a ready supply of manpower. The everpresent problem of peacetime Guardsman or reservist who wishes to continue to participate and collect points toward retirement is to "find a slot" or a "billet." Selective Service has always been a source of "slots" and training points, but to some it has been doubly attractive because a call to active duty would never entail the hardship of combat or place one in a war zone. In fact, active duty might scarcely disrupt the normal home life of the officer.

The paramilitary of the System's upper echelon constitute one of three closed personnel systems that are vital to maintaining the institution.[77] This personnel system that grew out of historic circumstances has been thoroughly institutionalized and now has a basis in the statute. It was first formally authorized as a Selective Service Reserve Program in 1947, but existed on an informal basis long before that. The University Military Training and Service Act states:

That any officer on the active or retired list of the armed forces, or any reserve component thereof with his consent, or any officer or employee of the United States who may be assigned or detailed to any office or position to carry out the provisions of this title — may serve in and perform the functions of such office or position without loss of or prejudice of his status as such officer in the armed forces or reserve component thereof...[78]

General Hershey and those on his staff handling personnel functions are able to maintain an autonomous personnel system in which they have control over recruitment and appointment, institutionalizing, training and promotion. Loyalty to the institution is thus nourished and maintained. Such men owe their jobs and status to no one outside the System, so there is no division of loyalty.

In fiscal 1965 the Selective Service Reserve program consisted of fifty-three National Guard units (each state, New York City, Puerto Rico and the District of Columbia) and eighty-one Reserve Training Units sponsored by all four of the armed forces. The program encompassed 761 Reserve Officers. The reserve program includes monthly meetings, two weeks' active duty, on-the-job training, correspondence courses, seminars, etc.[79]

Recruitment and the Selective Service Type

Because reservists are universally concerned about slots and points, there is a large pool of men available for recruitment into the Selective Service Reserve and thence into the System proper. Few are chosen, however, for the System is quite selective. An official involved in managing the reserve program remarked: "Well, we can be pretty picky. We get more volunteers than we need. We don't go looking for them."[80] Selective Service is not interested in recruiting the more adventurous reservist — the "combat type," who enjoys command, life in the field, or has a particular skill such as the fighter pilot. The System seeks a man that is attracted to the military, has Neo-Hamiltonian views and has high politico-administrative skills, but who will be content with the less exciting paramilitary role of Selective Service. The official quoted above described the type sought:

We usually don't look at a man till he is past thirty-five — mature, family man, settled in business, established in the community, etc. Maturity and experience are pretty important in the business of mobilization. A man has to deal with some high powered persons and groups and you can't have a kid doing it.[81]

Interviewees at all levels responded along similar lines when questioned on how they were recruited. All had been on active duty as officers in World War I, II, or in the Korean War, had liked it, and subsequently had resumed careers that seemed somewhat dull and unfulfilling after their military experience. Selective Service was a welcome opportunity to get close to the military again without being uprooted by a normal resumption of active duty. The reasons for turning to a Selective Service career varied. Some felt they were giving up successful careers in other fields to once again join the military and serve the nation; some seemed to feel they had reached a plateau of success in a civilian career or saw no great future prospects for advancement; others were simply looking for a good job that would not necessitate moving after the industry they were with closed down.

Martha Derthick notes that Guard officers (and presumably Selective Service officers) vary in their motivations for careers:

> Many top-ranking Guard officers have been prominent in their civil capacities, as professional men or business executives. For such men, membership in the Guard has been just one of many distinctions. But some observers feel that the Guard has also attracted men who, having in some degree failed in private life, seek alternative satisfactions in it. There they are endowed with the authority of rank and the prestige of the uniform of a United States Army officer. The satisfactions of Guard membership have not been available to them from any other source.[82]

Regardless of their motivations, all are drawn to "a desire for military service and the satisfactions associated with ... prestige of uniform and rank, involvement in a cause, excitement and a role to play in time of crises."[83]

> But there I was in 1943, the old warrior, in civilian clothes, while my children were in uniform. I had sons in the military and a daughter in the Nurse Corps. I ran into Colonel —— and I was saying, "I sure wish I could get into uniform." I was fifty-eight at the time and too old for anything. And he said, "Why don't you come down and join Selective Service?" And I said, "Why, I never thought of that!" So I came down. I thought they would give me a Major's rank but they started me out as just a Captain. A Captain at fifty-eight! You see, there is no age limit on a military man in Selective Service as there is in the regular military.[84]

Another officer recruited in peacetime was typical.

> Well, I worked for a while in Public Health after '45 but didn't much care for it. Seemed pretty dull. I guess to be real truthful I

missed the military. So I got to messing around with the National Guard. I was on the headquarters staff and they had a section working on Selective Service and I got involved in that. When the System started up again in '48 they offered me a spot so I came over. Been here ever since. Cuss it sometimes but I like it.[85]

The Selective Service Reserve is an excellent recruiting device. Not only does it provide an opportunity to train men but to screen them and institutionalize them as well. There is ample opportunity to see how interested the reservist is in the work, his attitudes, as well as capabilities. The active duty period when a reservist fills a position in the system for two weeks each year is particularly useful in this regard.

Functionality of the Paramilitary Cadre

What developed as necessity stemming from anti-militarism in American political culture has often turned out to be a virtue in the peculiar interface environment between the civil and military in which Selective Service operates. The System performs a military function (procuring military manpower) and responds to functional demands of the Military but simultaneously strives for acceptance by appearing to be civilian and responding to the demands of the civil society. Consequently an individual that can operate in a civil or military milieu with equal ease is desirable for smooth functioning of the System. One official in national headquarters put it this way:

> We are a bridge between the Military and the civilians. We live in both worlds. Local men [paramilitary in state headquarters] know their areas but they are military enough that they know what the Military is all about. Civilians don't fully trust the Military and the Military don't have any reason to trust civilians I guess. But we can speak the language of both — deal with the Pentagon and civilian local boards.[86]

The concern about "keeping out politics" is a natural one for a dispersed system which claims to operate on decentralized lines with formal "participation" of state governors and local residents. One way to avoid the introduction of ordinary political appointees is to rely upon the most surreptitiously political of institutions, the National Guard, for directors and headquarters personnel.[87] By always having on hand Guardsmen and Reservists that are trained in System processes, the already small temptation for politicians to use the offices as spoils is reduced almost to nonexistence.

Carrying out an informal manpower policy requires men that are not only mature and established but knowledgeable about various occupations and industries and in contact with them. But finding such men without their being overidentified with some segments of society is a problem. An official of national headquarters described the effort to obtain men from a spectrum of activities.

> We operate horizontally here — in other words — in mobilization everyone across a broad spectrum is affected. So we see if we have too many attorneys in one unit [Reserve and National Guard], we hold off on those and look for experts in other areas — agriculture, industry, etc.[88]

In reply to a follow-on question the officer gave the reason for relying on a paramilitary cadre drawn from functional segments of society to administer an informal manpower policy.

> Question: Do you ever hear criticism of using military officers in this civilian agency?
> Answer: Yes, some. The answer is that Military are not at issue. What counts is independence. You can't have a man appointed by the Secretary of Labor — 'cause then people would say he is a labor man — or some with agriculture or anything else.[89]

The paramilitary cadre is the perfect solution to the potential problems with interest groups in administering informal manpower policy. The military status of the cadre makes them invulnerable to charges of ties between them and interest groups, even though they may have been recruited from one of the groups with which they must deal. Their socialization to their role as military officers probably makes them largely impervious to blandishments of the groups they face.

Previous note has been made of the leverage the paramilitary status provides upper echelons in dealing with local boards. The local board members are heavily staffed with veterans who assume that the "military men" of upper echelons are experts and are more knowledgeable as to the needs of the Military and the national health, safety or interest than they are.

The paramilitary cadre are particularly important in setting institutional tenor. The members of Selective Service from local boards to national director are convinced they are performing a function that is indispensable to national defense. This feeling is enhanced by the paramilitary cadre. Clerks and board members enjoy contact with them and their feeling of participation in national defense is renewed and enhanced.

Institutional Adaptations to American Political Culture 81

One of the best manifestations of the spirit that the paramilitary cadre nourishes is a State Director Advice, which reads:

> The nature of the operation of the Selective Service System is unique in Government. In the type of its organization and in the composition of its membership, it cannot be compared with any other agency. As its name implies, it is a service organization with the responsibility for selection of men for the Armed Forces in accordance with laws and regulations that must be applied completely without partisan consideration. The members of the Selective Service System in many ways occupy positions similar to the uniformed members of the Armed Forces. The majority of those occupying executive positions in the Selective Service System are members of the Armed Forces. The duties performed by the members of the Selective Service System cannot be political in nature. Registrants must receive the same fair and just treatment that they would expect in a court of law.[90]

This sense of participation in a military organization or national defense effort was expressed often by board clerks. They were particularly fond of recalling the crises and long working hours of the Korean War or World War II. While they often began discussion in complaining tones, it quickly became evident that the quasi-military status of the System was a source of pride with them.

> We're just like the soldiers. I mean, we're on call whenever there's a crisis. Back during Korea and World War II, we worked like dogs, round the clock. Up before dawn and quit about midnight. 'Course, nobody's complaining. You know, it just had to be done and we're all responsible people.[91]

They clearly felt they were part of the national defense effort and above the ordinary routine of federal service.

The aura of temporariness that pervaded the System was another factor that made the cadre functional. If the System was dissolved or cut back, its personnel would carry on planning and training under reserve and Guard auspices without loss of expertise or it could perhaps even return to a voluntary basis as it had in the 1920's.

This touches upon another functional asset of the cadre — the Neo-Hamiltonian views of its members. With their commitment to a belief in strong national defense, they bring a sense of dedication and commitment to the institution that would be difficult to duplicate. This view assures that there will be no hesitancy or dissension within the System on the need for procuring manpower regardless of the foreign policy purposes to which they are put. And finally, Neo-Hamiltonianism assures the kind of dedication needed for System survival in the face of possible legislative discontinuance. It is doubtful that this institutional elan could be maintained without the paramilitary cadre.

In discussing World War II criticism of the paramilitary cadre a System monograph makes it clear that the most important functions of the paramilitary are its political impermeability, value to System survival, and the general advantages of a closed personnel system isolated from the rest of civil service.

> The inherent difficulty appears to be that while many points can be raised which support the reasoning for officer personnel as being highly desirable in the administration of Selective Service, none of these — training, security or discipline — are the ones normally applied to justify military personnel in nonmilitary agencies. In other words, the usual training of an officer does not necessarily fit him to be a valuable executive of the System. The matters dealt with are not of secret enough nature to require unusual security measures nor can officers be justified on the grounds that disciplinary action would be facilitated.
>
> The best rationalizations for officer personnel subsequent to their use to activate the System because of their training, were those related to *loyalty, detached and impersonal viewpoint, mobility and continuity of assignment, and freedom from influence or political pressure.*
>
> Civilian personnel, i.e., Civil Service appointees, offer nothing in the way of comparability here. The civilian staff of an organization undergoing liquidation is soon scattered to the four winds and, with no ready means of holding them, the maintenance of an organization is extremely difficult.[92]

Whether the changes in the Military outlined by Morris Janowitz mark a correspondent shift in civilian attitudes toward the military is not certain.[93] If so, it may be that the need to portray itself as a civilian agency is permanently past. But in any event, the paramilitary cadre has developed a functionality far beyond identification with political culture. It no longer merely aids the System in maintaining a civilian appearance but is crucial in maintaining a cadre of elite personnel and institutional elan.

Impermeability to Partisan Politics

The negative attitude of Americans toward "politics" is so well-known as to be axiomatic. Redford and Truman remark:

Institutional Adaptations to American Political Culture

The signs of our wholehearted commitment to Lord Acton's famous "law" of politics (that power tends to corrupt and absolute power to corrupt absolutely) are all about us. Few Americans are interested in assuming public office, and most parents would be upset were their children to embark on political careers. The notions that corruption, personal ambition, and compromise with principle mark the political life are commonplace.[94]

Despite the fact that localism has traditionally been viewed positively, the negative attitude is even more pronounced toward "local politics."

> When we think of local politics, the mind instantly fastens on certain emotion-charged terms: "the boss," "the machine," and "the courthouse gang."[95]

To most Americans "political" decisions mean partisan decisions. But decisions that respond to local customs, mores, and even the informal community power structure are not usually characterized as "political." As a consequence of this variable of our political culture, Selective Service has consciously striven to be "non-political" or non-partisan while at the same time being "decentralized" or responsive to local conditions.

It has been highly successful in this regard. There has been no major scandal with partisan overtones and in fact allegations of partisanship are virtually non-existent.[96] This is attributable to four factors: the closed personnel systems of the institution; conscious efforts to exclude partisanship; the system members' perceptions of social pressure; and the "hands-off" attitude of politicians at all levels of government.

The resistance to politics provided by the closed systems can be seen in the six and one-half years of operation in connection with World War II. A System monograph indicates:

> As would be expected, State elections during the period were accompanied by some change in Chief Executives (Governors) and upon occasions by subsequent changes in State Directors though very seldom among other personnel of State Headquarters staffs.[97]

The state director in this study remarked:

> I've been here under x Governors. I always make an appointment and go introduce myself and they say, "Well, I'll see you around." That's the last I hear from them. The state director's job is sort of like the board member positions. Nobody wants it very bad. It can do a man more harm than good, politically. So whatever their

[Governors'] party, I stay on and I'm a Radical Republican but nobody knows it outside this office. One of the strengths of the whole system is that it is above politics. Sometimes they [politicans] have to learn, though they usually leave us alone. I had some guy call the other day — he says, "I am ———, the Democratic ———." And I said, "Yeah, I know who you are." Shook him up a little bit. And I had one fellow a few years ago who introduced himself as ———, the Democratic ———, from the Democratic ———, in Old City's Democratic ———. I said, "Hold on a minute. Did you come breezing in here and use the word Democrat ten times in two minutes because you thought I might be able to do any favors for you? 'Cause if you did I'll have to disappoint you." He says, "Oh, no! No, General, nothing like that — let's go out to lunch sometime soon."[98]

Conscious efforts at non-partisanship have not required extensive guidance from national headquarters. The feeling seems to be that "this is the area where people will be most suspicious of 'politics' and it must therefore be avoided at all costs."

One of Donald Stewart's interviewees who claimed to have extensive experience as a member of a municipal political machine expressed the feeling encountered at all levels.

These local boards are political dynamite. Everybody around here knows that ——— has been stealing the taxpayers' money for years, and he is no worse than a dozen others I could name. Stealing money is one thing; fooling around with the lives of young men is another. It just isn't smart to play politics in a deal like this. "Let the chips fall where they may," we say, and that is what we always did. If the word had gotten around that deferments were being fixed, this thing would have gone sky-high and most of us with it. . . . I haven't run for office for a good many years and I may never run again, but if I do, no man will be able to say that I put him in the army because he was a Republican or kept somebody out because he was a Democrat.[99]

A System monograph discussed the governors' selection of board members in this way.

Something more should be said perhaps about the Governors' recommendations of citizens for appointment as local board members. The first time this arrangement comes to attention, there may be a tendency to think of it in terms of "politics." Almost never, though did it work out this way. Generally speaking the selection was bi-partisan and representative of the community.

Neither the act nor the regulations contained any reference whatsoever in these regards. It is known that in the so-called one-party

Institutional Adaptations to American Political Culture

States mostly members of the dominant political party were chosen for recommendation; in other States local board members were from both parties.[100]

One of several state directors who wrote histories of World War II operations in their state described the non-partisan plan developed by himself and the governor.

> That the local boards should represent both political parties, that there should be one Democrat and one Republican on each three-member board, but that none of the members should be men actively engaged as office holders, or contenders for public office; if a board member should become a candidate for public office, he would be required to resign; and that the majority of the board members should be veterans of previous wars of the Nation.
>
> In this manner we felt that there could be no charges of partisanship in connection with the classification or induction of citizens of the State.[101]

This and other accounts are consistent with the findings of this study, of Stewart's earlier work and of Davis and Dolbeare in Wisconsin, who found that among community activities board members engaged in, politics was quite low. Although Davis and Dolbeare found that two-thirds have had "some form of public office experience, relatively few have held partisan or elective office." The offices were "mostly appointive or 'good government' or non-partisan type."[102]

Constant awareness of social pressure to avoid "politics" is manifest and particularly at the local board level. The state director in this study was quick to point this out.

> Part of the answer [as to why conscription is accepted] is absolute honesty in handling things. Politics doesn't get into this at all. Board members know that if they don't handle a case with absolute honesty the word will get out. People are watching.[103]

Clerks of local boards quickly and without probing brought up the subject of social pressure and public scrutiny. "People call all the time — to complain about someone who is not being called when their boy is."[104] Another remarked:

> When we get mail back from an address and the other address on their card won't turn them up, we put their names in the newspapers. They print them as a public service. When Korea started up we had all those delinquents [holding up several typed pages] and we finally got all but fourteen.
>
> *Question:* You mean people called in and told you where to find them?

Reply: Sure. People are our biggest source of information — the neighbors. They never miss a thing.[105]

Boards also received anonymous letters offering information on missing registrants or complaining at their not being drafted like other boys.

Finally, one must consider the very important factor of the politicians' attitudes toward Selective Service. Evidence of their attitude clearly indicates that they prefer not to become enmeshed in trying to influence the decisions of the System. It is apparently viewed as a Pandora's Box which once opened can cause a politician little but grief. Stewart points out that the Mayor of New York had to make public appeals for volunteers to staff local boards in 1940.[106] A state director described the interaction of the agency with politicians in a manner that proved to be consistent throughout this study.

> *Question:* I get the impression from what you say that politicians are glad to have an honest system that gets them off the hook.
> *Reply:* Right! [excitedly] Look! [Holding up a stack of outgoing letters, he reads] "To the Honorable ———," "to Senator ———." Now this stuff comes in all day! *But* you know what happens? Well, a Congressman often calls and says, "Look, there's this constituent of mine that is driving me crazy because her kid's about to be drafted. Can we do something to get her off my back?" I say, "Sure! You send me a letter and tell me all about him and how valuable he is at home here, etc. and I'll send you a letter that speaks of all your efforts on his behalf but pointing out why he has to be inducted. I'll also attach a copy of the letter you sent me." And that's how it works. I never mind that. I tell a Congressman, "They are your constituents — and you are their elected representatives — and it is only proper that you do everything you can for them." But in this case they can't do much. We just make them look as good as possible.[107]

The System responds quickly within a specified number of hours to letters and calls from congressmen, senators, governors and the President. The author was permitted to read any of the letters from such sources and the replies as they flowed through state headquarters. This was done without any apparent embarrassment or effort to conceal anything on the part of the staff. A typical letter from a congressman read:

> Dear General ———,
> Mr. ——— feels that he should be deferred in the critical occupation category since he is vital to the operation of the family's farm

implement agency which serves the Blanktown area. Please do whatever is possible in this matter. Inform me of the action taken. I know you will do the best for everyone.[108]

The standard replies to such letters were as described by the state director and often they concluded by pointing out that the final decision was in the hands of the local board and that it had decided, etc.

The state director took delight in telling how he handled pleas to the governor for intervention.

> I used to have real fun when Governor ——— would send over some of the letters he would get and ask me to reply and write the letter for his signature. So I would "play Governor ———." "Dear Mr. So & So, I am delighted to know that you and your eight sons voted for me in the last two elections. Such loyalty is indeed heartwarming and hard to find these days. I have looked into the problem of your son James being drafted and have directed General ——— to review the matter thoroughly. He has reported to me that unfortunately the matter is in the hands of the local board and there is nothing we can do."[109]

This pattern of interaction between politicians and the System also held true at the local board level. During an interview a board clerk received a phone call. Upon hanging up she remarked:

> Well, that was Congressman ———'s office.
> *Interviewer:* I'll bet he makes it rough for your people.
> *Clerk:* Oh no, not really. They call over here sometimes but not often. Sometimes he's called himself. I suspect we only hear from them as often as we do because his office is over in the Federal Courts Building. But usually he calls because he's got someone raising a fuss in his office. All they want is information on the case so they know what they're up against. I've never had them try to influence a board. Most of the politicans know that if they are ever able to help out one person, they will be swamped with requests they can't handle.[110]

Some evidence of the caution with which congressmen approach Selective Service and the System's cheerful but limited cooperation is found in the following testimony.

> *Mr. Dulski:* I am going to go to a more sensitive area. Are your employees under the Hatch Act?
> *General Hershey:* Yes, sir.
> *Mr. Dulski:* I am going to develop some legislative history so that I can use it in answering some of my correspondence. Do your

boards resent if a Congressman mails in a letter asking for a review of a case?

General Hershey: A great majority do not, but I am sure that there are individuals that do. I have got the finest bunch of State directors in the world, but sometimes they resent the fact that I get into it. But on the other hand. I took an oath, and that is all there is to that. But human beings being what they are, of course we undoubtedly have some.

Now, that is not what we are looking for. It is just some of the shortcomings that we have in a thing that is operated by human beings.

Mr. Dulski: General, I know that many times an applicant, or shall I say, a draftee gets a card, and goes into the draft board. He is accepted. Right away mother and dad come down and say, visit your Congressman. Now, you know as well as I do that we have no authority. The only things we can ask is a review of the case, and that is the question that I have in mind. Is there any resentment on the local level and on the State level, or on the National level.

General Hershey: Well, I think probably that there are times that the National Director—he is one person—it is a little easier to fix responsibility by saying that he is snooping in the case. And I have never worried because people said that the Members of Congress were putting pressure on me, because they never have. They asked for information which they are entitled to. They are the one area where they are representing the people. And if they don't do what they can for them, I don't know what the people have a right to think.

So I have no worry about that.

But on the other hand, I am not going to say that—I don't have very many resignations. Once in a great while when I have taken issue with a local board and taken an appeal, after they made an appeal, I have had on occasion — over the last five years I suppose I can count the occasions on my fingers — but the great majority of them — even some that did resign resigned, I think, because they figured that they just about had to do it maybe with public sentiment worrying them a little, which happens at times.[111]

The previous discussion is not meant to imply that the System is not affected by external influences and pressures. But the System does *not*, as a general rule, respond to political pressure of the partisan variety that our political culture views negatively, nor does it appear that it is often called upon to respond to such pressure.

It would obviously be naive to assert that politics of the partisan variety *never* penetrate the System. Research and direct observation over six months revealed only one possible exception,

Institutional Adaptations to American Political Culture

however. The clerk of one board which was not observed claimed that her chairman who was an elected police chief used his position in a partisan manner. But this was notable for its uniqueness and in fact to find an office holder on a board was an exception to the general rule.

"Decentralization," as some of the instances mentioned show, is functional for dealing with partisan politics as well as interest groups. The peculiar quasi-state, quasi-federal nature of the System permits deflection of partisan political pressure. An excerpt from a history of state operations from 1940 to 1947 notes:

> Whenever the Governor received a letter pertaining to the Selective Service status of some particular registrant, the Governor immediately replied with the statement that, since Selective Service was under Federal jurisdiction, he was turning the letter over to the State Director, for whatever action was indicated according to the regulations.[112]

The comments of an officer in state headquarters confirm the above deflection pattern. "Because we are federal, the state politicians don't have any leverage on us. A few of the Congressmen do but not the state politicians."[113]

And as already noted, state and national headquarters both deflected pressure downward to the local boards, citing them as the final decision-makers. Local boards and clerks, in turn, referred pressure upward to state headquarters through regular or informal appeal channels, and so it went.

Proceduralism and Selective Service's "Pipeline"

Redford and Truman say of American emphasis on procedures or process:

> The public whose consent to being governed is essential appears uninterested, uninformed, and often unskilled in the role it must assume. It reserves its admiration and loyalty for symbolic and ritualistic articulation of moral purposes and not for the officials and machinery assigned the task of realizing the national destiny.
>
> Yet, a series of subtle and sensitive factors is at work to make our system operative. Essentially these are bound up in the American attention to process: to the extraordinary weight placed on the ways and means in which we work out our unarticulated compromises while continuing our grander rhetoric. Checks, balances, procedures, rules, regulations are all shrewdly built into the governmental structure, to modify the more general and grandiose expressions

of our style. This concentration on process rather than philosophy arises almost inevitably from the main components of our national character and the conditions of our environment.[114]

V. O. Key makes a similar observation and though he is speaking of political institutions it seems clear enough that proceduralism also is characteristic of administrative systems and accordingly lesser institutions such as Selective Service.

> Coupled with apprehensions about power are, of course, institutional procedures congenial to that attitude. American governmental procedures notoriously encourage delay — not only the delay necessary for full debate, but on occasion a delay of action for years on questions of great import. As delay occurs, popular attitudes do not necessarily remain constant. They may gradually assume a form that permits a settlement of the issue by predominant majorities, if not by universal consent.[115]

To minimize conflict, and maximize consensus and acceptability, Selective Service has developed an extremely elaborate set of appeal procedures. In addition, there exist equally elaborate *informal* appeal procedures which have been reviewed already in connection with control mechanisms. In the face of its sacrificial and contentious task it has developed an institutional ideology that might best be described as "find the path of least contention." It is always hoped that an appealing registrant will finally acquiesce and accept his fate.

If the registrant takes issue with his classification, his Notice of Classification informs him that he has thirty days in which to request in writing an interview with his local board. (Until 1967 he had ten days.) Clerks are particularly careful to see that a contentious registrant receives an interview with his board.

> I always tell them to request an interview with the board if they're unhappy. That way they can't complain later on. They get a chance to meet the board face-to-face and this helps a lot of them to accept the decision. They're more satisfied.[116]

The appearance before his board is not considered a formal appeal. The registrant may make his first appeal if he still takes issue with his classification after the board interview. Once again he has thirty days to file a written appeal with the State Appeal Board. The Appeal Board hears no testimony, reviews only the file, considers general information concerning economic, industrial or social conditions, recommendations of the Department of Justice and any reply the registrant might make to the same.

Institutional Adaptations to American Political Culture 91

If the State Appeal Board classifies him or upholds his classification as I-A, I-A-O or I-O and the registrant is still dissatisfied he may appeal to the National Appeal Board.[117] The appeal by a registrant or employer can be made on the conditions that the decision of the state board was not unanimous and that he make his appeal in writing through his local board. If the state board was unanimous his formal appeal process is at an end, though the state or national director can take his case to the national board. One exception to this pattern occurs in the case of a conscientious objector. If the State Appeal Board refuses to grant a request for I-A-O, or I-O the case is automatically referred to the Justice Department for a hearing. The Justice Department then makes a recommendation to the State Appeal Board which is not binding.

This elaborate machinery for formal appeals and the equally extensive means of informal appeals mount up to a rather high price the institution pays for minimizing conflict and the use of compulsion. Appeal board members are volunteers that meet once or twice a month. The appeal system is slow and cumbersome with channels that clog and overload quickly in a crisis. The institution must bear the burden of a long "paper pipeline" that complicates its task of meeting the functional demands made upon it by the Armed Forces.

In the spring of 1966 charges of inefficiency centered upon this clogged pipeline. Thirty Republican congressmen charged that "279,676 men were 'not available' because their papers are stalled in the bureaucratic pipeline." They called upon Congress to "examine this red tape jungle immediately,"[118] in an attack which was without parallel in the System's history. Undoubtedly the complaints stemmed more from dissatisfaction with the System's ability to meet societal demands like equity, uniformity, etc., than they did from its ability to perform efficiently. But significantly the complainants were able to attack Selective Service at the one point on which it had heretofore considered itself invulnerable — its ability to deliver the manpower demanded. This and other similar attacks were instrumental in forcing the House Armed Services Committee to hold hearings in a non-renewal year, an event that was also without precedent. The costs of acceptance were getting out of hand, and the appeals procedures were not delivering sufficient acceptance for such a high burden upon efficiency.

The point to be made here, however, is a simpler one. Selective Service has devised an extremely elaborate system for formal and informal appeals that permits delays of induction that sometimes seem interminable. The System also will not hesitate to stay an induction if it seems that contentious issues surrounding a case are not yet resolved. All this has been extremely functional in a political culture which places a high value on procedures and process to legitimate contentious decisions. Whether the appeals structure will remain functional under changing conditions remains to be seen.

Voluntarism

American political culture has placed a high value on voluntary action or performance of civic duty. Compulsion and coercion have naturally been viewed negatively and those who had to be compelled to do that which was accepted as civic obligation were held in low esteem. The review of the history of conscription makes this clear. The emphasis on voluntarism is manifest in our treatment of public officials whom we expect to serve at low salary or as dollar-a-year men. The positive value of it has plagued Selective Service and other conscription systems.

Selective Service has done its best to convert into advantages the liabilities imposed on it by voluntarism. First it has striven to portray itself as the stimulus for enlistments. Of the 1,090,000 men (excluding officers) who entered the service in fiscal 1966, 380,700 enlisted after they were examined and found qualified for induction.[119] It is impossible to tell how many of the other 366,000 enlistees were inspired by the draft but in the 1964 Defense Department opinion polls of service personnel, 43 per cent of the army respondents said their enlistments were "draft-inspired."[120] When under attack its final line of defense has been that without its pressure, enlistments would decrease dangerously. Postwar experience supports this claim.

The other attempt to glean some utility from voluntarism has been to portray the System as essentially a volunteer one — a grass-roots organization of dedicated, unpaid, volunteers whose only reward is the satisfaction of serving their country. As noted in discussions of the System's relations with Congress, the voluntary nature of the boards has been a bulwark of protection for Selective Service. Rarely have board members been criticized and in the few instances in which this has happened the criticism has been hedged about by praise for the sacrifice of board members. The following remarks on board members are typical.

The Chairman [Mendel Rivers]: The public ought to know what the country needs, and what these people whom you serve, what they are doing to merit the service you are giving this country, because you have built up a vast organization known as the Selective Service System. And these people whom the Governors appointed — and I think the Governors appoint all of them, don't they?
General Hershey: Well, of course, there isn't anything that you can give local board members and appeal board members who have worked, many of them, twenty-five years for nothing, there is nothing you could give them, except just a little regard.
The Chairman: Just a little backage.
General Hershey: And they haven't been getting that all the time.
The Chairman: I heard you say the other day that you stamp every day a silver seal on these letters.
General Hershey: Hundreds of them.
The Chairman: Of these men who serve twenty-five years on these boards, great and dedicated service doing a distasteful job.[121]

The gains of the institution from ties to voluntarism are heightened because of the generally materialistic and acquisitive nature of our society. Individuals that volunteer for non-compensated positions tend to be perceived as self-sacrificing and good. Local board members are aware of this outlook and find considerable psychic support in their voluntarism. Stewart found that only twelve out of 121 of his board member interviewees felt they should be compensated and ten of these indicated that they meant compensation for time taken from their business. The figures are even more striking because his respondents had worked from ten to forty hours a week during World War II.[122]

Conclusion

There are several points relevant for organizational theory and public administration that should be elaborated on in concluding this chapter. Selective Service provides an excellent example of what Orion White calls a political administrative system: one whose goals have lacked consensual unity from time to time. More specifically, in 1863 there was a lack of consenual unity of such cataclysmic proportions as to effect its administrative structure and processes down to this present day. Despite efforts to restrict dealings with its environment, to portray itself as a neutral instrument performing a carefully proscribed role, it has simultaneously been extremely sensitive to its political environment. On the basis of its leadership's perceptions of key values in American political culture, it has structured itself and developed processes and institutional myths so as to identify with such key values. The overwhelming impression conveyed is that environment is all important for the System. It is seen by members as ever-threatening, or hostile, a subject of conscious concern.

Mayer Zald would explain the phenomenon of adapting the institution to perceived political culture in terms of his concept of political economy and indeed it is an excellent tool of analysis for use on Selective Service. Zald feels that the key variable determining the structure and processes of an organization is the nature of the exchange between the organization and its environment.

The nature of Selective Service's exchange with its environment is revealed by the two variable equilibria with which the preceding historical chapter was introduced. Like any other governmental agency it must perform an assigned function — a function necessary for survival or well-being of the political system and the societal whole it serves. Selective Service's function is to conscript men — to compel men to serve with armed forces — which may at times involve the risk of life and limb. A more sensitive and controversial task could scarcely be imagined, yet this assigned function must be met. Selective Service must deliver men upon demand and maintain the civil economy or fail completely to justify its existence. It must be efficient, it must maintain control of lower echelons actions, it must produce.

The second variable grows logically out of the first. The compulsion of service must be carried out in a manner that is accepted as legitimate, authoritative and binding. Every society has certain expectations as to how government ought to be conducted; proper procedural norms must be followed. Every administrative agency must pay some attention to this societal or political culture demand if it or the political system is to endure for very long. But in the case of a conscription mechanism, the imperatives of political culture are of particularly acute importance. Administering a statute so sacrificial in nature necessitates careful attention to the means of carrying out the assigned function. The decision to induct or defer must be done in accordance with the relevant norms of political culture. Procedures regarded as "proper" must be followed, appropriate legitimating symbols must be invoked, the behavior of decision-makers must appear fair, and the resulting decision must be considered just.

The ends of public policy, i.e. the popularity of the war, are another facet of institutional equilibrium. A society also has expectations as to *what* government should try to do. Even the most scrupulous attention to *how* policy is carried out and the most strenuous efforts to identify with societal concepts of equity and legitimacy will be to no avail if the ends of a conscription system's function do not conform to norms of political culture, in other words if the war for which it is conscripting is considered unjust or unworthy. Similarly, if the war is popular the conscription system can, and in fact will, be expected to devote increasing effort to efficiency in meeting the demands of its functional task, while less attention is devoted to the equity norms of political culture.

The key values in American political culture that the System's designers and subsequent leaders have perceived to be important are decentralization, anti-militarism, negativeness toward politics, and voluntarism. Of these, decentralization has been most important and the most troublesome because it lies at the heart of the problem of maintaining equilibrium. The structure and processes which institutional leaders think have satisfied demands of political culture complicate fulfillment of the institution's functional task. Local boards, volunteer members, elaborate appeal procedures, etc. are by nature balky, lacking in uniformity, inefficient, slow and cumbersome. To offset these traits the institution has had to develop a wide variety of control mechanisms that generally enable upper echelons to prevail but preserve institutional myths intact.

To be sure Selective Service is only a case of an administrative system's reaction and adaptation to political culture. It may be that it is an extreme case but often it is only by relying upon the clarity of concepts that emerge from extreme cases that we are able to recognize that the same relationships are found in all organizations or institutions but in subtler forms.

Notes

[1] *Organization and Administration of the System,* Special Monograph No. 3, Vol. 1 (Washington, D.C.: Government Printing Office, 1951), p. 32.

[2] *Ibid.*

[3] The term "institutional myth" is taken from Philip Selznick who describes it as an effort "to state in language of uplift and idealism, what is distinctive about the aims and methods of the enterprise." See Selznick, *Leadership in Administration* (Evanston, Ill.: Row Peterson, 1957), p. 151. A myth is defined solely by function. It is neither true nor false, rational nor irrational.

[4] *Annual Report of the Director of Selective Service for 1965* (Washington, D.C.: Government Printing Office, January 1966), pp. 8 and 33; *Organization and Administration, op. cit.,* p. 3; or virtually any materials published by the System.

[5] Felix Nigro, *Modern Public Administration* (New York: Harper and Row, Publishers, 1965), p. 119.

[6] For a discussion of the weaknesses of the term see James W. Fesler, *Area and Administration* (Birmingham: University of Alabama Press, 1964), p. 52.

[7] Fred Riggs has discussed the potential and real conflict between different values of the same political culture. See "Structure and Function in Development: A Dialectical Approach" (paper delivered at the Chicago convention of the American Political Science Association, September 9, 1967).

[8] The reader is reminded that quotes such as these are part of the data collected in six months of study of local boards, a state headquarters and national headquarters. See preface.

[9] James Heaphey, "Spatial Aspects of Development Administration" (unpublished paper delivered at Seminar of the American Society for Public Administration's Comparative Administration Group, July 1965), p. 14.

[10] Selznick, *op. cit.,* p. 113.

[11] The details of the personnel systems will be discussed at later points.

[12] *Organization and Administration, op. cit.,* p. 60.

[13] Interview No. 35.

[14] Interview No. 36.

[15] Local Board Advice No. B-7-2 out of State in November 28, 1966. Operations Bulletin No. 296 came out of National March 31, 1966. Memo to Local Boards from State, May 3, 1966, Local Board Advice No. B-7-9 from State June 17, 1966.

Institutional Adaptations to American Political Culture   97

[16] Interview No. 15. It may or may not be significant that the author twice specifically requested that he be placed on the mailing list for *Selective Service* and though he was assured that he would be, no copies were ever received.

[17] Interview No. 37.

[18] Interview No. 22.

[19] The auditors referred to here should be differentiated from representatives of state directors that cover assigned areas of the state. The representatives of directors are much more important control mechanisms. Confusion often arises because these representatives are sometimes referred to as System Auditors (as in Wisconsin) or elsewhere as field representatives. The term field representative is most common and will be used throughout this study with auditor referring to the narrower less important position under discussion.

[20] *Review of the Administration and Operation of the Selective Service System,* Hearings before the Committee on Armed Services, House of Representatives, 89th Cong. 2nd Sess. (Washington, D.C.: Government Printing Office, 1966), p. 9689. Hereafter referred to as *Review.*

[21] Interview No. 20.

[22] Interview No. 22.

[23] Interview No. 1.

[24] Interview No. 37. The reference is to the director's decision to urge local boards to defer persons serving in the Peace Corps. As usual the vast majority followed the "guidance" and a few ignored it.

[25] Stewart, *op. cit.,* p. 116.

[26] Interview No. 36.

[27] Appendix B. Author's italics.

[28] Appendix C.

[29] State Director Advices Nos. 539 and 726 respectively. The most noticeable feature of the latter memorandum is that national headquarters failed to add any supporting comments as it invariably did when passing on guidance of which it approved. To persons accustomed to reading System documents this would immediately indicate that national headquarters did not enthusiastically endorse the President's views.

[30] Or see Local Board Bulletin #900, 2 June 1965, "Care and Repair of Typewriters."

[31] The reader may wonder at the absence of any discussion of the field representatives of national headquarters. Discussion has been postponed because they perform a system maintenance rather than "internal control" function. While field representatives of state headquarters have more control functions, and have been discussed here on that basis, maintenance also holds primacy at the state level.

[32] See Figure 1, p. 33 for place of manpower division in the System's organization.

[33] *Organization and Administration, op. cit.,* p. 61.

[34] Interview No. 36.

[35] In many instances the registrant may take all appeals available to him and still create difficulties. In the six-month period of this study such situations arose on a number of occasions—hysterical cursing mothers with teen-

age sons in tow, vice presidents of large industries, etc. Clerks would do whatever was possible to handle the situation but if it proved impossible, and a situation seemed imminent which could result in bad publicity or if it seemed that an influential party involved would go over the head of the clerk, the clerks would tell the party to call state headquarters. Such calls are routine part of state headquarters procedure and many were observed from that level of the System.

[36]*The Classification Process,* Special Monograph No. 5, Vol. I, Selective Service System (Washington, D.C.: Government Printing Office, 1950), 47. For an example of liberalizing and tightening of deferments see pp. 78-79 and *passim* in the above-cited work.

[37]Even during World War II when conditions were more favorable for relying on regulations, the System amended the regulations 550 times between 1940 and 1947.

[38]This is done to avoid telling the board and others about the registrant's work.

[39]Interview No. 21. Similar points were made by officials at national headquarters.

[40]Stewart, "Local Boards, A Study of the Place of Volunteer Participation in a Bureaucratic Organization" (unpublished Ph.D. dissertation, Columbia University, 1950), p. 58.

[41]It may also take an appeal to impart legitimacy to a contentious decision without really caring how it is decided, or to confirm a previous decision which is being attacked. In the latter instance, value integration may make it clear what decision is desired or there may be other means of transmitting cues. Since the National Appeal Board meets in the national headquarters and a similar situation exists in some states, the possibilities for transmittal are infinite.

[42]This conclusion is a major departure from the one reached by Donald Dean Stewart, *op. cit.,* p. 23. He felt that "generally this [uniformity and predictability] was accomplished by the elimination of alternatives open to the local board members in the judgment of individual cases until decisions had become almost automatic..."

[43]Interview No. 36.

[44]David B. Truman, *The Governmental Process* (New York: Alfred A. Knopf, Inc., 1958), p. 443.

[45]For a discussion of interaction between interest groups and the System during World War II, see *Problems of Selective Service,* Special Monograph No. 16, Vol. I, Text (Washington, D.C.: Government Printing Office, 1952), 197-218. Also see Stewart, *op. cit.,* p. 38.

[46]Interview No. 35.

[47]Interview No. 38.

[48]The list was developed by Interagency Advisory Committee on Essential Activities and Critical Occupations, Bureau of Employment Security, U.S. Department of Labor. Published by Selective Service as Operations Bulletin #18 amended 1955, and Operations Bulletin #228. Though rewritten in 1962 and amended in 1965 it was never considered very current even if boards had been inclined to use it.

[49]Interview No. 38. The List was officially dropped as a guideline in February 1968.

Institutional Adaptations to American Political Culture 99

[50] Interview No. 1. This controversy resulted in a 1955 amendment to the law which prohibited local boards from considering agricultural shortages or surpluses in making decisions. This restrictive proviso was dropped in the 1967 revisions.

[51] *Review, op. cit.*, p. 9639.

[52] *Ibid.*

[53] Interview No. 21.

[54] Interview No. 22.

[55] Interview No. 36.

[56] William S. White, *Home Place: The Story of the U.S. House of Representatives* (Boston: Houghton Mifflin Company, 1965), p. 5.

[57] Marion Irish and James Prothro, *Politics of American Democracy* (3rd ed.; Englewood Cliffs, N.J.: Prentice-Hall, Inc., 1965), p. 345.

[58] Interview No. 40.

[59] *Ibid.* Perhaps even better examples of the System's relationship to Congress were events surrounding efforts to amend the law in 1967. Despite the greatest pressure for change the System has ever faced, there were no changes in the law that had not already been effected by executive action or were not specifically desired by the System.

[60] *Annual Report of the Director, op. cit.*, p. 8.

[61] Irish and Prothro, *op. cit.*, p. 313. See also Donald R. Matthews, *The Social Background of Political Decision-Makers* (New York: Doubleday & Company, Inc., 1954).

[62] Irish and Prothro, *op. cit.*, p. 247.

[63] Redford and Truman, *op. cit.*, p. 212.

[64] See *Review, op. cit., passim.*

[65] *Compensation for Selective Service System Employees,* Hearing, House of Representatives, 89th Cong., 2nd sess. on H.R. 14357 (Washington, D.C.: Government Printing Office, 1966), April 18, 1966, p. 11. Hereafter referred to as Compensation Hearings.

[66] Alf Evers, *Selective Service: A Guide to the Draft* (Philadelphia: J. B. Lippincott Co., 1957), p. 38. While this book is non-academic, it is based on extensive research and interviews and contains considerable insights into Selective Service operations.

[67] *Ibid.*, p. 39.

[68] Memoranda to All State Directors, Sept. 30, 1940 to October 15, 1943 (Washington, D.C.: Government Printing Office), p. 3. The matter was turned over to state directors in April 1941.

[69] *Organization and Administration of the System, op. cit.*, p. 270.

[70] Correspondence with Alf Evers.

[71] *Ayers* v. *United States,* 9 Cir. 240 F 2d 802, cert. denied, 352 U.S. 1016, 77 S. Crt. 563 (1957).

[72] See *Organization and Administration, op. cit.*, pp. 259-71.

[73] *Report of the Director,* Office of Selective Service Records, 1947-1948 (Washington, D.C.: Government Printing Office, 1950), pp. 95-96.

[74] See *The Annual Report,* 1965, *op. cit.*, Appendix 6, p. 52.

[75] Martha Derthick, "Citizen Soldier on Capitol Hill: The Political Life of the National Guard" (dissertation, Radcliffe College, 1962), p. 42. Published as *The National Guard in Politics* (Cambridge: Harvard University Press, 1965).

[76] Interview No. 39.

[77] The other two are for board members and clerks and will be discussed later.

[78] Universal Military Training and Service Act of 1951, Section 10, para. 4 (b) subpara. 4.

[79] *Annual Report of the Director, op. cit.*, p. 10.

[80] Interview No. 35.

[81] *Ibid.*

[82] Derthick, *The National Guard in Politics*, pp. 4-5.

[83] *Ibid.*

[84] Interview No. 1.

[85] Interview No. 21.

[86] Interview No. 40.

[87] See Martha Derthick, *The National Guard in Politics, op. cit.* For a discussion of the Guard's unique qualities alluded to here see pp. 1-14.

[88] Interview No. 35.

[89] *Ibid.*

[90] State Director Advice No. 567, 13 February 1962.

[91] Interview No. 3.

[92] *Organization and Administration of the System, op. cit.*, p. 271. Author's italics.

[93] Morris Janowitz, *The Professional Soldier* (New York: The Free Press, 1960), pp. 8-11.

[94] Redford and Truman, *op. cit.*, p. 60.

[95] *Ibid.*, p. 172.

[96] There have been occasional resignations of board members who charged that they were overruled on partisan grounds.

[97] *Organization and Administration, op. cit.*, p. 132.

[98] Interview No. 1. The number of governors which the respondent served is marked with an *x* because the exact number was missed in the interview. Uncertain memory would place the figure at six.

[99] Stewart, *op. cit.*, p. 71.

[100] *Organization and Administration, op. cit.*, p. 191.

[101] *Ibid.* For another account of efforts at non-partisanship see *ibid.*, p. 133.

[102] James W. Davis and Kenneth M. Dolbeare, "Little Groups of Neighbors" (unpublished paper, University of Wisconsin, 1967), p. 16.

[103] Interview No. 1.

[104] Interview No. 3.

[105] *Ibid.*

[106] Stewart, *op. cit.*, p. 67.

[107] Interview No. 1.

[108] From a letter processed by state headquarters.

[109] Interview No. 1.

[110] Interview No. 5.

[111] *Compensation Hearings*, pp. 14 and 15.

[112] *Organization and Administration, op. cit.*, p. 133.

[113] Interview No. 21.

[114] Redford and Truman, *op. cit.*, p. 63.

[115] V. O. Key, *Public Opinion and American Democracy* (New York: Alfred A. Knopf, Inc., 1964), p. 45.

[116] Interview No. 5.

[117] In other words if he is classified as available for service, available for non-combatant military service or available for service in civilian institutions.

[118] *New York Times,* March 2, 1966.

[119] Annual Report of the Director of Selective Service for Fiscal Year 1966 (Washington, D.C.: Government Printing Office, 1967), p. 43.

[120] Review, *op. cit.*, p. 10038.

[121] *Review, op. cit.*, p. 9689.

[122] *Annual Report of the Director, op. cit.*, p. 8.

4

Local Boards: Mainstay or Weak Link?

Of the institutional adaptations to American political culture, the local boards and their quota system deserve special consideration. To the designers of the System they were the key element in relating to public attitudes and values, a legitimating link between the coercive power of the government and the individual citizen. General Crowder stated:

> The boards serve as a buffer between the individual citizen and the federal government ... the boards are the bearers of the burden of complaint and criticism and leave the government free to achieve war measures.[1]

The centrality of the local boards to the institutional character of the System has not diminished. The Annual Report of the Director of Selective Service for 1965 states: "The 4,016 local boards are the basic units where the fundamental operations of the System are performed."[2] The vast bulk of the decisions are formally made by the boards, and whether the decisions are more fundamental than the policy determinations that guide them is debatable. Nonetheless the institution's leaders have believed that the balance between political culture and the functional demands of conscription has rested in the boards. If problems have developed in maintaining that balance, logic would dictate scrutiny of the operation of local boards as a first step in determining the source of imbalance. And if it is true that the recent crescendo of criticism centers on how conscription is conducted, rather than whether it is conducted, no analysis of "how" can be complete without examination of the behavior of local boards, their structure and processes.

Staffing local boards with civilians indigenous to the boards' jurisdictions might not by itself have prevented the resistance to conscription in the America of 1863 but it would undoubtedly have had great appeal. The appeal was still very manifest in 1917 where rural and small town environs still predominated. Fitzpatrick, who was Director of Selective Service in Wisconsin during World War I, made clear the potency of local boards as symbols by his somewhat florid description.

> The civilians were neighbors. They were, as it were, indigenous to the soul. The men were well-known in the neighborhood. They were often personal friends or family friends of the men who were to be sent to war. They had the intimate knowledge of family histories and of individual histories.[3]

Does a local board of "friends and neighbors" seem "indigenous to the soul" in the America of today? The issue is at least doubtful and such empirical evidence as exists suggests the contrary. Perhaps boards that cover America's shrinking rural population still fit the somewhat idyllic image projected by Fitzpatrick, but America has undergone great change in fifty years.

Growing Anomie Over Function

General Hershey has often stated with disarming simplicity that the function of Selective Service is to provide men for the military. Such a depiction has certain tactical value in dealing with the System's environment but it is hardly accurate. It glosses over some very real questions of function that confront board members in their decisions.[4]

Adjusting the bureaucratic processes of government to the individual has always been complicated by another implied function of carrying out national manpower policy that no one admits exists. This situation has always made the role of board members a difficult one. For example, while the Armed Forces increased their demands for men in World War II, the War Manpower Commission charged with facilitating war production sought deferments for non-ferrous ore miners, workers in the airframe, the wood and wood pulp, and shipbuilding industries. Nevertheless the situation in World War II was less problematic than today for despite such competing demands there was little doubt that the needs of the Armed Forces came first. If the Military felt war production was threatened they could release or defer men to their original production jobs and in fact this was done in several instances.

Since the Korean War, however, there has been an overabundance of manpower that has made the demand by Armed Forces seem something less than urgent. More and more the considerations of the covert manpower policy have moved to the forefront in board decisions, not in any planned fashion but merely as a result of a lack of urgency of the military demand.

In 1951 Selective Service publications first began to use the phrase "channeling." The phrase became popular with the System not only because it offered justification for its continued existence but more importantly because it offered some rationalization for the liberal deferments the local boards were making. An official at national headquarters proudly claimed that he had conceived of the term.

> *Question*: I wonder if you can tell me something about the idea of channeling. I notice it pops up in the Annual Reports all of the sudden one year.
>
> *Reply:* Well, yes. [Smiling] I guess that was my idea. I think it is sort of a good one. It's a way of saying what we're really doing, you see. It's a pretty sure thing that the System encourages a lot of these kids to stay on and get some worth-while education. Sort of an indirect pressure, you know. It's a pretty good analogy.[5]

Selective Service System in press releases describes the development of channeling in this way:

> As early as 1950, it became clear that something had to be done to preserve and permit development of the embryonic scientists and trained people in all fields. With Congressional approval Selective Service adopted a system of testing students for aptitude, as a basis for deferment.[6]

Nor is the System modest in making claims for the benefits derived from channeling.

> The *only* reason the Nation is not short 40,000 or 50,000 engineers today is because they were among the approximately 1,100,000 students deferred by Selective Service in 1951, 1952, and 1953, during the Korean War. Similarly, these Selective Service student defer-

ments reduced what otherwise would have developed into more serious shortages in teaching, medicine, dentistry and every field requiring advanced study.[7]

If one finds deferments for scientists and engineers acceptable but questions the necessity of them for other fields, Selective Service has an answer: "It was not only scientists and engineers that Selective Service deferred; Selective Service played the whole field of learning, knowing not where, in this unpredictable age, man's searching and researching might break out anew."[8]

The remarkable thing about the channeling concept is that it can be found nowhere in hearings surrounding the System's establishment, in the statutes, or in the regulations. It is an institutional response to changes its environment wrought in its task, and an effort to legitimate the unusually liberal deferments that pressure of numbers was forcing upon it.

As a result of this semi-conscious drift into a changed priority pattern, the sudden demands of the Viet Nam War for military manpower were a real shock to the System. Specifically, this latest slackening and drastic tightening of military manpower demands seems to have created unusual strains upon board members' conceptions of their roles. In light of these strains, the most intense criticism in the System's history, and the centrality of the local boards in maintaining the institution's balance, it would seem relevant to focus upon them.

Capability for Decisions on National Health, Safety and Interest

Boards in this study spent the preponderance of their time arguing, discussing, and puzzling over the concrete meaning of "national health, safety, and interest." Selective Service regulations direct boards to make deferments on such grounds. But the vague phrase is found not only in the regulations. It is at the heart of board deliberations and behavior. The words were used constantly in granting or refusing deferments and registrants were often asked to show how their deferment would be in the national health, safety or interest.

Board Member: Well, I can see how valuable this man is to your pump company but I can't see how he is in any way vital to the national health, safety or interest.
Company Representative [appearing on behalf of registrant]:

Local Boards: Mainstay or Weak Link? 107

Could you give me an example of someone who is vital in such a way?

Board Member: [Smiling] No, no, I'm not going to walk into that trap. Would you rather have the man for six more months or ten days?[9]

Companies which had continuous contact with boards in seeking occupational deferments developed skillful letters built around the theme. An example was an air brake company seeking deferment for an employee.

> Braking systems for railroads and mass transit systems have been judged as essential to the welfare and safety of the nation and our contribution as a primary supplier has been considered vital for Selective Service purposes. Local boards have consistently granted the appropriate occupational deferment for our technical people.[10]

Selective Service is willing to take credit for the "fruits" of an implicit national manpower policy. For example, General Hershey testified in the 1965 Draft hearings that the channeling efforts of Selective Service had dramatically increased advanced degrees, male teachers, physicians, dentists and veterinarians, college graduates, etc.[11]

He concluded:

> I do not believe we are so rich in human resources that we can afford deliberately to ignore opportunities we have to channel people into training and the application of training. There are enough factors over which we have no control which interfere with the development of the potential of our citizens, and with the best utilization of that potential when it is developed. By deferment we can influence people to train themselves and to use the skills they acquire in work critical to the Nation, in civilian or in military life.[12]

Despite a willingness to take credit for this implied policy, when criticized for not making the policy explicit and for not applying it uniformly by clearer guidance to boards, Selective Service retreats to its original implied function of boards — adjustment of process to the individual on the basis of intimate knowledge of him and his environs. For example, in defending the lack of any System definition of a full or part-time student, General Hershey said:

> That is one of the reasons why the local boards could do things I could never do here, and nobody else could do because they know whether that is truth, and they know enough about him to know whether he is putting something over on them.[13]

Or he combines this traditionally implied task with manipulation of the frightening spectre of the computer.

> I don't know [why there is lack of uniformity between boards]. But I do have more confidence, and I am willing to put up with mistakes of the local board down there who can look into all the facts, than I have in a computer.[14]

The ambivalence and uncertainty as to the proper function of the boards extends to the board members themselves. In observing boards over a six-month period in 1966, it seemed that the frustration of the members over the lack of clear purpose increased markedly as the calls remained high, requests for interviews mounted, and letter requests for deferments poured in. Typical excerpts from discussion are:

> *Board Member A:* [looking at a letter] Here's a guy who's working on hydraulic pumps—an engineer. Company says it builds pumps for sewage treatment plants and for drainage systems in missile complexes — therefore, deferment requested because the job of the man is in the national health, safety, and interest.
> *Board Member B:* Sewage plants! Aw c'mon—the national health?
> *Board Member A:* H—, how do we know; maybe our national health is in jeopardy. How do they expect us to know?
> *Board Member C:* Yeah [with sarcasm]. Can't let our missiles get wet either — have enough trouble getting them to light as it is.[15]

Another board, which five months earlier had deferred without discussion all requests for critical occupational deferments that seemed to be in the field of science, began to manifest the symptoms of role conflict and confusion over their task.

> *Board Member No. 1:* Good Lord! I never saw so many men teaching grade school before [referring to files in front of him].
> *Board Member No. 2:* Might be the best thing that could happen to the schools.
> *Board Member No. 1:* Yeah, except that we don't want them teaching school just 'cause they are there to get out of the Army.
> *Chairman:* Well, I think the schools will weed those out for us.
> *Clerk:* We do have this advice from state headquarters saying it is policy to defer all teachers as critical.
> *Board Member No. 3:* Well, I think like [Board Member No. 1] we shouldn't be automatic on the teachers. I'm not that sure about schools weeding them out. They need bodies. Let's at least be sure that someone like the Superintendent of Schools puts out some effort to keep them.

Local Boards: Mainstay or Weak Link? 109

Clerk: Well, on these other occupationals you've been deferring them if they're scientific but I've had some that won't ask for deferment of a man. I've even written some and asked for a letter and they won't reply.
Several Members: Draft them! H——, yes—call them up.
Chairman: H——, we're fighting a war. If they can't take the time to write a letter draft them.
Clerk: O.K. and then there's ———company. They won't send a letter describing the man's job. They just send a telegram saying, "Please defer so-and-so. He is vital to our operations and we are in defense work." That's all. Nothing else. I've written to them and explained that we need more.
Chairman: [angrily] Draft them! These companies think they can impress you with a telegram instead of doing their job right! Well, I think it's about time we got tough on all these occupations. I've had a belly full of them. The military needs some of these skills too.
Board Member No. 1: Well, yeah but you can't get some of these men. Some of these skills are hard for an industry to find. Our job isn't to just ship them off—we're supposed to decide which ones are critical—aren't we?
Board Member No. 2: It says to let students get a degree in a normal four years—not to just let them move from a student deferment to an occupational.
Board Member No. 1: Well, I can see getting tough with the ones Mrs. ——— was talking about but I'm against getting tougher on all the rest.[16]

The interesting thing about the interchange, and indeed the entire meeting, was that there was no clearly discernible pattern to positions of the board members. They seemed genuinely ambivalent or confused as to their proper role and task. The perplexity was most sharply manifested in a new member attending his first meeting.

New Member: I'd like to ask a question if I might. We're supposed to decide these cases on the basis of whether deferment is in the national health, safety, or interest?
Chairman: Yes. That's what the regulations say.
New Member: How can we do that?
Chairman: Well, you get the hang of it after a while. You see, it's sort of like an accordion. Sometimes you stretch it out and get generous with deferments and then other times you squeeze it up tight.
New Member: Well, I guess I've got a lot to learn.[17]

The Chairman's reply is an excellent example of how the System responds to supply and demand. Its responses are just as simple and crude as his reply. All the perplexity and frustration was not confined to the new. One member of twenty-four years' service, after a forty-minute discussion of a case, exploded.

> If they expect us to decide what's in the national health, safety, and interest, why in the h— don't they give us something we can make a decision on — something in writing. They tell us one d— thing and then another and it's always "Headquarters says." Let's turn this down and if they don't like it, let headquarters appeal it.[18]

If one argues, as General Hershey has, that Selective Service is the best means of implementing a recondite manpower policy, then the question of capability must be faced. Observations throughout this study consistently and uniformly found open to question the capability of the board to decide cases on the basis of national health, safety, and interest. One need not claim to know what in fact is in the national interest to question the capability of the boards.

There is the matter of information. It would be reasonable to assume that if a local board of "friends and neighbors" is to decide questions of national interest, they would require considerable information from outside the limited range of their experiences. The information would provide universalistic, higher criteria for decisions. General Hershey, when pressed on this point, admitted that "the Board is entitled to the best information available,"[19] but as has been seen he also claims they have more information than they can absorb.

It is clear that boards do *not* have current information on national manpower needs, nor do they utilize well the little information which is available. They may well have more information than they can absorb, but capability to utilize information may be a function of the user as well as of the information.

There existed until 1968 an aging Critical Skills List first published in 1955, revised in 1962 and amended in 1965.[20] None of the boards observed in this study used the list at meetings; only two of them referred to it at all by asking the clerk to check later on an occupation. Some of the clerks in this study were not sure what it was; most knew of it but said they never used it or they were not sure where to locate it. It may very well be that the problems with interest groups discussed earlier may preclude providing better information, but the difficulty of providing information is quite a different matter from the question of decision capability.

For boards that grappled with the concept of national health, safety and interest, decisions flowed from their perceptions of these categories based on their limited frame of reference. Clerks often mentioned how board members were influenced by things they had read or heard and observation confirmed this.

> *Board Member:* Now here's someone who's really doing something! Listen to this [reads technical description of the registrant's duties. Registrant is an engineer supervising the loading and shipping of ammunition.]. Loading shells, now, that's pretty important. They say our boys over there don't have enough bullets. Read it in the paper just the other night.[21]

Another board considered the request from an engineering firm to grant a II-A to an engineer employed by them. The letter (read by a board member) stated that the firm was building steel mills in Greece and Turkey and thus contributing to American national interest.

> *Board Chairman:* Building 'em in Greece and Turkey! Now, what's that supposed to do for us? I don't see how that's in *our* national interest or how that's part of our defense effort. As far as I'm concerned we've put too much into those places already and they don't give us nothin' but trouble anyway. I don't give a d—— about 'em buildin' steel mills in Greece and Turkey. As far as I'm concerned that's enough to make him I-A right there. That man's not doing anything for this country so far as I can see. These companies tell you any kind of outrageous thing and expect you to swallow it.[22]

Another board referred two cases to the State Scientific Advisory Board but only after appearing very close to induction decisions because they were totally unfamiliar with the nature of the occupations and institutions. One registrant was a mathematician who had been hired by the Department of Defense to work in its National Security Agency and sent back to school for more graduate education. Board members had never heard of the National Security Agency and could not understand why a man the Agency considered critical would be sent back to school.[23] The other case involved a space suit technician involved in maintenance, repair, and testing of space suits with the National Aeronautics and Space Administration. Board members failed to see how a graduate of a two year technical school could be in a critical occupation.

The examples above are not cited because they were clearly instances where a registrant was in a critical occupation. The point is that the local board members did not know and that they perceived the national health, safety and interest through extremely limited frames of reference. They decided upon the basis of what they read or heard in the news, what they believed the national interest should be, or occasionally they were able to utilize knowledge based on their own occupational experience.[24]

Capability to Adjust Processes to the Individual

Unfortunately, the inability to decide what is in the national interest is not compensated for by the intimate knowledge of the registrants necessary to adjust the process of conscription to the individual and his locale. This study covered only a metropolitan area but the majority of Americans live in such areas. The boards which General Hershey has referred to as "little groups of neighbors" seem in urban areas to have lost every vestige of symbolic power that once derived from their "local" nature.[25]

In the six months encompassed by this study there was no instance observed in which board members knew a registrant or his family.[26] Board members clearly took pride in knowing the physical area of their jurisdiction. When a registrant appeared before a board, he was first asked where he lived or worked. Board members then proceeded to discuss this location until they had pinpointed it sufficiently for one of them to announce that "he knew where it was." Clerks often spoke of how their board members "knew their areas" but with only one exception questioning of the clerks revealed that they did not mean knowledge of the individual, his family, or personal circumstances.

None of the seventeen boards in the Hill City area had a map indicating the area of their jurisdictions. The lines of jurisdiction had been drawn in 1940 with only minor adjustments since then. The adjustments bore no pattern that would mark them as adjustments to socio-economic changes. So far as could be ascertained the 1940 lines were the same as those of 1917. The lines within the central city followed those of the wards. The only person among the seventeen boards who was cognizant of and conversant with jurisdictional lines was the mail clerk who served all the boards. He checked registrations to see that the registrants were assigned to the proper boards. He did this by using a city and county street map and a typed description of which wards and townships fell within which boards. He did not know the source of the typed description. Officials at state headquarters did not know how jurisdictional lines had been drawn and referred vaguely to the fact that it has been done "back in 1940."

Upon comparing addresses with jurisdiction lines it became evident that fully one-third of all the board members in the study did not live within the jurisdictions of their boards.

TABLE 3.   Residences and Jurisdictions of Board Members

Total Board Members for 17 Boards	74
Members residing in their jurisdictions	50
Members not residing in their jurisdictions but in a location that could be loosely construed as "in the area"	6
Members not residing in jurisdictions	18
Total	74

A major departure from the "friends and neighbors" concept was found in a board covering a Negro neighborhood. There were no Negro members on the board and none of the members lived in the jurisdiction. The Chairman who was the only member residing even in the "vicinity," lived in perhaps the last "all-white block" to be found near the neighborhood, and had stated on numerous occasions that he would resign before he would allow a Negro to sit on the board.

It should be pointed out that the centralized location of the seventeen boards in this study is not unique and therefore the loss of their "neighborliness" is not attributable solely to the change in location. More than half the metropolitan boards of the country follow such a pattern.[27] Location in the neighborhoods may have contributed to the meaningfulness of localism. But that contribution was probably greater twenty-one to twenty-seven years ago when there was much less mobility.[28] Evidence would indicate that there are other factors that have eroded the "little groups of neighbors" concept besides the mere physical location of board offices. Davis and Dolbeare point out that board members in urban areas have little contact with registrants. Of their large city respondents, 72 per cent indicated contact was "rare or none," 26 per cent "occasional," and only 3 per cent indicated contact was "frequent."[29] And the Report of the National Commission states that "urban board members usually work in anonymity — and indeed seem to look upon that anonymity as an advantage."[30]

Clearly local boards in urban areas do not have the capability to adjust the processes of conscription to the individual and his circumstances on the basis of their personal knowledge. Board members often complained that there was "no way to check on these stories," wondered "what the facts of the matter" were, and occasionally some were conscientious and frustrated enough to drive to a registrant's neighborhood or home to look into a matter.

One can legitimately ask whether the boards in rural areas do not still fit the "little groups of neighbors" concept. Not surprisingly rural boards *are* closer to the characterization and presumably they are consequently more capable of adjusting the draft to the individual. Davis and Dolbeare show more frequent contacts with registrants by rural boards. (See Table 4)

TABLE 4. Differences Between Urban and Rural Local Board Members in Contacts with Registrants, Wisconsin, 1967
(in percent)

	Degree of Urbanization			
	Large City (95% urban)	Small City (40%-70% urban)	Small Town (20%-39% urban)	Rural (below 20% urban)
Contact with Registrants[a]				
(a) Frequent	3	15	19	13
(b) Occasional	26	47	55	48
(c) Rare, none[b]	72	37	26	39
	N=39	N=91	N=100	N=84

[a] Measured by responses to question, "Some local board members frequently see registrants or get phone calls from them. Others hardly ever have contact with registrants except at board meetings. Would you say that you have contact with registrants (either in person or by phone) Rarely — Occasionally — Frequently — ?"

[b] Includes negligible number of nonresponses, which are taken to be negative answers. Responses were obtained from 314 board members, or 81 per cent of all board members.

Source: Davis and Dolbeare, "Who Gets Drafted," Institute for Research on Poverty, University of Wisconsin, Madison, 1967, p. 31.

Whether some of the effects of neighborliness are altogether felicitous depends on one's viewpoint. Davis and Dolbeare indicate that

> in some rural areas the draft has been converted (perhaps unconsciously) into part of the social control system of the community. Some board members will promptly and enthusiastically reclassify a man when a change in his status coincides with a violation of

community norms — as in the case of failure to keep up child support or not getting a job in timely fashion.[31]

Two things should be emphasized about the variation between rural and urban boards in their proximity to the friends and neighbors concept. First, the large majority of Americans now live in urban areas, *not* rural. So for the majority of Americans the concept has become a somewhat ironic myth devoid of the legitimating content on which it was originally based. The Report of the National Advisory Commission repeats one of the comments from nine students they asked to take soundings on campuses. "Identity of local draft boards," one of them commented sarcastically, "is one of the best guarded secrets in America."[32]

Perhaps the passing of the time when a local board in an urban area could know the registrant and his personal condition was best expressed by a clerk who was asked if board members knew many of the registrants. She replied:

> Oh no. They're familiar with the district, but they don't know the kids that come in. You know the induction notices used to read: "Your friends and neighbors have selected you" — and it got so it made people so mad that they dropped it. One fellow came in here boiling mad and said, "Who are these friends and neighbors? I want to see them right now."[33]

The second point to be made about the capabilities of urban and rural boards is that local boards, whether rural or urban, are now burdened with *two* task orientations — implementing national manpower policy and adjusting draft processes to the individual. No one is sure how much weight should be given each task. But given the mobility of our population and the condition of our manpower pool both must be faced. More importantly, boards have not been provided with decision premises that would enable them to adequately handle either task.

If one is willing to accept the claim that rural boards are capable of adjusting the processes to the individual, there is evidence that they are more incapable than urban boards of deciding what is in the national health, safety and interest. (As has been indicated there is little room for optimism concerning the capability of the *urban* boards on this point.)

Davis and Dolbeare note that the number of appeals to state appeal boards appears to be a reflection of a particular policy departure by a local board, such as classifying all teachers I-A, or taking a particularly hard line with engineers or students. In their

Wisconsin study the ten rural boards were high compared to the urban in incidence of appeals.[34] As they remark:

> If the local board ideal of familiarity with the registrant is measured at all by the incidence of appeals this finding would appear to be another refutation of the concept. In fact, anonymity may actually promote consistency of decisions and conformity with guidelines, with resulting lower incidence of appeals.[35]

It is possible that a high incidence of appeals is not, as Davis and Dolbeare suggest, a measure of misused familiarity with the registrant, but rather a measure of the inability of rural boards to handle national manpower decisions as well as the urban boards. It is true that it indirectly refutes the ideal that familiarity with the registrant contributes to the legitimacy of decisions. For it shows that this familiarity is useless under today's conditions unless complemented by a capability to handle manpower policy and unless bounded by proper decision premises.

Conditions Leading to Loss of Capability

The loss of capability to make national manpower decisions is easily explained and needs little attention. During times of crisis and mobilization that capability increases; first because national and state headquarters increase the specificity of guidelines, i.e., narrow control limits; second, the boards have little doubt about the overriding need for military manpower. A simple decision premise develops: "When in doubt, draft." With the growth of the manpower pool, decline in calls, and loosening of controls and guidelines, the capability for manpower policy decisions is lost. The Vietnamese War may temporarily arrest this general trend but will not reverse it.

The urban boards' loss of capability to adjust the draft to the individual arises from a somewhat less obvious source—recruitment and tenure practices of the boards against a backdrop of changes in population characteristics and living patterns in urban areas.

Recruitment and Tenure. The only legal requisites for board members are that they be male citizens of at least thirty years and residents of the county in which their board has jurisdiction. It is only *preferred* that they be residents of the areas over which they preside.[36] According to statutes the President appoints each board member on nomination of the governor. This of course is purely *pro forma* and the authority was delegated to the Director of Selective Service on nominations by governors. Most governors have delegated the matter of nominations to state directors, who in turn have developed a variety of means for securing nominees.

Jacobs and Gallagher indicate that in California Superior Court Judges recommend local board members to the governor.[37] Davis and Dolbeare point out that in Texas the recommendation is made either by the state director or by local committees acting in his name.[38] Stewart interviewed 155 board members in five mid-Atlantic states and in New York City in 1946. The board members *thought* they had been recommended to the director by a variety of sources. (See Table 5)

TABLE 5. Source of Recommendation for Local Board Appointment as Reported by Local Board Members in Five States

Political Leaders or Organizations	57
Non-Political Leaders or Organizations	46
Veterans' Organization Leaders	35
System Administrators or Local Board Members	11
Don't Know	6
	155

Source: Donald Dean Stewart, "Local Boards, A Study of the Place of Volunteer Participation in a Bureaucratic Organization" (unpublished Ph.D. dissertation, Columbia University, 1950), p. 68.

Stewart felt that far more than 11 had been recommended by other board members because 36 of his respondents said they had recommended others for membership.

In Hill City and apparently throughout Agdustria the boards are virtually self-perpetuating bodies. Board members recruit replacements themselves with the field representative of the state director making the intial review of the nomination and intervening only if it appears essential that a racial, ethnic, occupational or geographic consideration be given attention. Although the role of the field representative was described in the above way it was not possible to confirm it by observation. The only intervention observed was an instance when board members disagreed on whose turn it was to nominate a new man and the field representative tried to mediate the dispute.

It is probable, however, that a field representative does perform the role of reviewer and occasional intervener but that his power is quite circumscribed by board members' sensitivities and by lack of sufficient knowledge or contacts, especially in the complex urban area. The surprising lack of adjustment of Hill City boards to socio-economic patterns and mention made by headquarters personnel or other areas in the state that needed racial adjustment would indicate again the non-transitive power of upper echelons and the corresponding limits on the field representative's powers of intervention.

The Hill City field representative refused to say how she recruited board members. This might be confirmation that she had no significant role in the recruitment, or it might not. The state director described the process in this way:

> Well, I'm often asked, "How do you recruit board members?" Now the law says they are appointed by the President on the recommendation of the governor — but the governor delegates to the state director the job of recommending them. I, in turn, rely on my field representatives. There are seven of them, often former board clerks and they cover a number of boards and they know their areas well. They go around to civic and service clubs etc. and ask, "Who would be a good man to serve on a draft board?" Maybe she goes to the Kiwanis first and they say, "Gee, Bill Smith would be a good man for that. He's a veteran and a good man." And then the field representative might go to the Chamber of Commerce or American Legion, and ask them who would be good. And maybe they mention a few people, one of which is Bill Smith. So you see they begin to build up cross checks and build up a picture of a man and finally nominate the best one. They get someone who wants to serve his country, who can attend meetings once a month or more often if the calls go higher, and who is willing to serve without pay — no compensation — if he travels he will get travel only. And this is how you get pretty good people.[39]

The pattern described by Agdustria's director probably fits the less urban boards, for it sounds as though he is describing rural areas and small towns. It is in such environs that groups like the Kiwanis and American Legion assume greater importance in the life of the community. For example, though urban and rural Wisconsin boards have almost equal numbers of veterans, almost twice as many of the board members in rural areas said they belonged to veterans' organizations. This would confirm the pattern of recruitment described by Agdustria's director which suggests that in rural areas field representatives rely heavily on veterans' groups for nominations.[40]

Observation of the Hill City boards indicates that at least the metropolitan boards rely primarily on other board members to do the recruiting. Board members rely on professional, church and social contacts to recruit new men. Davis and Dolbeare also found that in metropolitan boards "39% said they had been recruited by the local board."[41] In Hill City it was not unusual to find a seat on a board which had passed from father to son, or boards where the majority (and in one case all) of the members worked for or had retired from the same company.

Tenure. Positions seldom become vacant except through death. Until the law was revised in the summer of 1967 there was no legal limit on the amount of time members might serve. The law as revised set retirement at the age of 75 or upon completion of 25 years' service. While this limit will force retirements it will not change the general picture. Members at the time of this study were, for the most part, of advanced years, many having served since 1940. Relatively younger men had been brought in since the Korean War and this was particularly true in Agdustria where state headquarters had tried to offset absentee problems among the superannuated by expanding the boards from three to five members. Nonetheless the generalization of advanced age still held true.[42]

The National Commission in 1967 reported the average age of the System members as 58. One-fifth of the members were over 70, and of these 400 were over 80; 12 were between 90 and 99.[43] It also reports that almost 50 per cent served more than 10 years and 8 per cent more than 20. Davis and Dolbeare compared the ages of Wisconsin board members with the state's population, the state legislature and the U.S. Congress. All were substantially lower in age than the local board members. (See Table 6) While the advanced ages of board members is only a concomitant factor of tenure and does not directly bear upon the loss of capability, it does have relevancy for the legitimacy of board decisions.

Board members are quick to point out how "thankless" their job is, its lack of remuneration, and the lack of public appreciation. Nevertheless, they obviously derive great satisfaction from the work. Some mentioned that they "enjoy comin' down and listenin' to these different cases" but most often they spoke of it as "a job somebody has to do" and seemed to be motivated by patriotism and a desire to be involved in matters of far more importance than their daily lives. Even though urban members are largely invisible and anonymous they feel they gain status from their membership.[44]

It would be an unusual individual who did not feel a sense of importance at participating in decisions so crucial to the lives of registrants. Each man seems to have his favorite story that reflects

TABLE 6. Age of local board members, compared to state population and selected other officials, Wisconsin 1967

Age Group	Local Board Questionnaire Respondents 1966	All Wisconsin Local Board Members 1966	Wisconsin State Population 1960[1]	Wisconsin State Legislators 1966[2]	U. S. Congress 1966[3]
30-44	16%	17%	38%	30%	29%
45-59	40	41	33	41	46
60-69	18	42[5]	17	21	19
70 and over	26		12	8	6
	100%	100%	100%	100%	100%
	N = 314	N = 389	N = 960,305	N = 117	N = 534

[1]Source: U.S. Census, 1960 (Male population over 30 used as base)
[2]Source: Wisconsin Blue Book, 1966 (N=117 because 16 members rejected because under 30 or age unknown)
[3]Source: Congressional Quarterly (1st session 89th Congress, N = 534 because one member under 30)
[4]In all instances, percentages are based on the population which are over 30 years of age (the minimum age requirement for service on a Local Board) in order to maintain compatibility.
[5]Figure includes all over 60.

Source: James W. Davis and Kenneth M. Dolbeare, "Little Groups of Neighbors" (unpublished paper, University of Wisconsin, 1967), p. 9.

the humor, pathos, and drama of the contacts with registrants. The cases often have all of the elements of the popular soap operas of radio and television.

> It used to be that we met out in the wards, and when it came time to induct this one boy his mother came charging in and she says, "——— you old son-of-a-———, if you take my boy I'm going to kill you!" I think she would have — I was scared. Lucky he was IV-F.

> Then we had this woman who asked us to draft her husband. Well, he was over 26 and we couldn't take him. I asked her why she wanted him drafted. She said, " 'Cause my roof leaks." I said, "What do you mean your roof leaks? What has that got to do with drafting your husband?" "Well," she says, "my roof leaks and when I ask him to fix it, he comes over and stays overnight and I get pregnant."

Why, I've got a scar on my arm I guess I'll carry to my grave. Got it from trying to protect the women in the office from some dope fiend that was attacking them.⁴⁵

Everything possible is done to enhance the feeling of participation in national defense and note was made earlier of the paramilitary cadre's contribution in this regard. Men with different lengths of service (ten, fifteen, twenty, and twenty-five years) receive certificates and pins often with proper ceremony. There is also constant reiteration of the importance of the boards and the theme that they are the System's sole and final decision-making authority. As indicated earlier this emphasis is often so effective that it creates control problems for upper echelons.

Socio-economic Changes in Jurisdiction

To understand the erosion of the friends and neighbors concept it is important to view the tenure pattern against the changes since 1940 in socio-economic complexion of metropolitan areas. Hill City has followed the typical pattern of an in-flowing Negro population that collected first in the lower class neighborhoods closest to the core of the central city and then began to spill outward, "tipping" white neighborhoods of successively higher socioeconomic status.⁴⁶

This trend had begun by 1940 but it can truly be said to have taken place since that year. The remarkable changes in urban living that are now receiving such widespread attention have taken place largely during the tenure of most board members. It is also likely that board members have experienced increases in their incomes over the years and have moved outward toward suburbs without resigning. Perhaps they did not move so far or so suddenly as to make them feel they had really departed "the neighborhood," and were accordingly obligated to resign. Despite their change of residence, there was probably no sudden change in their professional and social associations that would make them feel a severance.

The Negro neighborhood with an all-white board cited earlier is an example of how swiftly these changes have taken place. The neighborhood was a middle to lower-middle class white area that would fall in a third belt if concentric circles were drawn outward from Hill City's center. Negroes from the old second belt ghetto that had achieved some upward mobility moved out and "tipped" the new area in the time between the Korean War and the present.

Board lines seldom change, though populations of boards have changed greatly. But until the board member expires or (less likely) resigns, he will continue to make some critical decisions concerning his "friends and neighbors."

General Characteristics of Board Decisions

If boards do not have the capability to handle the two tasks thrust upon them by today's conditions, if they lack information for manpower decisions and the personal knowledge needed to adjust processes to individuals, upon what do they base their decisions? In general, their decisions were based on interaction of their socio-economic values and derived notions of national interest on the one hand, with the registrant or his file on the other. There seemed to be three major sources from which members derived such values and notions: sharply pronounced middle class values, a "legionnaire outlook" on military service and national security needs, and the lack of information and comprehensible criteria for decisions.

Middle Class Values

The predominance of middle class values and attitudes among board members is striking. Registrants were often lectured or quizzed on the values of thrift, hard work, obedience to the law, morality, concern for parents; aliens were shown little sympathy in classification actions; college education was highly valued; efforts at self-improvement, materially, socially, or education-wise were lauded. Members were cognizant of persons above them in class status — "the real wheels," "those who have real money," "the prominent families"; and manifested even more awareness of those below them in status — "the other half," "the poor devils."

The occupations of Hill City members revealed a heavy preponderance of those generally taken to be indicators of middle class status. They ranged from firemen up to a vice president of a medium-sized public utility company which probably represented the highest community standing found in this study. Most of them fell into the category of less-prominent attorneys, dentists, ministers, lower and middle management, small business owners, accountants, department managers in large retail stores, salesmen, etc. Though Hill City is noted for its heavy industry, only one board member was a blue-collar worker.[47]

Sociologists are apparently reluctant to divide occupational rankings like the 1947 North-Hall-N.O.R.C. study by class strata. It is instructive, however, that using the much-criticized list of occupations and their score as developed by N.O.R.C. the Hill City board members ranged from 90 to 67. This would probably place them in the middle class and upward.[48] Data reported by the National Commission confirms the observation of this study. Seventy per cent of all board members are in white-collar occupations and of these over 20 per cent belong to professions. A majority of the rest are farmers. Craftsmen, service workers, semiskilled workers and laborers are represented on local boards in far smaller proportions, less than 25 per cent of their presence in the general population.[49] (See Table 7)

TABLE 7. Occupation of Local Board Members in Metropolitan and Nonmetropolitan Areas (Nation-Wide) 1967

Occupation	Metropolitan		Nonmetropolitan	
	Number	Percent	Number	Percent
Lawyer	831	13.5	321	3.3
Other professional, technical	1,143	18.6	1,228	12.8
Salaried public administrators	209	3.4	504	5.2
All other salaried managers and officials	1,273	20.7	1,058	11.0
Self employed proprietors	568	9.2	1,150	12.0
Other proprietors, managers, and officials	272	4.4	598	6.2
Clerical and sales	1,071	17.4	1,340	14.0
Farmers, farm laborers, farm managers	233	3.8	2,387	24.9
Craftsmen, foremen, and kindred workers	309	5.0	554	5.8
Service workers	102	1.6	147	1.5
All others	134	2.2	306	3.2
Total	6,145	100.0	9,593	100.0
Not reported	365		535	

Source: National Advisory Commission on Selective Service, "In Pursuit of Equity: Who Serves When Not All Serve?" (Washington, D.C.: Government Printing Office, February, 1967), p. 19.

Education is also a classifier. While only 10 per cent of the general population of comparable age are college graduates, about 33 per cent of the board members fall into this category.[50] (See Table 8)

TABLE 8. Educational Level of Local Board Members in Metropolitan and Nonmetropolitan Areas (Nation-Wide) 1967

Educational Level	Metropolitan		Nonmetropolitan	
	Number	Per cent	Number	Per cent
Less than high school graduate	546	8.9	1,824	19.1
High school graduate	1,441	23.5	3,353	35.2
Some college	1,383	22.6	2,151	22.6
College graduate or more	2,752	44.9	2,204	23.1
Total	6,122	100.0	8,532	100.0
Not reporting	388		596	

Source: National Advisory Commission on Selective Service, "In Pursuit of Equity: Who Serves When Not All Serve?" (Washington, D.C.: Government Printing Office, February, 1967), p. 19.

The boards are almost exclusively white which does nothing to detract from their middle class character. Out of 16,638 local board members only 213 or 3.2 per cent are Negro. Negroes, of course, constitute roughly 12 per cent of the general population. As for other non-white groups, Puerto Ricans constituted 0.8 per cent, Spanish Americans 0.7, Orientals 0.2 (38), and American Indians 0.1 (16) of all board members. (See Table 9)

The differences between rural and metropolitan boards are not great. Metropolitan boards have roughly 10 per cent more lawyers, 9 per cent more salaried managers and officials and 21 per cent less farmers.[51] The only noteworthy difference seems to be the subtle one of status. Rural board members tend to stand higher in the community power structure, and participate more in civic and community affairs than their urban counterparts. They can thus be characterized more accurately as "influentials" and "notables" than can urban members.[52]

TABLE 9. Ethnic Status or Race of Local Board Members in Metropolitan and Nonmetropolitan Areas (Nation-Wide) 1967

Ethnicity or race	Metropolitan		Nonmetropolitan	
	Number	Percent	Number	Percent
Oriental	26	0.4	12	0.1
American Indian	—	—	16	.2
Spanish American	42	.7	72	.7
Puerto Rican	4	.1	122	1.3
Negro	178	2.8	35	.4
White or other	6,083	96.0	9,423	97.3
Total	6,333	100.0	9,680	100.0
Not reporting	177		448	

Note: Not surprisingly the Commission Report shows the following representation of Negroes on boards in some southern states:

State	% of Negro Board Members	% of State Population Negro
Alabama	0	30.0
Arkansas	0	21.8
Georgia	.2	28.5
Mississippi	0	42.0
South Carolina	.6	34.8
Florida	.9	17.8
Virginia	2.2	20.6

Source: National Advisory Commission on Selective Service, "In Pursuit of Equity: Who Serves When Not All Serve?" (Washington, D.C.: Government Printing Office, February, 1967), pp. 75, 80-81.

As noted above, middle class values and attitudes seem to be the most salient influence on board members' decisions. Stewart noted that the board member respondents emphasized that they were not straight-laced, that they were disinterested in morals. But Stewart points out:

> There was an observed tendency among board members to refer to the standards of middle class behavior in decisions... irregular work records, arrests, drunkenness, petty offenses were felt to be "better off in the Army." Marital unions not sanctioned by law were

disregarded in classification, even if it was of long standing and involved children.[53]

One striking example might be appropriate to conclude discussion of this variable of middle class values. A Hill City registrant sought a II-A critical occupational deferment to continue work with the Y.M.C.A. The registrant had all the qualities that board members viewed positively. He was pleasant, clean-cut, well-dressed, forthright, and confident but with respectful demeanor. Such characteristics were always looked upon as "presenting oneself well." During the interview the subject of social class was brought up.

> *Chairman:* What—a—sort of people do you try to reach with your clubs—are these the—a—lower classes—er—poorer...
> *Registrant:* [hesitatingly] Well—a—no. They're just middle class kids in the suburban high school. They're all basically good kids, but we feel that they need a program like this.

The board voted for deferment. When the researcher expressed his surprise to the clerk the next day she admitted that the decision had surprised her too.

> Well, I think they liked his personality. He sold himself well and I think mostly they thought he was doing some good work. That boy knew what he wanted to do. He wasn't just killing time like so many others. He'd turned down all those other jobs that offered more money and they probably felt that he was doing the community a real service in the long run. Don't you think he is? I mean, seeing those kids get into something worthwhile instead of becoming delinquents or something like that.[54]

The appropriateness of the classification is not questioned here. It is instructive to note that this deferment was granted by a board in the same office on the same day when another board had classified a graduate professional engineer I-A. Furthermore, the board was passing judgment on the value of a registrant to a community located 400 miles distant from it. Finally the registrant was the epitome of middle class ambition, assuredness, and goal orientedness that boards universally found appealing and looked for in registrants.

Veteran Status

The second major source of decision premises for board members stems from their status as veterans. Among the seventy-four board members included in this study, veterans outnumbered nonveterans better than seven to one. One clerk of twenty-five years experience admitted that until recently she had believed that the regulations required that members be veterans. Figures released in the National Commission's Report confirm that 67 per cent of board members are veterans. (See Table 10)

Veterans seem to possess outlooks on military service and the use of military power in pursuit of foreign policy that are functional for them and for Selective Service. One might label this set of attitudes as an American Legionnaire outlook. Veterans' groups, of course, run a gamut from moderate left to the far right, and "semihard" to "hard" on foreign and defense policy. But on atti-

TABLE 10. Military Service Experience of Local Board Members in Metropolitan and Nonmetropolitan Areas (Nation-Wide) 1967

Service experience	Metropolitan		Nonmetropolitan	
	Number	Percent	Number	Percent
None	2,393	37.9	3,064	31.0
World War I only	1,255	19.9	1,620	16.4
World War I and other	12	.2	16	.2
World War I and all other combinations	63	1.0	83	1.0
World War II only	2,205	34.9	4,391	44.4
World War II and Korean	50	.8	157	1.6
World War II, Korean and other	—	—	5	(*)
Korean only	157	2.5	267	2.7
Korean and other	2	(*)	4	(*)
Other only	153	2.4	261	2.6
Total	6,310	100.0	9,887	100.0
Not reported	200		241	

*Less than 0.1 percent

Source: National Advisory Commission on Selective Service, "In Pursuit of Equity: Who Serves When Not All Serve?" (Washington, D.C.: Government Printing Office, February, 1967), p. 75.

tudes toward military service and national security policy the majority of veterans fall on the Legion end of the spectrum. Gabriel Almond has said:

> The veterans' organizations in the United States have historically placed special emphasis on a strong national defense policy. Their general ideology has been nationalist and patriotic, and they have led in efforts to suppress subversive elements. As an aspect of their nationalism they have shown distrust of foreigners, and they have advocated the restriction of immigration.[55]

In the discussion that follows it will become evident that Almond has caught some of the main elements of the outlook of board members.

The term Legionnaire outlook is also fitting because of the high number of board members who belong to the Legion or other veterans' organizations. The history of Selective Service is one of close ties with the Legion, which in many areas was instrumental in organizing Selective Service for World War II.

A history of the Personnel Division of Agdustria's headquarters reveals that in 1940 the governor appointed Advisory Committees in each county to select board members, *but prior to selection* of board members the committees were furnished with names of individuals willing to serve. The lists had been provided by that part of the state staff of the Agdustria National Guard which had engaged in Selective Service planning.[56] One clerk that had been with the System since its 1940 beginning said that the National Guard had primarily worked through American Legion posts to develop the lists. She had been active in the Legion Auxiliary and had actually begun the operation of her board in the Legion post itself.

Presumably drawing on his experiences while working with national headquarters, Stewart notes that the director for one western state delegated the selection of local boards in 1940 to the county commanders of the Legion and stipulated that two Legionnaires should be placed on each three-man board. Stewart adds that "it was more common to consult with the American Legion and the Veterans of Foreign Wars in selecting board members."[57] The extent of such close collaboration is unknown but the American Legion would have been a natural ally for the National Guard to turn to in establishing the Selective Service System.

There were also cases in which the registrants who were aliens were quickly identified as such and I-A decisions reached with dispatch. Board members claimed that aliens were here to avoid the draft in their own countries. (Some of the countries in question have no conscription.) As for concern over subversives, conversations easily turned to such matters after meetings. There were discussions covering such matters as: the mistake of disarming after World War II; how General Marshall had "given away China"; MacArthur had the "right idea"; how America was being "suckered into all that foreign aid"; and how "the only thing those Russians and Chinese understand is muscle."

Partly as a result of the negative nature of conscription and partly as a result of their Legionnaire outlook, members viewed military service as "rites of passage," a manhood ritual all should go through; as a means of acquiring valuable skills and training that would be useful in civilian life; and above all as a service one owed his country. Stewart also found board members "inclined to regard such service as a not unpleasant citizen duty."[58]

Members, clerks and higher officials were proud of this preponderance of veterans because "no one can say they haven't served their country" and "they know what they are sending these boys off to." "The boys have more confidence in them." The status of a veteran is thus considered highly desirable for any man who must send others off to soldier and it becomes functional for legitimacy.

It also provides the System with the necessary stability in meeting the functional demand it faces—providing military power. No matter how controversial the war which requires conscripts, men with Legionnaire outlooks are unlikely to resign.[59] If board members reflected the same degree of division over the war as is found in the general population, it might be difficult or even impossible for it to perform its task. In six months of observation during the most controversial foreign war in which the United States has engaged there was no criticism of the application of military power in pursuit of foreign policy in Viet Nam. Stewart noted that all board members criticized something about the System but not one of his respondents questioned the assumption on which it was founded, i.e., that wartime conscription was necessary to secure an adequate supply of manpower for the Armed Forces and to organize civilian war production.[60]

Lack of Information and Decision Criteria

A third cluster of related variables influencing decisions is the peculiar lack of information, operational decision criteria, and confusion over the proper role of the boards. Without personal knowledge of the registrant, information on national manpower needs, or ability to investigate claims of registrants, the members are reduced to decisions that are non-rational in a Weberian sense.

To understand the difficulty of the boards' task and the operational meaning of the term non-rational, one must appreciate the dilemmas they face as decision-makers because of the lack of proper information and decision criteria. The functional imperative or the demand of the institutional task is to draft men or defer them in a way consistent with national health, safety, or interest. It is difficult for them to meet the demands of such a vague and nebulous imperative. Simultaneously they are confronted with a societal imperative that they draft and defer in line with societal standards of equity.

In years past, Selective Service operated in an atmosphere of crisis and total mobilization. Moreover it has always been viewed as temporary both by members of the institution and by the larger society. In such circumstances the tension between task demands and societal demands was greatly reduced. The meaning of national health, safety and interest was less obscure. Men were needed in uniform. In the case of those few with skills that might be critical enough to outweigh the need for them as soldiers, the policy guidance provided by higher echelons of Selective Service was sufficiently explicit to make deferment less problematic given the situational context. Now with a long-run plethora of manpower confronting the System the never-too-helpful decision premise of national health, safety and interest is of diminishing utility and in fact exacerbates difficulties.

If meeting the functional imperative is difficult, meeting the societal demand for equity seems doubly so. First, there seem to have been definite but scarcely charted changes in societal concepts of equity in our political culture. This is resulting in critical examination of formerly accepted procedures of Selective Service that once held legitimating power. But beyond this general difficulty over equity lies a more specific problem.[61] Equity has at least two facets: uniformity of treatment — that universal criteria be applied uniformly to all registrants; and particularistic consideration and adaptation of universal criteria to the circumstances of the individual.

Consider the difficulty of a board bent on uniformity of treatment. They would endeavor to determine what sort of registrant or type of case confronted them and then handle the matter in a way similar to all other matters of the same type. Such a handling of cases requires broad universal criteria that transcend the immediate and particular situation or the mere interaction between board members and registrant. The national health, safety, or interest qualifies as a universal and higher decision criterion but is inadequate because it is unintelligible to board members. They lack the kind of information that could make it a useful decision criterion that they could operationalize; or their attempt to apply it results in what seems to them to be an inequitable decision.

Uniformity of decisions is thus difficult, but particularistic adaptation of universal criteria to the individual is no less so. This is not to say that boards could not do this at all. A pharmacist facing induction who was a partner in the business was retained in a critical occupation category for four months until he could find a replacement; a man who claimed to be supporting his mother was given three months to find other relatives to relieve him of the burden, etc. Examples notwithstanding, boards were plagued by the fact that they were not really the "friends and neighbors" of the registrants. The fact remained that they had none of the first hand, personal knowledge that the institutional role demanded.

Grappling with these dichotomous demands of equity has probably always been part of the task of local boards. But the demands have become increasingly hard to reconcile as Selective Service drifted into an era of excess manpower and responded by expansion of deferments in an unplanned manner that grew out of the general aura of "temporariness" that has always pervaded the institution. The tensions over equity generated by the Viet Nam War are only an aggravating factor added to this fundamental problem.

Board members were constantly torn between trying to operationalize the impossibly vague criterion of national interest and adaptation of processes to the individual situation. Because they were expected to operationalize some nebulous national manpower policy they tried to act on the basis of national health, safety or interest and to treat similar cases in a uniform manner; but at the same time they felt driven to adjust the processes of Selective Service to individuals. Because they lacked informational resources to do either, they reacted in a disturbingly large portion of cases by treating registrants in accordance with the relationships they developed with them in the interview or from letters in the files. Consequently the seemingly insignificant things like posture and dress, and wording and signature of letters become inordinately important in decisions.

An example of a board attempting to reach a decision on the basis of a higher criterion was one that proceeded through a stack of files, granting occupational deferments as usual until they began to encounter requests for deferments from men who had just joined firms after leaving college.

> *Board Member 1:* I can't see letting these guys dodge their commitment like this. You know what they're gonna do — get kids or stay there till over 26. I don't think it's fair.
> *Board Member 2:* Well, I agree but some of these guys are going into defense work.
> *Board Member 1:* [referring to a file] This guy's going to work at GM auto engineering and testing — how in the h—— is that connected with defense? And besides — how critical can any man be just out of college and on the job three weeks? You can't tell me these guys are critical to anyone — defense or not.
> *Chairman:* Thing we have to remember is that Colonel ——— (state headquarters) said to let these guys go from college to industry and get started.
> *Board Member 1:* I know. But it doesn't make sense to me. H—— yes, he'll be valuable to someone after he's on the job a while.[62]

The argument continued at some length and grew quite heated before the board agreed to defer such men. Thus they had struggled to operationalize a higher criterion but found themselves confounded by a vague suggestion from state headquarters that made no sense to them on the basis of their information, and was leading them to a conclusion that seemed unfair to them.

Their frustration, however, was not yet at an end. As they proceeded through more files they were confronted with requests to defer men on the basis of jobs they would accept within a month. At this, the whole argument erupted again with one board member angrily declaring, "I'll be d—— if I am going to defer some man as critical who isn't even on the job yet!" He then launched into a long and bitter tirade against "sending all these poor kids from the West End of town while all these others with money go to college and then get into a critical occupation." He concluded flushed and angry with: "I've had it! I say turn down this request for deferment. If headquarters doesn't like it that's too d—— bad. I'm not afraid to tell them where to go! I told F. D. R. I'm ready to tell them."[63] Finally the chairman brought all of them back to the frustrating reality that went with trying to apply higher criteria uniformly when he said, "Well, we let all the others go — how are we going to treat this one any differently?" Of course, they couldn't.

In this case the board stuck with uniform application of a vague higher criterion but not without frustration. Certainly it is hard to see how the board arrived at any satisfying degree of equity despite all the frustration they endured in reaching decisions. Boards just as often balked at the apparent inequity that seemed to lie at the end of such a course or despaired of finding the information needed for a decision, and resorted to personalistic interaction between themselves and the registrant for decision premises. For example:

> *Board Member 1:* A deferment to study architecture in graduate school!?
> *Board Member 2:* Isn't this the rich kid that's given us all the trouble?
> *Clerk:* That's the one.
> *Board Member 1:* As far as I'm concerned he shouldn't be allowed to keep going to school. It's so obvious he's trying to get out of serving! Remember that bad knee story he came in here with?[64]

Often they reacted in a personalistic manner to such things as the official title of the person seeking a deferment for an employee.

> Look at this [holding out a letter] — a personnel officer signs it. Now you know what level a personnel officer is in a company — he's just a flunky. Probably does this for everyone in the company as a matter of course. I don't think we ought to give a deferment to a company that handles it this way.[65]

Or they reacted strongly and punitively to the wording of letters which seemed to imply disrespect for the boards. More often they reacted in a personalistic and particularistic way to the registrant in his interview with the board.

> *Clerk:* If you're ready I'll bring Mr. X in.
> *Chairman:* [with a smile] Has he gotten rid of this? [gesturing to indicate a beard]
> *Clerk:* Oh, yes—slick as a whistle. [other board members chuckle][66]

Or another board:

> *Chairman:* [holding up a file and speaking to the researcher] You ought to see this guy. Were you ever in the military, Captain? [sic] Well this is the sort of guy you would take down to the latrine and scrub down with a wire brush. I mean, I've seen these Hell's Angels out in California — seen them on the television and he's worse looking than any of them. Just plain scurvy. [to the clerk] Let's make this baby I-A. We'll fix his trolley.[67]

Discussion following an interview often dwelt only partially upon the possible applicability of higher criteria to the case. Much time was frequently spent in particularistic commentary.

"Nice looking lad."
"Makes a good appearance."
"That's a wonderful press job on that shirt."

"Leaves a good impression."
"Clean cut lad. Dresses and carries himself well."

[Board member to a clerk] "What's the attitude of these two boys when you've seen them? Were they smart allecky? or belligerent?"

In the absence of useful guidelines and information, dress, mannerisms, bearing, forthrightness, grooming etc., all took on exaggerated importance. Because manpower demands changed constantly and because higher criteria were not understandable, clear, or manageable, they often seemed inapplicable. Obviously, the board members themselves did not consider national health, safety, and interest to be useful criteria.

One Hill City board had developed its own higher criterion and thus solved the problems that plagued the others. Its higher criterion was that "everybody had to serve." No one was in a critical occupation for any longer than it took to replace him and an employer was given a specified time to do just that. Deferments, they said, were deferments, *not* exemptions. Considerable tension existed between the board and state headquarters as a result of this drastic method of simplifying decision rules. Probably the most exasperating thing to state headquarters was the fact that the board's interpretation of the law and regulations was perfectly legitimate.

The difficulty the board faced was manifest in their efforts to acquire information of any sort that might help them reach a decision. The search for information often only heightened their dilemma because they were seldom sure what information was relevant which was in turn a consequence of their inability to decide which criterion they could or should use. If one is to apply some sort of higher criterion then only a restricted range of information is relevant because concern with the registrant is limited and significance found in limited bits of information.

The operational failure of any higher criterion was evident as board members probed into irrelevant aspects of the registrants' lives in an effort to find something on which to base a decision. Typical queries were such as these:

"What do you do with your spare time?"

"You don't like to submit to authority, do you?"

"What kind of car do you drive?"

"Were you ever in the Boy Scouts?"
"Where do you do your loafing?"
"Does your father have a problem with drinking or anything?"

If one cannot somehow limit the scope of his concern with an object he cannot apply higher universal criteria with uniformity. Diffuse probing and interest is more justifiable when attempting to adjust universal criteria or administrative processes to the individual, but even this function would seem to require more limits of specificity than the boards manifested. It may be that with more and more people deferred for ever-vaguer reasons, boards must be increasingly diffuse and broad in their concern. Depending on the situation and line of questioning, any of the above *might* be relevant but disturbingly often the relevancy was not evident. In any event, the diffuseness of the questions points up the lack of personal knowledge the institution claims that board members have.

The National Commission's Report has provided information that verifies the ambivalence and frustration of board members observed in this study. Board members were asked the following: "In deciding about deferments, would you prefer more specific state and national directives, less specific directives, or do you feel the amount of guidance provided to local boards is about right?" Nearly 46 per cent of boards responding wanted more specific guidance on occupational deferments. Forty per cent wanted more on student deferments, and 29 per cent wanted more on hardship deferments. Less than 5 per cent felt they received too much guidance from upper echelons.[68]

The Commission also sought to ascertain how board members rated the importance of several different factors in reaching decisions on hardship and student deferments. There was substantial agreement among boards as to which factors were most important, reflecting the uniformity that the various control mechanisms discussed previously are able to produce among 4,070 boards. But there were also some surprising disagreements of the sort that make for some of the much-criticized lack of uniformity and inconsistency. In a student deferment case 25 per cent of the boards thought that the fact that a student is working was a very important factor in deciding about his deferment, while 23 per cent thought it should not be considered at all; nearly 38 per cent felt his level in school was of great importance while 21 per cent felt it was not very important and almost 15 per cent would not consider it at all. Though upper echelons have given no guidance as to which fields of study are to be given priority, 33 per cent felt it was a factor of great importance, 23 per cent felt it was not very important and 16.4 per cent would not consider it at all.

In hardship cases, 21 per cent thought the level of calls should be an important consideration while 36 per cent felt it should not be considered at all.[69] These figures lend support to this study. Boards are confronted with contradictory demands, and are inadequately equipped to meet any of the demands or a combination of them. The fundamental uniformity produced by control mechanisms is marred by glaring disuniformity of action. These areas, while perhaps slight in terms of an efficiency price, are becoming extremely costly in political effectiveness under today's conditions.

Board Decisions and the Clerks

The role of the clerks deserves special attention for several reasons: (1) much criticism has been leveled against them; (2) their role in decision-making is misunderstood because of institutional myths; and (3) the clerks themselves serve to deflect or blunt hostility directed at the institution.

The clerks often describe themselves with some accuracy as part clerk, social worker, top sergeant, policeman, recruiter, and substitute parent. They are overwhelmingly women, mature in years, with a devotion to their work that is incredible.[70] They comprise one of several insulated and autonomous personnel systems within the Selective Service System,[71] which make possible a highly selective recruitment and extensive institutionalization. In the case of the clerks it places persons in positions of far greater responsibility and power than most of them would ever expect to achieve given their socio-economic background, educational level, or their salary of 4,600 dollars.[72] Clerks constantly referred to themselves as "responsible people," and said they liked "being their own boss." This would seem to reflect the fact that those who elect to join the System are totally immersed in their roles and relish their work. Many work late into the night and on weekends despite low pay, a lack of ingrade pay increases, no overtime, and more compensatory time built up than they can ever be permitted to use.

The basis for the closed personnel system is the fact that the clerks are non-classified civil service. The Universal Military

Training and Service Act of 1951 authorized the President (who authorized the Director of Selective Service)

> to appoint, and to fix, in accordance with the classification act of 1923, as amended, the compensation of, such officers, agents, and employees as he may deem necessary to carry out the provisions of this title: provided, that the *compensation of employees of local boards and appeal boards may be fixed without regard to the classification act of 1923 as amended.*[73]

This means that because the positions are not classified salaries are controlled by the director and the clerks do not receive automatic merit salary adjustments or pay increases; and other civil service personnel cannot transfer into the System and "bump" clerks. Originally the clerks were not civil service at all. National headquarters *recommended* only that they have a high school education, three years clerical experience, ability to file and type, loyalty and good character. Regulations prohibited the hiring of a relative of a board member who was related as close or closer than a first cousin.[74]

The position was "exempt" from civil service as part of the "decentralized" stance of the System. National headquarters has always emphasized the importance of having the clerks, along with all the other persons connected with the local board, identified with the community served. System spokesmen have insisted that one of the most important ways in which this identification could be attained is by compensating the clerks in accordance with community standards rather than standards established for federal employees generally.[75]

In recent years the position was placed under Civil Service but it was not classified. Clerks must pass what is essentially the test for the lowest clerical skill level in civil service. Persons hired from such a non-classified list are largely used by agencies for temporary or seasonal work. This means that in most cases the System hires assistant clerks (or occasionally clerks) from the non-classified list. There is a high turnover among such persons but interestingly enough the System regards this as an acceptable price for an extremely functional recruiting mechanism. Though there is a very high turnover and a local board may have to go through several assistant clerks or clerks, they eventually turn up the unusual individual the System seeks who will be completely dedicated to the job. Since clerical skills are only one of the traits considered desirable, the System can afford to wait until the exceptional individual they seek turns up on this low-skill list.

A state headquarters official put it this way:

> We have a big turnover in the assistant clerks we hire off the list. Mostly because they come in under some clerk who has been there a long time and is going to stay a long time. The new gal often sees it as a dead end. But this is O.K. It sort of sorts them out and leaves only the dedicated. They'll work like religious fanatics.[76]

And General Hershey has testified:

> Well, in the first place, we do have to get them off the register. And they do have to qualify. But I think with some pride I would say that we do not consider every one competent to be a local board clerk that could qualify for a clerical classification perhaps comparable to what we would get, because they have got to have some rather peculiar qualities of getting along with the communities and the registrants and registrants' parents where they happen to work.[77]

Selective Service has consistently opposed classification of the clerks. There have been several studies on the subject and sentiment for classification within the Civil Service Commission but it has always backed down on pressing the matter in the face of resistance from the System, and often from Presidents who were convinced by the System's argument.[78]

What type of person is recruited? Allusion has already been made to their dedication, a quality desirable in a System that has had to operate on an emergency or crisis basis on occasion. They must also be something more than "8 to 5" workers in order to work with volunteer boards that often meet at night. Beyond this they project a completely civilian image of the System and an image that tends to deflect hostility. For they might best be described by the term "grandmother type." As a generalization this is not inaccurate. Most of them are of middle age and beyond in years.[79] They do *not* project an image of cold efficiency and aloofness even though they represent the most bureaucratic element in a consciously non-bureaucratic system. Many of them are grandmothers, unassuming and "homey" in appearance. They are tolerant and philosophic about registrants. Many refer to them as "my boys." They are hardly a suitable object of hostility or criticism.

> *Question:* Do you ever get any that refuse to register or cause trouble?
> Clerk: [mother of two teenagers] Oh no, not really. I guess this morning there was some trouble with some fellow who was tongue-tied and the other kids were giving him a hard time. But you don't

take them seriously, or at least I don't. They're just kids — just babies. If you've got kids of your own you know what they're like and you couldn't take them serious.⁸⁰

Another clerk who had been with the System since 1942 and had two children of her own said:

My boys [her registrants] are all good boys. Oh, I don't mean good with the law — they're always in trouble with the police and things but they're good in that they're ready to go. Sometimes you have to chew a boy out. I had a little fellow who the police picked up with seven draft cards on him. I told him, "Nothing else — not another thing from me!" Now if he comes in and sees me he ducks back out.⁸¹

And another clerk in a typical gesture manifested some of the psychic rewards gained from the position.

I must show you a picture one of my boys sent me. This little fellow is a guard at Arlington and sent me a picture of Kennedy's grave. This is the sort of thing that makes the job worthwhile. You wouldn't do it just for money — but when they do this or come in and see you. . . .⁸²

The image the clerks project is a vital one, for relatively few registrants will have contact with board members. The clerk can never be anonymous and invisible. A better image, more attuned to political culture could scarcely be devised. General Hershey acknowledged this.

But our clerks are the individuals that have made the image of the Selective Service System, because they are the individuals that have met the registrants.⁸³

The National Commission acknowledged a widespread belief among registrants that clerks "run the boards."⁸⁴ And Congressman Chet Holifield of California during the 1966 draft hearings said:

The Civil Service Commission clerks are running these boards, not the members . . . the bulk of the work, I would say 85% of the work of screening and classifying these boys are done by Civil Service clerks and then when the board meets that night, they hand it to them and they run through them and the clerk says, "this bunch on top ought to go" so they sign their names and they go. In many instances we are not achieving the principle that we thought we were achieving of having local businessmen and leaders in the community express evaluative judgment on the merits of specific cases. It is being done by low paygrade clerks.⁸⁵

Does the research support his conclusions? Basically, yes, but some explanations and qualifications are in order. Complaints such as those above stem largely from a misunderstanding of the nature of the boards' task. This misinterpretation is an outgrowth of the institutional myth the System has fostered that "each case is handled individually" or "each one is decided on an individual basis."[86] By attempting to identify so closely with the individualism of our political culture, the System left itself open to criticism when the clerks assumed ever-increasing importance as the System became more permanent and there were years of slack calls. Sooner or later the discrepancy between institutional myth and reality was bound to be pointed out.

First the volume of classification is so great that a board could not possibly handle all cases, even in a cursory way, let alone review each one extensively. There is no way to tell whether a classification action required discussion or was reviewed by a board. There is no requirement that board members sign board actions although clerks are urged to obtain their signatures.

Nevertheless, the vast majority of classification actions are so routine that they are quite unlikely to have received board review. For example, the following routine classifications make up the great numerical bulk of classification decisions.

I-A	reclassified IV-F (unfit) or I-Y (available for emergency)
III-A	(dependency) reclassified to V-A (over-age) or any other classification changed to V-A
I-Y	reclassified to IV-F (or any other change to IV-F)
I-A	reclassified to I-D (reserves), or I-C (active duty)
I-D or I-C	reclassified to IV-A (veteran)
I-A	reclassified to I-SH or II-S (students)
I-SH	reclassified to II-S (high school to college)

Some boards process certain classifications routinely without review while other boards might not follow such procedure. For example, some boards had instructed their clerks to automatically grant anyone working in the field of science an occupation deferment so that all their I-A's or II-S's in the field of science applying for reclassification to II-A were not reviewed. These same actions might have been carefully gone over by another board. Or a I-A seeking a III-A (dependency) might have been reclassified automatically by one clerk on the basis of a pregnancy slip or birth certificate while the case might have been thoroughly discussed by another board. The following were most likely to receive review of a board:

I-A seeking a I-O or IA-O (Conscientious Objectors)
I-A claiming a III-A (dependency)
I-A seeking a II-A (critical occupation)
I-A asking for II-C (agriculture)
II-S claiming a II-A (student to critical occupation)

The public record of board classification actions gives no clues as to how a classification was made but the total number of actions for each meeting offers evidence that the majority are never reviewed by the boards.

Several Hill City boards of varying sizes were selected at random and a review of classification actions over five months was made. The volume of classification actions was relatively uniform for all. Typical was a board with 13,000 registrants which had 215 actions in March, 176 in April, 219 in May, 348 in June and 217 in July. The size of these totals clearly shows that they were not all reviewed in a two to three hour monthly meeting. The largest board among the seventeen was the second largest in the state. It had 24,000 registrants and met twice a month. Its monthly classifications ranged from 450 to 1,334, obviously beyond the ability of any board to discuss each case thoroughly, even in two meetings.

The typed minutes of board meetings kept by clerks are not public records. They give no clear indication as to whether a board reviewed the cases and made a decision, but usually a clerk noted on it those that she felt were important enough to take into a meeting even if the board never discussed all of them. A board rarely was able to conduct interviews with more than three or four registrants in a meeting. The number of files they were able to review depended on whether they divided the work, how well they worked together and the types of cases. Many boards divided files and each member decided the cases in his stack. Others divided them and each man presented a summary of each case to the others and they indicated approval or disapproval of his proposed actions. Generally, of the twenty to thirty files a clerk would carry into a meeting, ten to fifteen might be discussed for widely varying amounts of time and there might be three or four interviews. The other files might be signed without discussion or perhaps even this would not be done. Clearly, 175 to 350 cases were not reviewed.

The Report of the Special Commission probed this matter and its findings confirm those of this study. Boards were asked the following question: "Some cases are virtually automatic from the regulations or other facts, and others require more consideration. In your September 1966 board meeting, how many men did you classify or reclassify?" As indicated by Table 11, 62.9 per cent indicated that they classified or reclassified forty-nine or less men. As for the 9.6 per cent who said they had classified or reclassified from 200 to over 600 men, the kindest thing that can be said is that they misinterpreted the question.[87] The Commission made particular note that 17 per cent of the boards said that 90 per cent or more of the classifications were automatic. The Commission noted that this figure was confirmed by their interviews with board members.[88]

The second qualification that must be made is that it is unnecessary for a board to discuss most cases separately. The great majority of classifications are absolutely routine and automatic. When a man sends in a pregnancy slip he can only become III-A; papers proving enlistment in the Active Armed Forces can only result in I-C; the Reserves, I-D; over 26, in V-A, etc.

Third, the clerks *do* sort and stack files for board meetings, and some lightly pencil in a recommended classification on the file cover, but they do not necessarily place on top the ones they feel "ought to go." Rather they usually set aside for first consideration those that are most contentious or sensitive whether they seemed headed for induction or deferment — cases they would not dare handle automatically or routinely because an appeal will probably be taken and they want legitimation by the board. It should not be assumed that the clerks have a bias that favors induction. Though their exasperation at the registrant whom they feel is clearly trying to evade his obligation may tend to make them "pro-induction" toward such individuals, these instances are exceptions. Generally a clerk has a thoroughly bureaucratic (in a non-pejorative sense) outlook toward the registrants and wants only to put them "into some slot." In other words, they are not as concerned over seeing a man inducted as they are in seeing that he is no longer problematic for them.

It is entirely possible for clerks to influence decisions. But the clerk's intervention was not always detrimental to the registrant. As one clerk said:

> You have to protect the registrants from the board as much as you do the board from the registrants. They [members] can't keep up with the rules and regulations. They only come in once a month and

TABLE 11. Volume of Classifications Reported by Local Boards

Question: "Some cases are virtually automatic from the regulations or other facts, and others require more consideration. In your September 1966 board meeting, how many men did you classify or reclassify?"

Number classified or reclassified	Number of local boards					
	Classifications			Reclassifications		
	Total	Metropolitan	Non-metropolitan	Total	Metropolitan	Non-metropolitan
Less than 20	1,224	157	1,067	227	24	203
20 to 49	1,072	353	719	593	36	557
50 to 99	630	322	308	903	131	772
100 to 199	380	203	177	943	374	569
200 to 299	151	94	57	481	297	184
300 to 399	76	55	21	230	154	76
400 to 499	43	33	10	125	100	25
500 to 599	29	22	7	71	56	15
600 and over	46	40	6	126	110	16
Total	3,651	1,279	2,372	3,699	1,282	2,417
Percent distribution						
Less than 20	33.5	12.3	45.0	6.1	1.9	8.4
20 to 49	29.4	27.6	30.3	16.1	2.8	23.1
50 to 99	17.3	25.2	13.0	24.4	10.2	31.9
100 to 199	10.4	15.9	7.4	25.5	29.2	23.6
200 to 299	4.1	7.4	2.4	13.0	23.1	7.6
300 to 399	2.1	4.3	.9	6.2	12.0	3.1
400 to 499	1.2	2.6	.4	3.4	7.8	1.0
500 to 599	.8	1.7	.3	1.9	4.4	.6
600 and over	1.2	3.0	.3	3.4	8.6	.7
Total	100.0	100.0	100.0	100.0	100.0	100.0

Source: National Advisory Commission on Selective Service, "In Pursuit of Equity: Who Serves When Not All Serve?" (Washington, D.C.: Government Printing Office, February, 1967), see table 7.1.

maybe they read something in the paper like a lot of boys getting shot in Viet Nam or how badly men are needed, that made them decide — "no more grad students deferred." Well, you can't have that sort of thing. We're supposed to report things like that to headquarters but you can't do that either. You have to live with these men. So I pull files like that one out and say they are held for further information, or I say, "We have a new regulation on that." Then when they have cooled down I take them back in another time. Every clerk has to do things like that.[89]

Most board members made comments about how much they relied on the clerk. Clerks were in a position to control information that came to a board. Before each interview clerks customarily briefed the board on the contacts and experiences she had had with the registrant, or recalled the highlights of any past interaction between the registrant and the board. In doing this she could (and from observations often did) set the general predisposition of the board toward the registrant.[90] Throughout this study, however, there were no briefings that seemed to prejudice a board in any direction that they would not otherwise have taken after the interview. This is probably attributable to the fact that the clerks hold the same attitudes and middle class values as the board.

The role of the clerks can be summarized by saying that they were far more significant in classification decisions than is admitted by spokesmen for the System, who deny that they have any part in classification. However, the clerks' role did not introduce a serious bias in board deliberations. Though the potential for such an occurrence exists it is neutralized by the automatic nature of most decisions and the shared values of clerks and board members.[91]

Inasmuch as this discussion of boards as part of the linkage to the values of localism has revealed that this tie between the institution and its environment is in trouble, it should be said that the clerks have probably spared Selective Service more criticism than they have attracted. If the analysis of this study is correct, American political culture has undergone a change in the direction of legal-rationalism and away from traditionalistic legitimation of decisions. Roger Little caught the sense of the clerk's role in the midst of this change in political culture:

> With respect to the Clerks, they apply the criteria fairly and objectively. If I had to go through the ordeal of being classified again, I would rather that it be done by the Clerk than by the Board. The misfortune is not in the decisions they make, but rather that the ambiguity of some rules requires that she refer some cases to

the board for decision. Because of her long tenure and day-to-day involvement in the classification process, she is more likely to have developed expert knowledge of the system and its jurisprudence. She is probably the only expert in the board room when it meets. The effect of her presence is to make the system work more according to the rules than local folklore.[92]

Board Decisions—The Problematical Classifications

As indicated, necessity and common sense dictate that boards handle only problematical or contentious cases. These tend to be hardships, occupationals, conscientious objectors, and with the manpower buildup for Viet Nam — students.[93]

Hardship-Dependency

The boards were most effective and their decisions contained less logical contradiction in deciding if the degree of dependency warranted a III-A deferment. They were relieved of any pressure to search for and apply higher universal criteria. Here they were clearly adapting general process to the individual and both particularistic concern about his situation and wide-ranging inquiry were more clearly acceptable patterns of action and decision. It is true that Hill City boards lacked any knowledge of the individual and little of his environment, but they did humanize by inquiry a sensitive area which a thoroughly bureaucratic approach might have aggravated by impersonality. Their inquiry was unlimited and they felt no compulsion to be anything but diffuse. Furthermore, the variables in a dependency case are so great, and the exigencies of situations so numerous, that efforts to make more rigidly bureaucratic decisions would have created hostility. It is impossible to see how rules could be written and universally valid criteria applied in these cases. The boards probably do less than a perfect job but they undoubtedly surpass in equity a bureaucratized approach.

> Is a widowed mother financially secure but emotionally dependent on her son?
>
> If the family that lost a father does not need the oldest son financially, do the younger children still need him as a form of father substitute?
>
> A well-to-do widow may have enough money to live on without her son's support but at what level should she be forced to live? If she is used to living at $15,000 a year, should she have to live on half that? Sell her house?

The boards' capabilities in dependency cases would have been improved by better information. Often the decision to induct is centered around whether or not dependents would receive as much support in the form of military allotments as they did from the registrant as a civilian. Yet some boards seemed to be unaware that allotments were paid; others did not know how much they amounted to.

Conscientious Objectors

There are not many such cases. Only a few were observed. Clerks offered information on other cases. Persons seeking a I-O or I-A-O whose denominations have a long history of pacifism are processed routinely and from the information obtained, the deferment is granted without board interviews. Jehovah's Witnesses were invariably spoken of deprecatingly. Perhaps this was a reflection of their socio-economic status, perhaps the perceived extremity of their views and a belief that they had an uncooperative attitude toward Selective Service. The biggest problem was that all of them claimed deferment as ministers. This was viewed as troublesome by the System but if they had certification as a minister of certain rank, they were readily deferred on that basis. If not, they were handled like other conscientious objectors. Davis and Dolbeare found that many Wisconsin boards almost automatically rejected deferments for conscientious objectors because they knew they would be further appealed.[94]

Board members and clerks who had Negro registrants within their jurisdictions spoke often of Black Muslims who sought deferments as conscientious objectors and did so in a painfully guarded way which seemed to indicate they felt the claims were illegitimate but that one could not openly say so.

> Have you seen any of the Black Muslim cases? No? Oh, you have to see one of those. I have a lot of them. They're really something. Always done up to a T, just as properly dressed as you please. No smoking or drinking. It's against their religion to fight in something like Viet Nam but it's all right to get some little girl in trouble. Oh, yes, they're very good at that.[95]

The impression gained from limited observation and interviews is that conscientious objectors who do not fit established and accepted patterns, such as the Muslims, are brought before the boards as the first test of the religiosity of their objection.

Board handling of these cases is hard to fault, not because they have any more information about the individual or his circumstances but because they have a somewhat more manageable higher criterion to guide them. The conscientious objection must be based on religious grounds rather than a mere objection to a particular war or foreign policy. Board members are possibly as capable as anyone else of determining the sincerity of religious beliefs. There also are a variety of indicators that society accepts as evidence of religious conviction — church membership and attendance, ability to cite biblical passages or religious doctrine that supports pacifism. However, the boards showed no awareness or understanding of the Seeger case which broadened the basis for conscientious objection from "belief in a Supreme Being" to beliefs that prompted his objection to all wars and that "occupy the same place in his life as the belief in a traditional deity." (Congress sought revision of the draft law in 1967 to restrict the basis for conscientious objection once again.)

If one does not have sublime confidence in the theological sophistication of board members, or in their knowledge of Supreme Court decisions in this area, there is the assurance that a case taken on appeal will eventually come before a Department of Justice hearing officer. Thus, it will receive a review that differs from the one given other cases which go to the appeal boards; for the latter do not differ fundamentally from the local boards except that more effort is made to see that members are drawn from different functional or occupational groupings.

Students

The boards did not view the student classification as problematic until the demands of Viet Nam grew more acute. In 1966 the boards were directed both formally and informally to "tighten up" on students.[96] Thus, during the period of this study, students began to request board interviews in large numbers.

In the observed cases the boards bent over backwards to permit a man to stay in school. The function of the interviews was, according to clerks and board members, to "scare" the marginal student into enlistment or into full commitment to his studies. Boards were extremely sympathetic and manifested the high regard of the middle class for education. It might be argued the boards probably were as competent as anyone outside of professional educators to listen to the reasons for a registrant's failure to progress at a "normal" rate of speed toward a four-year degree.

The real problems of the boards' handling of students lie not in the board decisions but in the all pervasive, indiscriminate pressure of the draft and in the variability of guidance from different state headquarters. The guidance to tighten up on students in Agdustria included specific directions to cancel induction orders if a student had returned to or entered a school and was in good standing at the time he was called. However, this information was never transmitted to the thousands of registrants who were ordered for pre-induction physicals unless they asked. Assuming that induction was inevitable, many (there is no way to know how many) rushed to enlist or volunteer for induction. Undoubtedly, this did serve to "pick up" students of marginal commitment but there is no way of knowing how many serious students were panicked into enlistment.

The field director for the state pointed out that by reviewing reports of local boards he could quickly spot a situation where a board was making inequitable decisions or decisions that were contrary to policy.[97] This might have been true for non-voluntary induction (though the claim is debatable) but there is no way of detecting the indirect pressure that causes enlistment and volunteering for induction.

As for other states, Missouri's headquarters reportedly directed the classification of all graduate students as I-A. The order was later modified but not until some graduate students had been inducted.[98] Indiana local boards are said to have informed students that only graduate students in engineering and science would be deferred. (The form that guidance from headquarters took is not known.)[99] Some states told local boards that the scores of college qualification tests were advisory only, other states told boards to classify on the basis of the scores. States differ on the definition of a "full load" and the status of students in trade schools.[100]

On the advice of the National Security Council the System in June 1968 terminated deferments for graduate students with less than two years of study. This move stirred criticism in the academic community but this was probably offset by general satisfaction on the part of the public. It is safe to say that the deferment of graduate students in fields other than medicine and dentistry enjoyed only limited popular support under the conditions created by Viet Nam. Local board members in Hill City frequently spoke critically of such deferments. As one put it, "I'm all for a kid going to college but I think four years is enough for anyone."

While the regulations made it clear that graduate students with less than two years work were to be drafted, there remained a host of difficulties that made students problematic for boards. There was still the task of pressuring and judging marginal students. But efforts to draft graduate students also seems certain to result in a flood of requests for interviews, delays to complete the semester in which they receive induction notices, and in appeals.[101]

The end of deferments for graduate students created some resentment but left untouched the politically explosive question of deferments for millions of undergraduates. The undergraduate student population represents 6 million politically articulate individuals, a figure that might be tripled if the reactions of parents were included.

Occupations

In the matter of critical occupations (II-A) the performance of the boards has been most open to criticism. Some boards deferred anyone whose employer requested it; others had the clerks automatically defer anyone in science and engineering. Some boards inducted professional engineers with graduate degrees, but others forwarded all requests from the scientific field to the State Scientific Advisory Board. While some were trying to induct all teachers with the exception of those teaching science, still others were deferring all teachers. The Critical Skills List was rarely used. Some boards felt that a critical occupation deferment should never be for more than six months. There was no easy way to document such lack of uniformity — there simply was none. As has been shown earlier, the II-A's have never constituted a large number of registrants but they have been a major source of institutional posture and style.

Complicating the problems with occupationals was the mobility of the registrants seeking this deferment. They often attended college some place other than their board of registration, perhaps graduate school somewhere else, and then were moved to still another location by a company. Their local boards, which always remained the ones of their registrations, might know little and care less about how critical their occupations were. Local boards might be unconsciously tempted to fill a quota with someone distant, remote and unlikely to create unpleasantness in face-to-face contact.[102]

In February 1968, the National Security Council advised the System that neither the Armed Forces nor the civilian economy required occupational deferments such as were on the lists of essential activities and critical occupations.[103] The director subsequently ordered the lists suspended, but significantly his memo pointed out that each local board was left "with discretion to grant, in individual cases, occupational deferments based on showing of essential community need."[104] The door was far from closed on occupational deferments. Nor did it necessarily mean that deferments would be ended. About half of the 339,474 occupational deferments were based on the boards judgment of essentiality to community rather than the critical occupation list. Local boards were required only to review some of the II-A's and either end them or change the basis for them. Occupational deferments were therefore to remain problematic and a major source of institutional "posture" for the boards.

From Mainstay to Weak Link

The purpose of this discussion of local boards and how they make their decisions is not to pass judgment on their quality. Since there are no objective criteria for such a judgment this would require use of subjective criteria. The purpose of the foregoing discussion is (1) to point up the fact that there *are* no objective criteria; (2) to explore the degree to which the reality of decision-making corresponds to the institutional myths; and (3) to describe the conditions that serve as the sources of challenges to legitimacy of board decisions.

It may be useful to point up a preliminary conclusion at this point. It is not the reality of the way boards make decisions that is a source of threats to legitimacy, rather it is the institutional setting, the premises or lack of premises for decisions, certain institutional norms and personnel practices, and the disparity between institutional myths and reality. A board of volunteer laymen which sought to base its claims for legitimacy on more realistic grounds than presently used might be a perfectly practicable and successfully legitimate decision-making mechanism, but such a board would require some drastic alterations of the conditions that have been explored. Perhaps the positive aspects of local boards as decision mechanisms will never outweigh the negative, or it may be that the dubious assets of such boards would not be worthy of the efforts needed to secure them.

Under present conditions the boards, which were once believed crucial for identifying with key values of political culture thereby contributing to the balance between demands of task and demands of political culture, now add to the strain on that equilibrium by attracting challenges to the legitimacy of decisions.

Quotas

One of the mechanisms Selective Service has always perceived to be essential in tying the institution to localism is the quota system, the direct descendant of bitter controversy during the Civil War. One of the most contentious issues of the first federal draft of individuals was the equity of manpower contributions by states. Those that had sent thousands of volunteers or conscripted militia units off to war were angered by the conscription quotas levied against them by the new draft of 1863. The resulting political clamor over this and the riots over conscription left a deep imprint on draft administrators of that day and those that came after.

The quota system that was subsequently developed was designed to equitably divide the national call not just among the states but right down to the individual board. It must be said that the system is as fair and equitable as is possible under Selective Service's present "decentralized" structure.

The calls are levied against the number of I-A's estimated to be available for service in a state. The state headquarters in turn levy a call against those estimated to be in each board's pool. The I-A's available are those registrants remaining after deferments and credits for enlistments are subtracted. Each board receives credits for enlistments in the regular, reserve, and National Guard forces, though such figures are quite late and inaccurate. The biggest difficulty lies in the fact that circumstances change constantly making registrants eligible for deferment, meaning the number of I-A's available in any board's pool varies daily, hourly, and virtually by the minute. As the induction orders go out, the reasons for deferment come in. Thus, I-A's are not handled as a national manpower pool but as 4,070 different pools, and as General Hershey has said, a pool is a poor analogy — a river in constant flux is more descriptive.[105]

Quotas may be sent out with the intention of inducting only single men who are I-A but the single I-A's may suddenly disappear in board x as pregnancy slips, requests for occupational deferments by employers, and other bases for deferment pour in. The board must then return to its manpower "river" and dip lower in age or perhaps into its childless married men. It must once again send out induction orders and await results. Depending on when its quota was mailed and considering that every inductee must have ten days notice, a board may have a mere ten to twenty days to meet its call.

Notice that throughout this allocation process the figures used are dated or obsolescent. Because statistics gathered are obsolete the minute they are recorded, the number of I-A's available nationally, by state, or by board are merely approximations. There is inevitably a statistical lag. General Hershey's testimony on the process confirms this.

> We are normally supposed to get the calls about 2 months ahead, and if we have our information that is a month old at that time we are probably rather lucky. So, therefore, we are forecasting 3 months ahead of time the numbers of I-A's there will be in each draft board in the United States.[106]

At all levels quotas rest upon forecasts that are based upon outdated information as to what I-A's are available in each board and how many enlistment credits each is due.

It is conceivable that automatic data processing could shrink the lag but reliability of the prediction probably does not vary greatly with time. The prediction can probably be just as faulty based on data that is "days" old as it can that which is "weeks" old. Moreover, the critical period comes as induction orders go out; it is then that the "river" fluctuates so wildly. It is hard to see how the small improvement in the reliability of prediction could be worth the staggering cost of ADP equipment needed to cut the lag.

Moreover, there are other factors working to destroy the uniformity of inductions. The Selective Service System has always relied heavily on appeals as an element of institutional style. It is, in crude terms, a vast system of appeals. Its institutional posture has always been one of indirect compulsion and it will do anything possible to have a man enlist rather than induct him. It has consciously striven to align itself with one of the most powerful symbols of our political culture — voluntarism.

In keeping with this posture it permits a man to enlist in the active armed forces even after he gets his induction order.[107] In fact a man may enlist on the same day he is to report for induction. Until mid-January of 1966 the same thing was permitted for enlistment in the National Guard and Reserves. Given the extensive recruiting programs of the Services, the small number of men being drafted from the large pool, and the wide number of options in fulfilling a military obligation, a man has every incentive to wait until he receives his induction orders before he makes a final decision. Virtually all the clerks in this study said that registrants who responded to an induction order by enlisting were doing so (according to the registrants) on the advice of the recruiters.

As long as the many variables involved operate to create an institutional policy of simply "getting a man into the Service," regardless of how or in what form, there will remain fluctuations in the 4,070 manpower rivers that occur between the levying of the call and delivery; and there will remain the resulting lack of uniformity in call-ups. No speed-up in data processing seems likely to change that.

It should be said that Selective Service does meet its *state quotas* with amazing accuracy. In the state of Agdustria from 1948 to 1965 deliveries were 104.8 per cent of the quotas levied. All other states were quite close to 100 per cent with variations between 118.4 per cent and 93 per cent. Most never varied more than three to four percentage points.[108] This accuracy stems from experience factors used in computing quotas. From past experience the Manpower Divisions know they must overcall by certain percentages depending on the time of the year. Many local clerks also know roughly how many extra men they should order for induction in order to meet a call.

While state headquarters successfully use the experience factor, the clerks show no consistent use pattern. Some call only as many as the quota levied against them, some over-call to offset attrition, others wait to see how many men they can line up on the basis of the first batch of orders and then call more to make up the difference. This lack of uniformity was true despite directions from headquarters to continue calling until their quotas were met precisely. As many pointed out, there simply was not enough time between receipt of a call and the deadline to follow such a procedure. Thus the variety of clerk responses to quotas contributes to the lack of uniformity in call-ups. The end result of the quota system is one board drafting married men while an adjoining one does not.

The belief is widespread among clerks that the differences in their work procedures contributes yet another component of variability. Since quotas are levied against the I-A's available, the clerks feel that those who work to keep their pool up-to-date are penalized. Clerks feel that those who diligently and promptly process new men or changes in status of others will have a larger number of I-A's available and thus have a heavier quota levied against them. State headquarter's officials admitted that this possibility for variability exists. There would be no way for this to show up in any statistics. Donald Stewart found the same complaint among clerks in 1946.[109]

Clearly the equitable uniformity of the quotas is lost between the calculation of board quotas by state headquarters and delivery by the boards as a result of fluctuations in manpower "rivers" and differing responses of the clerks. If there is equitable uniformity at state level there is little at board level. Between the accuracy of meeting national calls and the uniformity of sacrifice among the states on the one hand, and the quotas that fall on the boards on the other, there are many unfortunate inequities stemming from a lack of uniformity.

Conclusion

This chapter has discussed local boards as an institutional adaptation to what the System's designers and administrative elite perceived to be key values of American political culture. It may be useful to conclude it with an effort to capture a summary picture of the sort of institution that emerged from the critical decision to base the System on such an adaptation.

Local boards began as friends and neighbors of the registrant, supposedly able to adjust the processes of the System to the individual. This theoretical function became an institutional myth which now draws criticism. It is clear to everyone including board members and registrants that local boards cannot perform such a function. Over the years as manpower became more plentiful and draft calls lower, the function of making decisions in the national health, safety, and interest has grown up as a parallel institutional myth. As analysis shows the boards do not have the capability to credibly live up to this myth either.

Recruitment and tenure practices that were a natural part of institutionalization, that helped develop the System's dedicated cadre and peculiar institutional elan, have now put it hopelessly out of touch with its environment and have destroyed any capability to make decisions, either in the national interest or in order to adjust the processes to the individual.

Board decisions rest upon middle class values, a legionnaire outlook, and upon diffuse and particularistic interaction with the registrant or his file. These are not decisive premises that enable the System to live credibly close to its institutional myths. The discrepancies between myths and realities are embarrassingly evident to increasing numbers of the public.

Institutional myth claims that each case is handled individually. The claim is remote from reality with clerks playing a major role in the bulk of the decisions. Boards are only able to concentrate on a few problematic classifications.

Local Boards: Mainstay or Weak Link?

The local board quota system that had such symbolic importance in earlier years now creates inequity and disuniformity. Since the institution has come under attack, General Hershey has tended to emphasize the efficiency of Selective Service in carrying out its functional task.[110] Critics have often countered by saying that "consistency and uniformity are being sacrificed for efficiency." Or put another way, acceptance is being sacrified for efficiency.

This direction of the dialogue is a confusing change in the nature of criticism the System was designed to deflect and it has tended to obscure the fact that consistency and uniformity were always sacrificed, not for the sake of efficiency but for the sake of acceptance. When Selective Service was designed, acceptance did not rest on consistency and uniformity as much as on adaptation to local and individual idiosyncracies. Selective Service was structured primarily to gain acceptance and it was assumed that efficiency, albeit at a much reduced level, would emerge. In other words, it was designed to be primarily legitimating and secondarily efficient. But the structure of the System is a century old in design. A structure adapted to the political culture of 1867 (or even 1917) may not be well adapted to its political culture a century later, particularly if one is speaking of a society as fluid and dynamic as America's.

Those familiar with the writings of Max Weber on legitimation of authority will recognize that the organization of Selective Service lies somewhere between the traditional and the legal-rational means of legitimating decisions. The board of non-expert friends and neighbors lies closer to the patriarchal society's means of legitimating decisions than it does to the modern society's. Modern society relies upon "the organization of a rationally oriented officialdom whose exercise of administrative functions is dependent upon central authority," in other words a bureaucracy.[111] "Decentralization," "little groups of neighbors," "local board autonomy," all are conscious efforts to deviate from the bureaucratic ideal-type as Weber described it. The purpose was to tie the conscription mechanism to some elements of the much more traditionalistic political culture of mid-19th century America and thus overcome resistance growing out of other elements of that same political culture, like anti-militarism, individualism, etc.

Political cultures usually contain elements that are competing or in conflict in given circumstances. Some elements are in ascendance while others are in decline. American political culture is no exception, and decentralization is a good example. The concept of "keeping decision-making close to the grass roots" still has great appeal, particularly in Congress, but increasingly the American positive view of the nebulous concept clashes with results of decentralization in certain circumstances that are felt to be objectionable.[112] Our positive view of decentralization collides head on with the fact that the concept has contributed to our staggering urban problems. Direct federal aid to cities runs counter to decentralization but continues to increase rapidly because it seems to be the only solution to many persons.

There is some evidence that the whole cluster of values represented by local boards is definitely in decline in American political culture. If local boards are the embodiment of localism, traditionalism, proceduralism, and voluntarism, the available evidence suggests that this has no significant positive effect upon the public.

Selective Service insists unflaggingly that local boards are the key to acceptability for conscription and that they result in better decisions because of their specialized local knowledge. They hold on to this claim tenaciously and for understandable reasons. Local boards are the key to the institution's ideology, structure, processes, to its reason for existence. To admit that local boards attract criticism would be to admit that the entire System as constituted has outlived its usefulness. Institutions — organizations suffused with values and specifically their elites — are unlikely to accept such evidence even when it is irrefutable. The institution and its ideology are articles of faith, not fact.

But the findings of Davis and Dolbeare in Wisconsin suggest that local boards do in fact detract from the legitimacy of conscription decisions. Statewide opinion sampling of adults in September, 1966, revealed that only 52 per cent of those interviewed were even aware that conscription was handled by local boards. Of the respondents who did know it was conducted by local boards, 53 per cent considered the System to be working fairly; but of those who did not know local boards were involved, 57 per cent believed the draft was working fairly. In other words, a slight majority of the public is totally ignorant of local boards. If those who know about local boards are contrasted with those who do not, ignorance of local boards enhances acceptance.

Interesting results were found when ignorance and knowledge of local boards was paired with approval-disapproval. Of those who knew about local boards, 52 per cent disapproved of the concept of local boards making decisions, the others who were ignorant concerning local boards when informed of the concept disapproved of the idea by a ratio of two to one.[113] It is impossible to see how such an opinion structure supports acceptance of conscription.

Other institutional ties to political culture are less troublesome and still appear to be functional. Efforts to avoid the appearance of political partisanship, appeal systems that encompass proceduralism, and efforts to appeal to voluntarism, though they create certain problems, are still functional. Efforts to associate with voluntarism created difficulties when inductions were stayed to permit enlistment in the National Guard and Reserves but this was a result of Selective Service's tactical blunder in trying to benefit institutional allies. Criticism developed only because the Guard and Reserves were never mobilized and there were long delays in sending men to basic training during a war. There is no evidence that voluntarism has declined in its importance in our politcal culture and there has been no criticism of staying induction to permit enlistment for active duty.

The efforts to appear to be a civilian institution have not caused much trouble for the System. It is not clear whether the absence of difficulties arises from public ignorance of the paramilitary cadre or from the fact that American attitudes toward the military have undergone change. The more likely hypothesis is that attitudes have changed. Selective Service does not make any extensive effort to hide the paramilitary nature of the upper echelons. So long as it does not do so or make blatant claims of being civilian there would seem to be little trouble or embarrassment that could result. Analysis has shown that local boards and quotas as means of binding the institution to localism are in serious trouble. Where once these were mainstays of equilibrium they now threaten it.

The previous analysis of board behavior in decision making suggests that the dilemmas of board members are traceable to a growing gap between Selective Service's traditionalistic structure and processes and society's shift in concept of legitimacy toward legal rationality. The search of board members for practical higher decision criteria and their perplexity in trying to limit meaningfully their concern with the registrant would seem to be manifestations of a need on their part to move toward bureaucracy and legal rationalism. The institution that is the result of efforts to adapt to political culture of earlier days is one that is traditionalistic in a Weberian sense; acutely sensitive to what it feels is a threatening environment; highly prone to the use of informal communications and ad hoc policy guidance. It is decentralized largely in appearance but centralized in responsibility for decisions and in outlook of System members. The System is formally civilian but paramilitary in staffing, attitudes, and operating norms. Organizationally it appears to be a confusing melange of federal, state and local government, though essentially a federal program under federal control.

In order to maintain an equilibrium between functional and cultural demands it has developed a "satisfice" attitude toward equity for registrants. Its members feel that a concern about equity for each individual is unrealistic and unnecessary to achieve acceptance. This means that unintentionally the articulate and higher strata registrants are the recipients of as much concern for equity as the System can afford to dispense.

Finally, it is a System that has changed scarcely at all since 1940, in fact, very little from 1917, while the political culture and the conditions in which it operates have changed a great deal.

Notes

[1]Provost Marshal General, *Second Report to December 22, 1918* (Washington, D.C.: Government Printing Office, 1918), p. 277.

[2]*Annual Report of the Director of Selective Service, 1965* (Washington, D.C.: Government Printing Office, 1966), p. 8.

[3]E. A. Fitzpatrick, *Conscription and America* (Milwaukee, Wis.: The Richards Publishing Inc., 1940), pp. 46-47.

[4]It also ignores the problem of institutional balance alluded to in this study.

[5]Interview No. 15.

[6]"Selective Service," Office of Legislative Liaison and Public Information, March 1, 1965, National Headquarters, Selective Service System, p. 2. James Gerhardt in correspondence with the author says that Congressional approval of testing and deferring students took the form of a House Committee on Armed Services report describing in favorable terms the System's plans for handling students in this manner; and rejection by the House Armed Services Committee, the House and the Conference Committee of a Senate-approved alternative method for handling students that the Department of Defense had backed.

[7]*Ibid.*

[8]*Ibid.*

[9]Observation Report No. 19.

[10]From a letter to a local board.

[11]*Review, op. cit.,* p. 9622.

[12]*Ibid.,* p. 9623.

[13]*Ibid.,* p. 9694.

[14]*Ibid.,* p. 9634.

[15]Observation Report No. 8.

[16]Observation Report No. 18. This interchange also points up the typical role of the clerk, which will be discussed further at another point.

[17]Observation Report No. 4.

[18]Observation Report No. 17.

[19]*Review of the Administration and Operation of the Selective Service System,* Hearings before the Committee on Armed Services, House of Representatives, 89th Cong. 2nd Sess. (Washington, D.C.: Government Printing Office, 1966), p. 9697. Hereafter cited as *Review.*

[20] Some letters from companies requesting II-A's mentioned the 1962 revision, others seemed unaware of revisions after 1955.

[21] Observation Report No. 10. The registrant was deferred.

[22] Observation Report No. 5. Registrant classified I-A.

[23] National Security Agency is a part of the Department of Defense and engages in coding and decoding operations and electronic surveillance for intelligence purposes.

[24] Stewart noted that only a small proportion of his interviewees had occupational activities that were related to war effort in a way that would give them information useful for decisions.

[25] Davis and Dolbeare have used the phrase "little groups of neighbors" for the title of their book. It is taken from Hearings before a Subcommittee of the Committee on Appropriations, House of Representatives, 89th Cong., 2nd Sess., February 1, 1966, p. 19.

[26] Clerks and board members occasionally cited situations (perhaps ten) in which members knew registrants. All but one of these references were part of reminiscences of World War II operations when board offices were located in the jurisdictions rather than centralized. The exception referred to was a case during the Korean War. Donald Stewart's study in 1946 found very few board members with personal knowledge of their registrants. "Local Board, *A Study of the Place of Volunteer Participation in the Bureaucratic Organization*" (unpublished Ph.D. dissertation, Columbia University, 1950), pp. 77 ff.

[27] National Advisory Commission on Selective Service, "In Pursuit of Equity: Who Serves When Not All Serve?" (Washington, D.C.: Government Printing Office, February 1967), p. 21. Hereafter referred to as *Commission Report*.

[28] It is true that Selective Service had trouble with registrant mobility during the war but this was considered a temporary "war problem." The mobility of today is a fundamental part of American culture; neighborhoods are not.

[29] Davis and Dolbeare, "Who Gets Drafted," Institute for Research on Poverty, University of Wisconsin, Madison, 1967, p. 31.

[30] *Commission Report, op. cit.,* p. 20. One of the constant complaints made of the System is that it refuses to divulge the names and addresses of board members. In February 1967 national headquarters finally ordered local boards to respond positively to requests for such information.

[31] Davis and Dolbeare, "Little Groups of Neighbors," (unpublished paper, University of Wisconsin, 1967), p. 22.

[32] *Commission Report, op. cit.,* p. 20.

[33] Interview No. 8; the form was SS252, printing date of 1951.

[34] Davis and Dolbeare, "Who Gets Drafted," *op. cit.,* p. 35.

[35] *Ibid.*

[36] Regulations say they shall be residents of the county and "if at all practicable" of the area in which their board has jurisdiction. Code of Federal Regulations 1604.52.

[37] Clyde E. Jacobs and John F. Gallagher, *The Selective Service Act: A Case Study of the Governmental Process* (New York: Dodd, Mead and Co., 1967), p. 125. Superior Courts of California are the state's court of original jurisdiction with at least one in each county.

Local Boards: Mainstay or Weak Link? 161

[38] Davis and Dolbeare, "Little Groups of Neighbors," *op. cit.*, p. 3.

[39] Interview No. 1.

[40] Davis and Dolbeare, "Little Groups of Neighbors," *op. cit.*, p. 18.

[41] *Ibid.*, p. 4. Stewart also found a great deal of recruitment by board members. See Stewart, *op. cit.*, p. 75.

[42] One state official explained the lack of a retirement policy by pointing out that the state director was nearly 85 and that he didn't feel he could rightfully ask a board member to resign. In fairness to Agdustria's Director it should be said that he has the physical and mental capabilities of many men half his age.

[43] *Commission Report, op. cit.*, p. 19. See also Stewart, *op. cit.*, p. 66 for confirmation on superannuation.

[44] *Commission Report*, p. 73. Also see Stewart, *op. cit.*, p. 66.

[45] Interviews, and Observation Reports.

[46] There are many descriptions of this pattern of change. Typical is Martin Grodzins, "The New Shame of the Cities," in *Politics of Metropolitan Areas*, ed. Philip B. Coulter (New York: Thomas Y. Crowell, Inc., 1967), pp. 13-27.

[47] Donald Stewart found similar occupations and middle class predominance. See Stewart, *op. cit.*, p. 64.

[48] The North-Hall-NORC study is mentioned in virtually any treatment of stratification. See Robert Hodge, *et al.*, "Occupational Prestige in the United States," *American Journal of Sociology*, LXX (November 1964), 290.

[49] *Commission Report*, p. 19.

[50] *Ibid.*

[51] *Commission Report*, p. 75.

[52] The difference alluded to here is based on our observation and Davis and Dolbeare's study. Hill City board members were never the prosperous, exceedingly busy, professional men, or those highly placed in companies. They were the "not quite successful," or "not quite notables." Davis and Dolbeare noted the difference. See pp. 21-22 of "Little Groups of Neighbors." As they indicate, the identification of "influentials" is a subject of academic disagreement. For a survey of the literature see Wendell Bell, *et al.*, *Public Leadership* (San Francisco: Chandler Publishing Co., 1961).

[53] Stewart, *op. cit.*, p. 150.

[54] Observation Report No. 7.

[55] Gabriel Almond, *The American People and Foreign Policy* (New York: Frederick A. Praeger, Inc., 1960), pp. 171-74.

[56] Report on the Administration and Operation of the Personnel Division of the Selective Service System of "Agdustria," 27 April, 1946, p. 1, from files of Agdustria Headquarters.

[57] Stewart, *op. cit.*, p. 74.

[58] *Ibid.*

[59] Resignations have taken place on rare occasions. One instance cited in a Report of the Director predictably occurred because several board members felt the U. S. should use atomic weapons "to end the fighting in Korea."

[60] Stewart, *op. cit.*, p. 89.

[61] Some may recognize an attempt to utilize the pattern variables of Talcott Parsons. See *Toward a General Theory of Action* (New York: Harper Torchbooks, 1965), pp. 53-110.

[62] Observation Report No. 9. They were deferred.

[63] *Ibid.*

[64] Observation Report No. 19. Registrant classified I-A.

[65] Observation Report No. 16. Deferment denied.

[66] Observation Report No. 4. Deferment granted.

[67] Observation Report No. 14.

[68] Commission Report, p. 184.

[69] *Ibid.*, pp. 186-87.

[70] Sixteen of the seventeen in our study were women. See also *Compensation for Selective Service System Employees*, Hearing, House of Representatives, 89th Cong., 2nd Sess. on H.R. 14357 (Washington, D.C.: Government Printing Office, 1966), April 18, 1966, p. 6. Hereafter cited as *Compensation Hearings*.

[71] The other systems are the Reservist and National Guard officers, that staff state and national headquarters, and the board members.

[72] This is an average figure for the nation. See *Compensation Hearings*, p. 9.

[73] Universal Military Training and Service Act, Sect. 10, para. 4 (b), subpara. 4, p. 85.

[74] *Organization and Administration*, p. 200.

[75] See *Compensation Hearings*, p. 27 and *passim*.

[76] Interview No. 19.

[77] *Compensation Hearings*, p. 4.

[78] Interviews with Agdustria Headquarters. See testimony of John W. Macy, *ibid.*

[79] Donald Stewart found 85 per cent of the clerks in his 1950 study were females, middle-aged or older. See Stewart, *op. cit.*, p. 113.

[80] Interview No. 6.

[81] Interview No. 7.

[82] Interview No. 9.

[83] *Compensation Hearings*, p. 5.

[84] *Commission Report*, p. 21.

[85] *Review, op. cit.*, p. 9764.

[86] Selective Service publications and uncritical books written about it use such phrasing repeatedly. See also *Review, op. cit.*, pp. 9623, 9624, 9667.

[87] *Commission Report*, p. 183.

[88] *Ibid.*, p. 178.

[89] Interview No. 7.

[90] Donald Stewart felt the role of the clerks was "usually of significance" and "influenced decisions by method of presentation" (*op. cit.*, pp. 112 and 126). He did not elaborate on what this meant.

Local Boards: Mainstay or Weak Link? 163

[91] Davis and Dolbeare reached a conclusion that is quite similar. See "Who Gets Drafted," *op. cit.*, p. 29.

[92] June A. Willenz, ed., *Dialogue on the Draft,* Report of the National Conference on the Draft, Nov. 11-12, 1966, Washington, D. C., American Veterans Committee, p. 26.

[93] This study turned up information on agricultural deferments in three states. In all three agricultural deferments were few in absolute numbers and were governed by elaborate criteria developed by the state headquarters in conjunction with interest groups. X number of points were given for x bushels of wheat marketed, eggs, feed grains, etc. Under this sort of arrangement the cases could be handled in virtually an automatic way.

[94] Davis and Dolbeare, "Little Groups of Neighbors," *op. cit.*, p. 26.

[95] Interview No. 10.

[96] As is customary in Selective Service, this informal direction came from a variety of places. It was implied in the directions on drop-outs, transfers, etc., word-of-mouth from state and national headquarters, and in General Hershey's editorials in *Selective Service.*

[97] Interview No. 21.

[98] *Dialogue on the Draft, op. cit.*, p. 49.

[99] *Ibid.*

[100] *Commission Report, op. cit.*, p. 27.

[101] As of this writing System officials were insisting that local boards would not be able to grant such delays.

[102] A registrant residing away from his board can take an appeal to the appeal board of his new place of residence. Davis and Dolbeare felt that the appeal boards in Wisconsin spent much of their time correcting the induction bias of a mobile registrant's "friends and neighbors" back in his home town. Davis and Dolbeare, "Who Gets Drafted?" p. 34-35. Observations in this study lend support to the suggestion that local boards are sometimes tougher on distant registrants with occupational deferments.

[103] For the texts of the document see the *New York Times,* February 16, 1968, p. 10.

[104] *Ibid.*

[105] *Review, op. cit.*, p. 9638.

[106] *Ibid.*, p. 9662.

[107] Selective Service System Operations Bulletin 257 and 287 and *Review,* p. 9626.

[108] Unpublished data from Agdustria State Headquarters.

[109] Stewart, *op. cit.*, p. 109. Stewart found state headquarters officers who expressed the belief that local boards "kept two sets of books — one for themselves and one for us," p. 111. Stewart says that several board member interviewees reported they had heard of such practices and one was able to describe the techniques in some detail. *Ibid.* No evidence of this sort turned up in the Hill City study.

[110] See *New York Times, op. cit.*

[111] "Bureaucracy" is used here in an analytical and descriptive way and denotes a "type of organizational structure resting upon and associated with

ideas and institutions tending toward the modern and rational." See an essay on "Bureaucracy" by Dwight Waldo, *Collier's Encyclopedia,* (1962) ed., Vol. 4, p. 732. Also Reinhard Bendix, *Max Weber: an Intellectual Portrait,* (New York: Doubleday Anchor Books, 1962), p. 38 and pp. 417-30.

[112]Lectures by Professor Roscoe Martin delivered at San Diego State College in Spring 1967 pointed this up. The literature on federalism and intergovernmental relations is replete with examples.

[113]James W. Davis Jr. and Kenneth M. Dolbeare, *Little Groups of Neighbors: The Selective Service System* (Chicago: Markham Publishing Co., 1968). See Chapter 7.

5

Other Institutional Defenses

Identification with what were felt to be key values of political culture has been one of the major defenses of the Selective Service System but there are others that deserve attention in any analysis.

Weighted Power Relationships with Registrants

It might be logical to start with the defense that is most closely related to the local boards. The Universal Military Training and Service Act was written so as to further weight relations between the boards and registrants in the boards' favor. Power relationships between citizens and a government agency are seldom if ever so heavily weighted as they are in the case of Selective Service. As one government appeal agent testified "the Selective Service law is monstrously weighted against a registrant who seeks a classification other than I-A."[1]

The Act exempts the local boards from the Administrative Procedures Act of 1946.[2] This act is considered the foundation of administrative law and was intended to assure the individual some of the same rights he enjoys in ordinary law and a certain amount of protective power in relationships with government agencies. It was to specify the procedural rights of private parties including the right to be informed of the organization, procedures, and policies of the agencies; to be made aware of new agency rules and to participate in their formulation; the right to counsel and to issue legal subpoenas; and the right to file exceptions to agency decisions. It also broadened provisions for a resort to judicial review of formal agency decisions in the courts.[3]

Because local boards are exempted from the provisions of the act there are no particular procedures that they must follow in handling witnesses, admitting or considering evidence, interrogating, etc. They need not reveal the basis for their decision or how they reached it.

Only the individual has the right to appear before the boards. The boards may consent to have others appear on the registrant's behalf but they are in no way required to do so. They may also call in anyone they wish to question, have testify or present information, but the registrant must have the board's permission to do the same. Needless to say the meetings are not open to the public in any way. Presumably the largely moribund Government Appeal Agent can appear before the boards any time he wishes to do so. The agents until recently have been almost totally "paper positions." General Hershey informed a Congressional committee that the agents were obliged to inform on their clients if they told the agent in confidence they had broken the law. The General claims that because the agent had taken an oath to support the laws of the United States, a failure to inform on his client would constitute conspiracy with him. Lawyers who felt this violated their professional ethics would have to resign he claimed. General Hershey also claimed that allowing lawyers to appear before draft boards would "offer literally millions of opportunities for delays."

> You just can't apply judicial procedures to a call-up. If you're going to let the court decide when there is an emergency instead of a military commander, then the court should be responsible when the war is lost.[4]

The effect, of course, is to relieve the lay, volunteer members from being burdened with legal intricacies with which they are not familiar. This is understandable. But the exemption from the normal constraints of administrative law also has the effect of reducing the board interview to a confrontation between the individual and his board, a confrontation in which he is divested of any procedural safeguards, or representation by counsel or by any group of which he is a member.

No judgment of the propriety of this situation is implied and there is no evidence that boards abuse this power. There are things to be said both for and against it. While this situation probably weighs heavily against the lower class individual who lacks articulateness and confidence, it probably is also effective in reducing the power of those of higher status who have means of influencing the System at other than local board level.

It is, however, a fact of the relationship between the individual and his board that he is reduced strictly to his status and his articulateness as an individual (except where national policy favors characteristics of his strata). This would seem to be a distinct defensive advantage for the System and an aid to legitimation. It makes it difficult for groups and individuals to bring pressure to bear upon decisions. The area of uncertainty or discretion that constitutes the boards' power is difficult for an individual to penetrate or influence.

A part of the power relationship between the individual and his board is the fact that Congress has limited the courts' power to review the findings of local draft boards. The Deputy Director of Selective Service describes the situation in this way:

> The courts have held that they have no authority to weigh the evidence to determine whether a classification is justified, if there is any evidence or basis in fact to support it. Unless it is shown that the board's action was arbitrary and capricious, or based on bias or prejudice, or that the registrant was denied a procedural right and that such denial was prejudicial to his substantive rights, the courts will not interfere.[5]

Field Division Representatives as Institutional Sensors

National headquarters has twelve field representatives covering the United States. Unlike field representatives or auditors at the state level these national field representatives are not primarily control mechanisms. Their function is more appropriately identified as system maintenance. They operate as sensors, serving to detect threats and opportunities for the System.

There are twelve representatives covering six army regions in the country. They are high ranking paramilitary officers (colonels or Navy captains). They act as sensors for the System in its relations with other federal agencies, the Armed Forces (particularly the Armed Forces Examining and Induction Stations), the governors, and state directors.

Because of Selective Service's unique structure that follows the pattern of the states rather than regions, it could find itself out of touch with events that could affect it within the rest of the federal administrative structure. The field representatives help to prevent this by attending meetings and maintaining contact with federal offices in each region. The Annual Reports of the director always attempt to relate the System to the current administration's programs and policies as long as it seems that identification will not hamper relations with Congress. For example, the System emphasized its role in civil defense when the latter was the subject of favorable attention in the early 1960's and it quickly emphasized its role in the War on Poverty when it first got under way.[6]

The importance of the sensor role was alluded to by General Hershey when he remarked:

> I've done everything but intelligence [in my military career]. H——, talk about intelligence. There is a lot of it done around here to keep tabs on what these other agencies are up to.[7]

The field representatives are important to the System in their ability to maintain important contacts with the Armed Forces with which there are several points of tension. There is, for example, endemic friction between the System and the Armed Forces Examination and Induction Stations (AFEIS). This arises because Selective Service, after working hard to meet its quota, may see that quota decimated by AFEIS examinations.

Problems are also created for Selective Service when famous professional athletes, classified by a local board I-A, are rejected by AFEIS. Selective Service mistakenly bears the brunt of public criticism, and as a local board clerk pointed out:

> We may ship some kid off and the next day he's out strutting around in the neighborhood telling how he "got out of the draft" and implying he knows someone on the board who did him a favor. He doesn't want to admit he's IV-F you see. So we catch all the h—— for that.[8]

There is also a considerable amount of paper work friction between the two organizations.

The Field Division also handles the Selective Service Reserve program for recruitment and institutionalization of the paramilitary cadre. In this connection they need to know base commanders and directors for the reserve programs of each Service on a first name basis. For the System must rely upon the hospitality of the Armed Forces for training facilities and the contacts with the active establishment important in maintaining morale of the System's paramilitary cadre, such accoutrements as officer's clubs, post exchanges, etc. As a Selective Service official pointed out: "We are military on EAD [extended active duty] but we have no post, or station."[9] Field representatives keep open the kind of contacts that can give the paramilitary cadre access to the regular military establishment.

The relations of the field representatives with governors and state directors are also highly important since their power is not formal and highly tenuous. Some directors, because of long association with General Hershey, have little to do with the field representatives. Agdustria's director was an example.

> I just by-pass them. General Hershey commands me directly and no one is between. If I want to find out what is going on I just go on down to Washington and mosey into one office and then another, picking up bits of information — like a spy — I just snoop around.[10]

An officer in national headquarters described the sensitive task of the representatives this way:

> Our field reps are like stock salesmen selling an idea of the Old Man's [General Hershey] to the directors. Often the state director has already made up his mind in a different way. But when we say, "General Hershey wants this" or "it is his idea" that usually clears things up. Going against you is the fact that you have no formal authority but going for you is the personality of the General.[11]

If their power is tenuous it is no less critical to system maintenance. Occasionally in some states a highly partisan political situation develops and a new governor may "clean house" and in the process turn out the state director. Directors who are simultaneously serving as Adjutant Generals of a state may be quite vulnerable to such a turn of events. As has been indicated in discussing the System's avoidance of partisan politics, this usually does not happen, but when it does it is a serious disruption of normal institutional patterns. The closed personnel system of the paramilitary cadre may be penetrated and someone placed in the System who has not been institutionalized. Two examples were the politically forced resignations of the Adjutant Generals of Iowa in 1950 and West Virginia in 1956. In such an event the field representative strives to heal the break in normal patterns and see to it that the "alien" to the institution is either given "quick-course" institutionalization or that any potentially dysfunctional aspects of his presence are neutralized. A national headquarters official described the plight of the "alien" and the resulting entree for the field representatives.

> When a politician "cleans house" and puts his man in as director, it is not going to be long before the poor soul is going to start looking around for help. All of the sudden he's in a federal organization, he's dealing with military men and matters or he's got federal civil service personnel to contend with, etc. He's pretty glad to see our field rep when he walks in the door.[12]

At times the field representatives help the governors who have no interest in filling the position of state directors. A former field representative related an incident which illustrates the role of the field representative and also the successful insulation of the System from politics through its confusing quasi-federal nature.

> A few years ago General X, our state director, passed away down in one of the southern states, and the governors always call General Hershey right away and ask him to recommend someone. Well, we didn't hear from the governor and we didn't want to seem pushy so we waited for his call. Finally weeks went by. So General Hershey sent me to see the governor. When I walked into his office he grabbed my hand and said, "Well, I'm sure glad to see you. I wondered when General Hershey would appoint a replacement.[13]

Differential Impact on Strata As a Defense

One of the most controversial aspects of the operation of Selective Service has been its impact on socio-economic strata. It can also be said that this debate has been a very poorly informed one, primarily because neither the Armed Forces nor Selective Service have kept the sort of data that could lead to proper analysis.[14]

It is a widely accepted popular notion that "the draft falls heavier on the lower classes." Everyone from *Life* magazine to congressmen have made the claim.[15] The immediate concern of this study is with the differential impact on strata as a natural (unplanned) defense for the Selective Service System. The primary concern therefore, is not with the causes for such impact or its equity and possible consequences. The concern is limited to whether in fact there is differential impact and its possible meaning for the environment in which Selective Service must operate.

As early as 1955 Mayer and Hoult had shown that the higher the socio-economic status of a population grouping, and the lower its proportion of non-whites, the lower its casualty rates in the

Korean War.[16] Their figures, however, included both draftees and enlisted personnel. Further, their study did not sufficiently separate the differential impact of the draft on strata from the effect of manpower utilization by the Armed Forces.[17] The difficulties of the Mayer and Hoult study have plagued all discussions of the draft and strata that have followed.

Lower educational levels and "soft skills" inevitably result in men of lower socio-economic standing being placed in higher risk positions with greater possibility of participation in combat operations. Also adding confusion is the fact that Negroes are found in large numbers in Viet Nam and suffer heavy casualties because they perceive the military, especially the army combat units, to be one of the best career opportunities available and accordingly reenlist at more than double the rate of whites.[18] Clearly such matters as enlistment, reenlistment, serving in commissioned status, and manpower utilization patterns of the military, must be separated from the question of the impact of the draft on strata.

Finally one must be quite specific about what he means by "impact of the draft." For example, one can take the matter of draft impact on Negroes which is closely related to the matter of stratification. General Hershey has always been quick to point out the fact that while Negroes constitute 12 per cent of the total population they constituted only 10.4 per cent of the inductees.[19] This figure is deceptive, however, as far as "impact" is concerned.[20] There is little doubt that as the Special Commission says, "The Negro does not serve in the Armed Forces out of proportion to his representation in the population as a whole."[21] But the Special Commission went on to the matter of impact in a way that General Hershey pointedly did not. The Report points out that though the Negro is rejected at double the rate of the white registrant and the resulting percentage of Negroes qualified for service is thus considerably smaller, *still* in proportional terms almost twice as many *qualified* Negroes are inducted as *qualified* whites. When one uses the term impact to denote contact between Selective Service and registrants and the latters' perceptions of the institution, obviously the draft has far greater impact on Negroes; and given the societal status of most Negroes it is safe to surmise a greater impact on lower socio-economic strata.[22]

A favorite ploy used by General Hershey to avoid the question of impact is to point out that "of the people we defer for college, about 56 per cent of them get into the service, and only 43 to 44 per cent of those who do not go to college get into the service."[23]

This, of course, completely skirts the important issue of whether they got into the service through enlistment, Reserves, officer programs, National Guard, or draft.

As the Special Commission pointed out, Negroes have one-third the chance of getting into the Reserves that a white youth does; and only 0.2 per cent of the total non-white population and 0.4 per cent of those non-whites qualified, enter officer programs as opposed to 3.3 per cent of the total whites and 4.3 per cent of the qualified whites.[24] Clearly race (and strata) have very real implications when it comes to the impact of the draft or who gets drafted. It is true that the whites who ended up in the Reserves or officer programs had contact with the Selective Service System and like all males had to be concerned about their classification. Still, its impact could never be the same. For the whites there were options, for the Negro (and it would seem for lower classes), there was the draft. The Selective Service System, for all its circumspection, is still one of the most direct and explicit applications of compulsion in our society and exactly who feels this compulsion and their reactions are questions of great relevancy.

Davis and Dolbeare have made the only attempt to trace the impact of draft on socio-economic strata. They correctly point out that only in focusing on the operation of different deferments can the impact be ascertained. The largest deferment classifications in Wisconsin, and nationally, are hardships (or dependencies), IV-F's and students. The most significant thing about these deferments is the range among boards with respect to the proportions of men in each of these classifications.

> The highest board [in deviation from median per cent of eligible age group found in each classification] has ten times as many registrants in II-S and I-D (Reserves) as the lowest board; in both cases, the highest board is in a wealthy urban area and the lowest in a low income, Negro area. The norm is for the percentage of the highest boards to be two to three times that of lowest boards in a classification.[25] [See Figure 2]

They found further that enlistment rates were *lower* in low income areas at the same time inductions were higher. Low income areas therefore did not receive as many credits for enlistments and thus their calls were higher. Higher income areas had a reverse pattern with high enlistments and low inductions.[26]

Here again a defender of Selective Service would probably point out that "the important thing is that the registrants in higher income areas served." The importance of this depends entirely on one's point of view. It is *not* the most significant point in consider-

Other Institutional Defenses

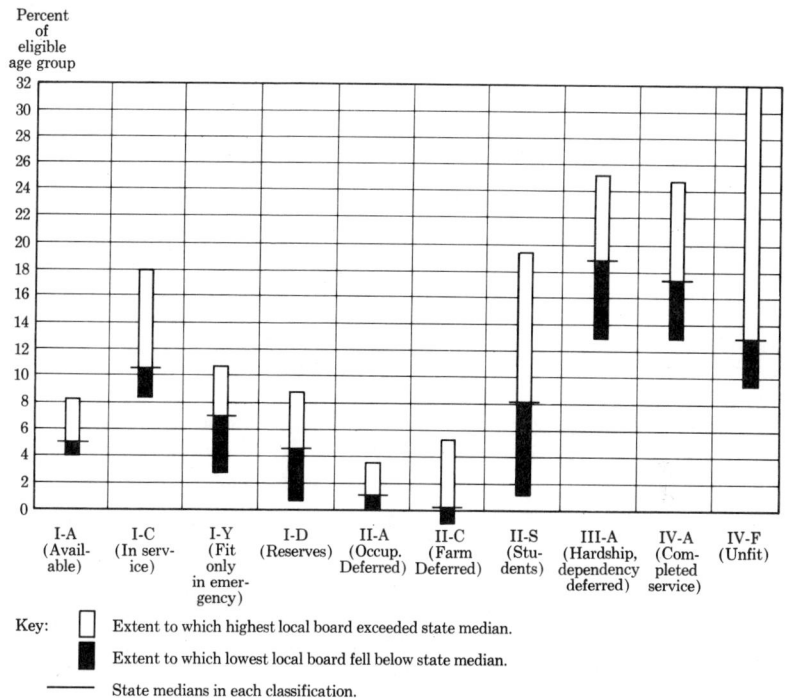

Source: James W. Davis and Kenneth M. Dolbeare, "Who Gets Drafted," Institute for Research on Poverty, University of Wisconsin, Madison, 1967.

Figure 2. *Variation of Local Boards from State Median Selected Classifications, 1966, Wisconsin (Highest and lowest boards in terms of deviation from median percent of eligible age group in each classification in the state)*

ing the *impact* of the draft or answering the question, "who gets drafted." Registrants in higher income areas have options of ways to serve and with student deferments they have options as to timing of service which can be a very important point when the nation is involved in a "shooting war." Davis and Dolbeare noted a 40 per cent increase in student deferments between 1965 and 1966 in Wisconsin. This is dramatic evidence of using the advantageous option of timing.[27]

Presumably many of those registrants moving into II-S (student) would eventually be drafted if the 1965 and 1966 level of commitment to the Viet Nam War were to continue. The United

States, however, has seldom remained committed at such a level for periods in excess of four years. Whether this situation will hold or not remains to be seen. In any event it is likely that most students will enter service through some route *other* than induction.

In the case of reserve deferments (I-D) there was a proportionate increase in Wisconsin between 1965 and 1966 similar to that

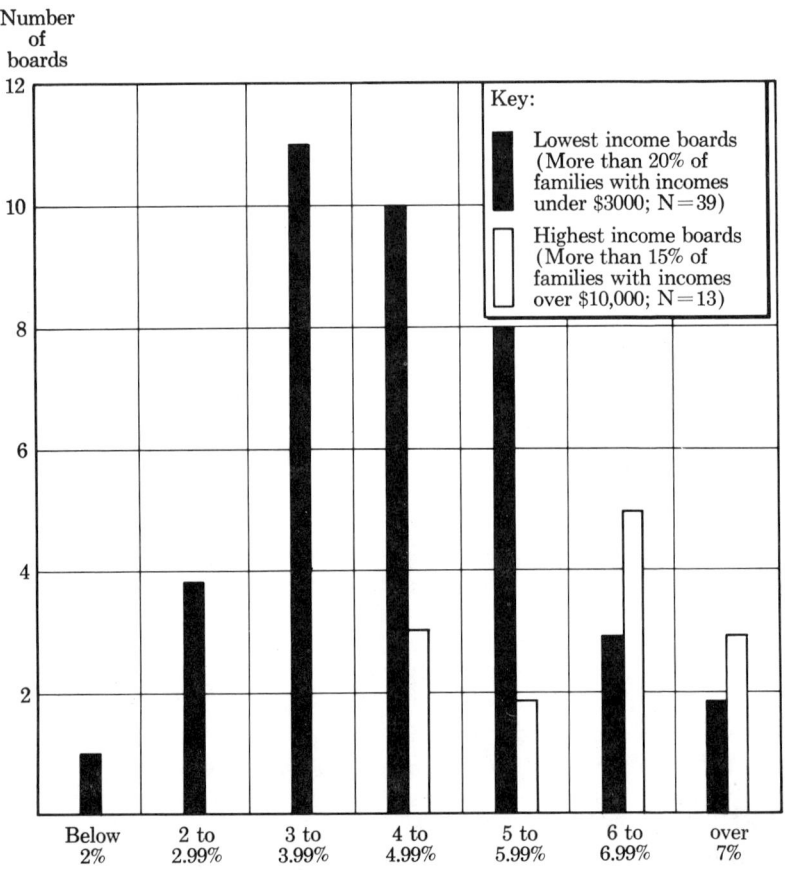

Percentage of Eligible Age Group in I-D (Reserves)

Source: James W. Davis and Kenneth M. Dolbeare, "Who Gets Drafted," Institute for Research on Poverty, University of Wisconsin, Madison, 1967.

Figure 3. *Reserve Classifications, Highest and Lowest Income Areas (Wisconsin, 1966)*

in the student categories, with the greatest increase in higher income areas. Figure 3 shows the much greater proportionate use of the Reserves by registrants in higher income areas.

Davis and Dolbeare found only one exception to the general pattern of "the higher the income, the lower the service experience, and the lower the income the higher the service experience." The exception which supported rather than detracted from the pattern was for three boards that were Negro, low-income and urban.

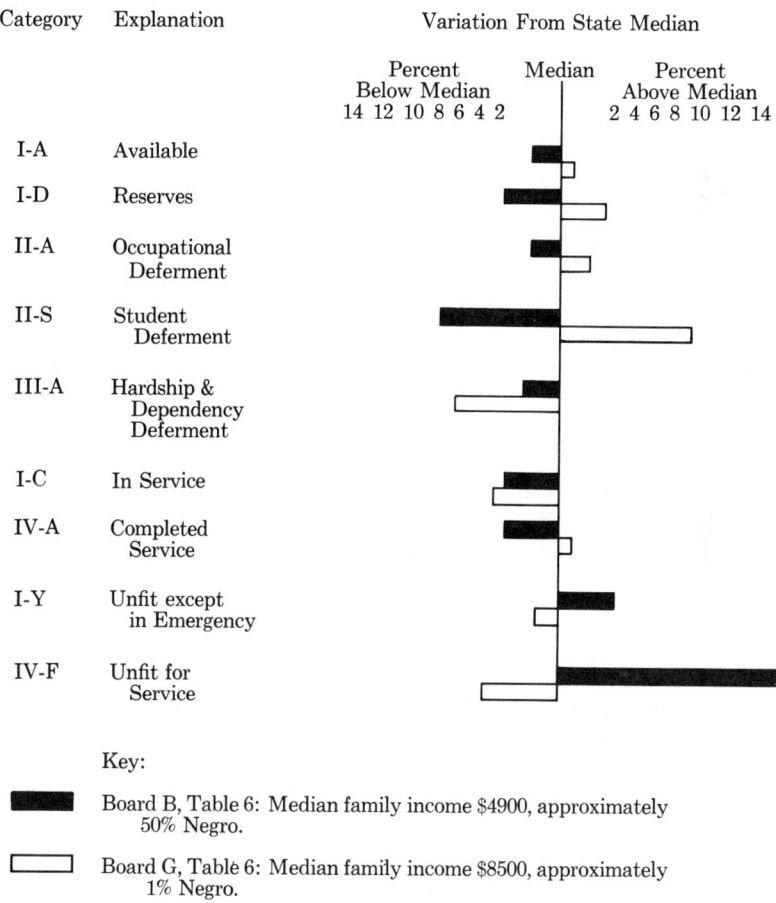

Source: James W. Davis and Kenneth M. Dolbeare, "Who Gets Drafted," Institute for Research on Poverty, University of Wisconsin, Madison, 1967.

Figure 4. *Comparison of Proportions of Registrants in Selected Classifications, Two Boards (Wisconsin, 1966)*

They contrasted a higher income urban board with one of the lower income Negro boards on each classification and in doing so found that the Negro area with a smaller number of acceptable men made nearly the same contribution to the Armed Forces, primarily by induction. (See Figure 4)

The differential impact of the draft tends to decrease as high calls continue and the age of induction drops. The desirability of the Reserves as a deferment might be drastically altered if they were activated but despite the actuation of some units in reaction to North Korea's seizure of the U.S.S. Pueblo the possibility of a large scale call up remains remote. Because Congressional renewal of the draft law in 1967 did not include an alteration of the undergraduate student deferment this classification will apparently remain a haven from the draft for higher strata for some time to come. Thus the differential impact of the draft on strata which Davis and Dolbeare have shown seems likely to continue with only slight changes.

The opinion of local board members concerning the impact of the draft on strata may not be the most significant of findings but is certainly one of the most interesting. Davis and Dolbeare asked for local board members' responses to the two evaluative statements about the System. The responses are rather startling:

"The Reserves and National Guard are frequently a means whereby registrants successfully avoid the draft."

31% Agree strongly
43% Agree
11% Don't know, depends
10% Disagree
3% Disagree strongly
2% No Response
100%
N=314

"Registrants from wealthier families are less likely to be inducted under present policies than registrants from less favored families."

17% Agree strongly
30% Agree
11% Don't know, depends
24% Disagree
16% Disagree strongly
3% No response
100%
N=314[28]

Other Institutional Defenses

Even though the *Selective Service Newsletter* continually takes a defensive position against the two statements above and seeks to refute them, apparently local board members have not been persuaded by their own "in house" organ.[29] Local board members are privy to no special information that would result in their responses. The responses therefore must stem from their personal experiences, and awareness of complaints.

The aim of this section is to indicate how the differential impact of the draft on strata serves as an unplanned defense for Selective Service. The greater proportional impact of the draft on lower economic strata has not resulted in some inexorable Marxian build-up of class hostility and resentment. Aside from the "black power" advocates among Negro groups there has been little criticism of Selective Service from lower strata. In fact, the sources of criticism are quite the opposite and come from middle class and higher strata. It should be noted, however, that even this criticism is a historic novelty and stems from factors that will be outlined in the next chapter.

It is the conclusion of this study that the draft's proportionally heavier impact on lower classes has been a positive factor working for acceptance of the System rather than a negative one. For the pattern of impact means that those who feel it the most are also most favorably disposed to military service, feel the Selective Service System is fairest, and possess less of the sophistication and articulateness necessary for effective criticism of the System.

Karen Oppenheim has provided some evidence of this in a study done for the National Opinion Research Center in 1966. Level of educational attainment and particularly college attendance is highly related to family income and therefore to stratification. For example, the 1960 Census showed that in families with incomes under $5000 only 19 per cent of the persons between 16 and 24 had attended college. But in families with income between $5000 and $7500 the percentage rose to 33 per cent, and in the $7500 to $10,000 income range the percentage of attendance rose to 49 per cent.[30]

Oppenheim's study shows that the lower the education of those sampled, the greater the percentage that thought the draft was fair. (See Table 12) Bearing in mind the correlation between education and stratification it can be seen that acceptance is higher in lower strata. A similar effect is seen when the responses are

TABLE 12. Per Cent Who Think the Draft Fair, by Level of Education (Nonveterans Only) (National, 1966)

Level of Education	Per Cent	Base N
Less than twelfth grade	81	1,928
High school graduate	77	1,060
College experience	63	1,485

Source: Karen Oppenheim, "Attitudes of Younger American Men Toward Selective Service," Military Manpower Survey, Working Paper No. 5, National Opinion Research Center, University of Chicago, March, 1966, p. 15.

broken along the lines of the amount of education planned rather than the amount attained. The same trend held when the responses were broken along lines of actual educational destination (level of education the respondent was working toward) rather than mere plans. (See Table 13)

Moving away from education plans to the next logical consideration of planned occupation the National Opinion Research Center data shows the acceptance pattern to hold. There should be no need to review the correlation between occupation and stratification. If we substitute the words upper, middle and lower for the first three categories of persons on Table 14, we see that the lowest strata find the draft most fair. Farming occupations disrupt the trend because they generally, despite lower status, represent high financial and physical investment that the draft would threaten.

TABLE 13. Per Cent Who Think the Draft Fair, by Amount of Education Planned (Nonveterans Only) (National, 1966)

Amount of Education Planned	Per Cent	Base N
No more planned	85	1,445
High school	81	674
College	65	2,244

Source: Karen Oppenheim, "Attitudes of Younger American Men Toward Selective Service," Military Manpower Survey, Working Paper No. 5, National Opinion Research Center, University of Chicago, March, 1966, p. 15.

TABLE 14. Per Cent Who Think the Draft Fair, by Occupation Planned (Nonveterans only) (National, 1966)

Occupation Planned	Per Cent	Base N
Professional, top business	65	1,314
Nonprofessional white-collar job	79	143
Blue-collar job	82	668
Farming occupation	78	126

Source: Karen Oppenheim, "Attitudes of Younger American Men Toward Selective Service," Military Manpower Survey, Working Paper No. 5, National Opinion Research Center, University of Chicago, March, 1966, p. 17.

Thus a fairly clear picture emerges which indicates that the lower the class strata the more acceptable the registrant finds the draft. This evidence might reflect an awareness that the military may afford career opportunities and a chance for upward mobility, though no firm evidence of this was uncovered in the course of this study. The strong impression gained from observing board interviews involving registrants who were below middle class in strata, is that such individuals *do* perceive the service as an opportunity. The high reenlistment rates of Negroes supports this impression. Another probable reason for the acceptance has been mentioned. That is an apathy born of lack of political articulateness that would follow from a lower educational level. But probably the most important reason for the pattern of positive and negative responses is that lower class individuals have less to lose by being drafted while the reverse is true of higher classes.

Oppenheim feels that this is the most important reason.[31] If drafted, these higher classes with greater investments in education and careers stand to lose two years of substantial material gains that their better jobs and careers would offer over military pay. If drafted they are less likely to be able to utilize skills and education acquired or to gain more than would be of use to them. (Most draftees go to the Army, particularly the infantry.) And of course, the better educated, higher class individuals are more capable of viewing the draft critically and expressing their criticism.

In times of relative quiet in international relations, the draft falls lightest on those persons potentially most critical of Selective Service, most likely to take issue with board decisions, or most likely to become part of an articulate political force against it. If Selective Service can defer such persons (as it has been able to do until quite recently) it diminishes threats and hostility to itself. The potentially hostile usually can move with confidence and relative security through student deferments to different options of enlisted or commissioned service, occupation, and dependency/hardship deferments.

Finally, it might be noted that observation of the boards leaves the strong impression that personal interaction between the boards and interviewees was made easier for board members by strata differentials. Most of the registrants that were observed coming before the boards seemed to be either upper-lower class or lower-middle class.[32] They came, in other words, from those strata that are generally felt to be the most ambitious in efforts at upward mobility, who are most anxious to achieve the status of middle class. They consequently seemed to be the most impressed with "their betters" that made up the local board; they seemed most prone to accept the homilies, lectures on hard work and thrift, and other striking manifestations of middle class attitudes by the boards; and they seemed to perceive the Armed Forces as less threatening than did the registrants of higher classes.[33]

Registrants from such strata may meet with the boards in greater numbers because many registrants wait until they have taken their preinduction physical and found themselves still I-A before seeking a board interview. This means that many extremely lower class registrants were eliminated as IV-F or I-Y. Persons of higher strata seeking occupational deferment seemed to appear less frequently in person; and students who had not dropped out of school to work, changed schools, or received poor grades, were usually secure and did not appear before boards. Those students who did appear often seemed to fall into the upward striving strata mentioned. It could be that the upward striving, somewhat articulate but not critical individual, is most prone to end up in an interview with his board.

The observations in this study were too limited and the evidence too impressionistic to state the point in more than a hypothetical form, but the impression gained is that the individuals seeking interviews with the boards came from strata most prone to see the boards and the System as fair and legitimate. If this is so it would certainly facilitate the operation of the boards and reinforce the boards' self-images as fair, equitable, and prestigious mechanisms.

General Hershey's Leadership as a Defense

Considering the fact that the Selective Service System has so many of the attributes of a voluntary paramilitary organization and is more traditionalistic than bureaucratic in structure and character, it is perhaps to be expected that its director has many of the charismatic qualities evident in General Hershey. In the literature of management and administration the distinction is often made between formal and informal leadership. The latter, says George Homans, "is the man who comes closest to realizing the norms the groups value highest."[34] If one is uneasy with a characterization of Hershey as charismatic perhaps the term informal leader is more acceptable. Felix Nigro says that "sometimes the happy situation exists of a formal head who is also accepted by the group as its informal leader."[35] Certainly these things are true of Hershey and his leadership of Selective Service.

One of the most striking things to emerge from interviews conducted at state and national levels during this study is the outpouring of praise for the General. The simplest of questions is likely to trigger a eulogy from the respondent. For example, the first interview with Agdustria's director began with what was thought to be a general probing question.

> *Question:* How have we managed to come from conscription riots of the Civil War to a system that has such wide-spread acceptance as the Selective Service System has in American life?
> *Reply:* Well, it all can be traced back to one man — one man with great wisdom and foresight. You see, back in the 1930's ... [There followed a fifteen minute eulogy and life history of General Hershey.][36]

This response was not just an isolated happenstance. Rather it was typical among respondents at state and national headquarters. Interviews seldom progressed far before discussion involved the Director and his qualities of leadership. As the study progressed it became clear that there was considerable accuracy in the assertion of Agdustria's director that "it can all be traced to one man." Selective Service is a product of historical events in interaction with political culture, but inevitably it must be admitted that a great deal of what Selective Service is can be traced back to one man, and a great deal of its past ability to deflect hostility and criticism sprang from the same source.

Criticism of General Hershey began in 1967 and eventually reached the status of a minor campaign issue for most of the candidates for presidential nomination. This, however, was a situation unique to the history of Selective Service. Rather than contradicting the fact that Hershey's leadership has been an institutional defense it confirms the loss of institutional equilibrium and the institutional isolation the System has suffered.

The System's past ability to deflect criticism and hostility depended on Hershey's leadership for three general reasons. First, because Hershey's personal philosophy concerning the role of the citizen in national defense has coincided so well with American political culture. That philosophy or cluster of values consists of: the citizen-soldier concept; admiration tinged with skepticism for the "Regular Military"; belief in the efficacy of the grass-roots democracy of the small town; a preference for voluntary action to achieve a common goal; negativism toward partisan politics; a belief in the desirability of compromise and "hearing the other fellow out" which coincides with American proceduralism and pragmatism; acceptance of the propriety of the judicious application of compulsion to achieve goals that involve national defense; and a faith in the tonic effect of short duration military training for the average citizen.[37]

The correlation of Hershey's philosophy with the various institutional mechanisms that tied the System to political culture was not coincidental. In a large part Hershey (and thus the System) have been so successful because they both embody those norms of American political culture that relate to the compulsory service by the citizen in defense of his country.

The second reason that the System's ability to defend itself rested in large part with Hershey, is the fact that he has many personality traits that in American culture evoked admiration and deflected hostility. He is extremely warm and witty with an earthy Indiana humor complete with Hoosier patois; he is the epitome of small town America that so many Americans seem to nostalgically identify with regardless of where they live; he is the small town boy who made good, and while he never lets one forget his humble origins, he never parades his success; he is modest and self-effacing to an extreme and he is disarmingly candid. All of this means that he has generally been an extremely poor target for criticism and attack.

His identification with the System, the esteem in which he was held, and his invulnerability to criticism were comparable only to

J. Edgar Hoover and the Federal Bureau of Investigation. Even more remarkable was that Hoover has the perfect basis for building such a reputation — he was a crime fighter; Hershey on the other hand built his position upon the administration of an unpopular law and in carrying out a negative task. And in the final analysis Hoover was subjected to criticism from the liberal periodicals long before Hershey. The attacks on the General were also much milder.[38] Hershey is the antithesis of an impartial, efficient, impersonal, expert "bureaucrat" (in the popular negative sense).

The third general reason that Hershey's leadership served to defend the System is that he is an extremely skillful institutional leader of the type outlined by Philip Selznick. As opposed to an organization which is "a technical instrument for mobilizing human energies and directing them toward set aims," the institution is "a natural product of social needs and pressures — a responsive, adaptive organism."[39]

Selznick's institutional leader is a fusion of politician and administrator.

> We have argued that policy and administration are interdependent in the special sense that certain areas of organizational activity are peculiarly sensitive to policy matters. Because these areas exist, creative men are needed — more in some circumstances than in others — who know how to transform a neutral body of men into a committed policy. These men are called leaders; their profession is politics.[40]

They have also been referred to as political executives, and Philip Kronenberg has referred to them as interface leaders who must span the boundary between politics and administration.[41]

Selznick defines four key tasks for the institutional leader:

> 1. Definition of institutional mission and role — discovery of the true commitments of the organization as set by effective internal and external demands.
> 2. Institutional embodiment of purpose — to make policy and build it into the organization's social structure.
> 3. The defense of institutional integrity — maintaining values and a distinctive identity.
> 4. Ordering of internal conflict — seeing to it that a balance of power is achieved among competing internal interest groups that is appropriate to fulfillment of key commitments.[42]

General Hershey performs the tasks of an institutional leader with consummate skill. In defining institutional mission and role he has carefully circumscribed the System's task, seeking to portray it as having a simple, neutral, and instrumental role of "delivering men to the Armed Forces." He has not hesitated to identify the System with currently popular themes like the War on Poverty but he has been careful to see that this never involved more than a superficial commitment of the institution. He has evidently felt, and correctly so, that the role of a neutral instrument would in the long run be the safest for the institution. In discussing critical decisions for an institutional leader, Selznick notes:

> Cooperation with other organizations is another field of administrative action fraught with policy implications. Cooperation threatens a loss of control, since commitments in action tend to spill over the limits of verbal agreement.[43]

And as one of the officers closest to Hershey remarked:

> All these agencies are always trying to use us for welfare, correction and everything else, but we figure it is safest to stay in our own territory. We've had advice from all these outfits that have no responsibility for our job — Justice, Labor, H.E.W., etc. They're pretty free with their advice. If their advice goes sour they're not responsible but we *are*; we're left holding the sack. If things are *sweet* they look good.[44]

Previous analysis has revealed Hershey's success in embodying purpose in the institution. His success in building policy norms or decision premises into the organization's social structure is manifest in the uniformity that over 4,000 local boards achieve despite the lack of uniform guidance and such structural difficulties as the quota system and fluctuating demands.

Throughout the System there is a "family atmosphere" that sustains the embodiment of purpose and stems from Hershey's skill. Respondents in interviews spoke openly of the feeling.

> I've been with six different agencies in my career. There's none where you feel the impact of the head man like you do here. It's like a family. I like it — I suppose a lot of people wouldn't.[45]

And the General himself has acknowledged the "family atmosphere" that he in large part has created.

> Personally, I think we have had the greatest stability. And I rather challenge any other — of course, we are a smaller group. We tend to know each other personally quite a little more ... But just the same we are more of a family than any other agency I know of.[46]

It is in the defense of the institution and its integrity that Hershey has been most notably successful. Given the sensitive nature of the System's task, its Director must be acutely aware of environmental threats. It is in this realm that the political half of his institutional leadership role has been most functional in defending the System.

Like many Americans (and many military leaders) who scorn partisan politics, the General is highly skilled at resolving conflicts of interests and the achievement of consensus, skills which Americans do not always recognize as political. His non-partisan political skills are immediately evident in an interview or in Congressional testimony. He can swiftly elicit facts from the background of the person with whom he is dealing and use them to establish rapport and identification. He also has the politician's talent for cataloguing and remembering such items as names, home towns and other related personal data. He described some of the origins of his political acumen in an interview.

> Well, I lost my mother when I was 4 — went mostly with my Dad, fortunately or unfortunately. Started going to county caucuses with him right away. Dad was a simple man but he always dabbled in politics of all kinds. He was a County Registrar, an Assessor, and a Sheriff. I saw at an early age people with different opinions getting together and hammering out differences. Well, all these things you just don't forget. They become a part of you.[47]

"These things" have been successfully used in developing institutional allies. Hershey has succeeded in securing and maintaining as allies some of the most powerful interest groups on the American scene. The National Guard, the American Legion, and the Veterans of Foreign Wars are widely acknowledged to be among the most powerful and successful of interest groups. Scarcely less impressive are the Air Force Association, the Association of the U.S. Army and the Reserve Officers Association. And though the friction between the System and the Armed Forces and Department of Defense is sometimes open and sharp (often by Hershey's design) nonetheless the Armed Forces can be expected to support the System out of sheer necessity.

An example of how the support of the Guard is secured is the repeated work of the General to defer Guardsmen from the draft and to cancel induction if a man would enlist in the Guard. The deferment of Guardsmen early in the Korean War was done despite considerable criticism and pressure to which he finally had to yield.[48] The stays of induction were also given up only after criticism had become well developed during 1965. The General has also found positions on the national staff of Selective Service for politically deposed Adjutant Generals.[49]

The close relationships with interest groups can also be seen in their testimony supporting the renewal of the Universal Military Training and Service Act from 1951 to 1967. A reading of the testimony of these groups in each quadrennial renewal shows a remarkable similarity in their testimony. Comment was made on this to an official of national headquarters:

> *Researcher:* I've noticed there is quite a similarity in the language different groups use in testifying for renewal. I've often wondered if you people had anything to do with that.
> *Respondent:* [smiling] You needn't wonder any more. Sure, we help them out by providing them with some stuff.[50]

The extremely close relations with Congress based on decentralization have been noted. The institution relies heavily upon Congress and has managed to make itself nearly as responsible to the legislative branch of government as to the executive. While much of this lies in Congress's interest in anything so close and important to their constituents as the draft, still much of it rests in Hershey's skill in handling Congress. William S. White has described the approach a witness should take before the Senate. (He might have included the House of Representatives with equal accuracy.)

> Then it is necessary to approach the place with a blend of confidence and of deference, of assertiveness and of care. The agent of the Executive must (or ought to) come forward prepared to yield much but to hold on to the bitter end to the core of his principle and purpose. He must make clear, at once, the permissible area for bargaining and the area that is out of bounds for compromise. But he must do all this subtly, neither belligerently nor fearfully, for Senators react with anger to the one and with contempt toward the other.[51]

Few men can match Hershey in following White's prescription and defending their agencies before Congress. As one student of Selective Service remarked, "The dialogue between Hershey and a committee is a verbal love feast."[52] General Hershey employs several standard stratagems.

(1) Identify with and relate to an attacker's constituency:

> *Mr. Henderson:* [opposing Hershey on keeping board clerks nonclassified] It is most unusual, isn't it? [Selective Service's relation to states.]
> *General Hershey:* It is a most unusual one. I am quite familiar with the Old North State. I have a daughter-in-law that comes from there. [Henderson is from North Carolina.] And I knew General

(2) Constantly acknowledge the unique expertise and wisdom of Congress:

> *Chairman:* I think this is a fine tribute to the foresight and the patriotism of the War Department, Major.
> *Major Hershey:* I think it is also a tribute to the foresight of Congress, sir, in 1920, when they resolved that never again should we be in the situation we were in 1917.[54]

(3) Admit easily to a lack of knowledge or that you could be wrong:

> *General Hershey:* But I could easily be wrong. I had that experience many times.... Now I would agree with you wholly. And not only that, I have the greatest respect for people who disagree with me. But on the other hand, the only thing I can do is to react to the problems as I see them.
> *Mr. Henderson:* Mr. Chairman, I would like to say how refreshing it is to have a witness even suggest that he might be wrong — especially when he has such a record of being as right as he has been for so long. Let me tell you that I feel more kindly toward you after your testimony this morning. I think your response to the gentlemen from North Carolina was a heartwarming experience for me. I want to commend you for your presentation.[55]

(4) Play the role of Hoosier Sage to rationalize conscription and inequities:

> Ninety-nine per cent of things I have done in a rather long life have not been voluntary. I merely was choosing what seemed to me the better of things that I did not like.[56]

While the General can be most lavish in his praise of Congress he is never servile or intimidated. If pressed hard by an attacker he is capable of incisive counter blows that are camouflaged by sufficient humor to avoid the appearance of belligerency:

> *Mr. Pike:* General, we are going to the wisdom of the local board now.
> *General Hershey:* Right.
> *Mr. Pike:* A member of a local board must be a male, he must be 30 years old and he must reside in the county. Does he have to be a college graduate?
> *General Hershey:* No, sir, he doesn't.
> *Mr. Pike:* Does he have to be a high school graduate?
> *General Hershey:* No, sir.

Mr. Pike: Does he have to be a grade school graduate?
General Hershey: No, and not only that there are many other occupations that we have in Government for which people are chosen that do not have to be ... [Laughter][57]

A Congress barraged with experts, criticised for obsolescence and doubting its own utility must indeed find the General to be a solace. He "talks their language" and the local boards he represents make the kind of decisions congressmen and senators feel is one of their few remaining claims to expertise. The board decisions are crucial to many people but must be made on vague if not useless criteria. A congressman can understand such decisions and is likely to feel that they cannot be made much differently. The failure of Congress in 1967 to revise the draft law so as to affect local boards in any way, despite recommendations to the contrary from the Special Commission, speaks eloquently on the above points.

One of the most interesting pay-offs for the affinity Hershey has developed with Congress is the permanency that his agency was able to develop by careful amendment of the Universal Military Training and Service Act. As previously mentioned, Selective Service has always been afflicted with an aura of impermanence. As one officer said: "We were always bugged by someone like the Bureau of the Budget. They'd say, 'Who are you anyway. You may not even be around next year.' "[58]

Selective Service found a way to alleviate this around the time of the Korean War, by playing upon the negative feelings of key committee members toward student deferments. These congressmen were concerned that the students might escape the draft. A committee member suggested that the law be amended to extend deferment to age 35 for those who obtain a deferment. Selective Service of course supported this, but quietly let it be known that this still might not prohibit escape. When concerned members asked why, it was pointed out that if the law expired the students might "get away." Selective Service thereupon provided pleased congressmen with amendments which were adopted, assuring that only the power to induct could expire — not the power to register and classify.

Selective Service officials felt that even the power to induct continued in a slightly limited form. Late in 1966 the Deputy Director of the System pointed out that in the unlikely event Congress took no action, "The Selective Service System would operate ... exactly the same as it does now, except that no one would be ordered to report for induction who had not been deferred previously under section 6, and whose basis for deferment had ceased to exist."[59] In

Other Institutional Defenses

other words even inductions could have continued by drawing upon anyone who had received a deferment and whose basis for a deferment either ran out naturally, as in graduating students, or whose basis for deferment might be removed by the President through Executive Order. Thus Selective Service achieved a permanency that few people outside the System realize. There was some consternation when the System's interpretation of the law was revealed in 1966, for it was widely assumed that the entire act and Selective Service System would expire on July 1 of 1967.[60]

General Hershey summarized his attitude toward Congress which has served him and the System so well.

> Congressmen are just plain ordinary people and you should never make the mistake of talking down to them. We have one fellow around here — heads a powerful agency. Supposed to be one of the most brilliant minds around. He's always getting himself in hot water with Congress. Just seems to go out of his way to do it. Now I don't know how that kind of mind works — who am I to say? But it don't seem like the way to me.[61]

In addition to an ability to garner and maintain institutional support, the General is astute in selecting scapegoats for deflecting hostility directed against his institution. Despite his own close ties to the regular military (he began his career in the National Guard but became a regular officer) and the ties of the paramilitary cadre, he constantly criticizes and attacks the military establishment and tries to make clear his institution's independence of it. Any independence of Secretary McNamara that the General could manifest also paid off handsomely with Congress:

> *Mr. Hebert:* May I also congratulate you on your again-demonstrated courage in challenging something Mr. McNamara has proposed as not being the right thing?
> *General Hershey:* I thought I was joining with the people that might be present.
> *Mr. Hebert:* Even to raise the questions against the "infallible one" is a mark of courage.[62]

Independence of the "Pentagon" is "coin of the realm" in Hershey's world and he spends it freely, secure in the knowledge the regular military need his institution too much to do anything but tolerate him. He prides himself on being "about as popular as a b—— at a family reunion with the military."[63]

Attitudes like the ones expressed above and skills like those demonstrated are the sort that mark General Hershey as the epitome of an institutional leader; a man whose sensitivity to his political environment along with other leadership skills, still has to be counted as one of the major defenses of the Selective Service System despite mounting criticism.

Conclusion

As an institution — a product of social needs and pressures — an adaptive organism, Selective Service has developed a variety of defenses that protect it. Adaptations to what the designers and leaders felt were key values of political culture remain among its major defenses, but others include:

(1) a carefully weighted power relationship between the individual registrant and the boards which favors the latter;
(2) institutional sensors which keep the consciously isolated System supplied with intelligence from both the federal and state levels while maintaining vital relations with the Armed Forces;
(3) the operation of policies and procedures that result in the major impact of the System falling upon those strata which are least articulate and least critical of it;
(4) the extremely skillful institutional leadership of General Hershey.

Notes

[1] Testimony before the Senate Committee on Administrative Practice and Procedure, as reported in the *New York Times,* May 16, 1966.

[2] U.S. *Universal Military Training and Service Act,* Section 13, para. (b). For the *Administrative Procedures Act,* see U.S. Codes, 60 Stat. 237.

[3] Charles E. Jacobs, *Policy and Bureaucracy* (New York: D. Van Nostrand Co., Inc., 1966), p. 89.

[4] *New York Times, op. cit.*

[5] Col. Daniel O. Omer in June A. Willenz, ed., *Dialogue on the Draft,* November 11-12, 1966, American Veterans Committee, Washington, D.C., pp. 13-14. See also Clyde E. Jacobs and John F. Gallagher, *The Selective Service Act: A Case Study of the Governmental Process* (New York: Dodd, Mead & Co., 1967), p. 145.

[6] The System participated in an "early examination program in 1965 to help identify educational and health problems and refer registrants to other agencies such as Job Corps for remedial assistance. The emphasis on the program waned and was for all practical purposes dropped with the intensification of the Viet Nam War.

[7] Interview No. 39.

[8] Interview No. 11.

[9] Interview No. 35.

[10] Interview No. 1.

[11] Interview No. 35.

[12] Interview No. 35.

[13] Interview No. 40.

[14] For a discussion of some of the difficulties in obtaining data see Davis and Dolbeare, "Who Gets Drafted," Institute for Research on Poverty, University of Wisconsin, Madison, 1967, pp. 1-2.

[15] See *Life,* Vol. 60, No. 17, April 29, 1966, p. 4, and *Review, op. cit.,* pp. 9662-64.

[16] Albert J. Mayer and Thomas Ford Hoult, "Social Stratification and Combat Survival," *Social Forces,* XXXIV (December 1955), 155-59.

[17] One of the most extensive explorations of *military service* and stratification unfortunately did not single out the impact of the draft on strata. See Albert D. Klassen, "Military Service in American Life Since World War II; An Overview," National Opinion Research Center, University of Chicago,

September 1966. Some data is given on the per cent drafted and deferred of those entering active service by father's education, and occupation, but it is not satisfyingly clear cut. It would seem that some of the data fails to reflect the impact of the draft on lower classes because of the older age of some of the respondents. Men over 30 would have been caught up in the high calls of Korea and its aftermath. High calls tend to erase differential impact. See pp. 236, A-VI.2b; 250, A-VI.5a; 252, A-VI.5c.

[18] For a summary description of this see National Advisory Commission on Selective Service, "In Pursuit of Equity: Who Serves When Not All Serve?" (Washington, D.C.: Government Printing Office, February, 1967), p. 26. Hereafter cited as *Commission Report*.

[19] *Review, op. cit.,* p. 9650.

[20] It also leaves unanswered the more salient question as to what proportion of the draft age population is made up of Negroes.

[21] *Commission Report,* p. 22.

[22] For a fascinating example of General Hershey trying to side-step this point under penetrating questioning by Congressman Otis Pike of New York, see *Review of the Administration and Operation of the Selective Service System,* Hearings before the Committee on Armed Services, House of Representatives, 89th Congress, 2nd sess. (Washington, D.C.: Government Printing Office, 1966), p. 9665.

[23] *Ibid.,* p. 9642.

[24] *Commission Report, op, cit.,* p. 22.

[25] Davis and Dolbeare, "Who Gets Drafted," *op. cit.,* p. 6.

[26] *Ibid.,* p. 15.

[27] *Ibid.,* p. 16.

[28] James W. Davis and Kenneth M. Dolbeare, *Little Groups of Neighbors* (Chicago: Markham Publishing Co., 1968), p. 29.

[29] *Ibid.,* pp. 28 and 29.

[30] U.S. Bureau of Census, *Current Population Reports, Population Characteristics,* Series p-20, no. 110, July 24, 1961, Table 10, p. 15.

[31] Karen Oppenheim, "Attitudes of Younger American Men Toward Selective Service," Military Manpower Survey, Working Paper No. 5, National Opinion Research Center, University of Chicago, March, 1966, pp. 16-24.

[32] The point being made here is a small one and the evidence impressionistic. It is therefore not worthwhile to elaborate on the definition of the class strata mentioned, but it is based on father's occupation, education, dress, place of residence, and speech patterns. The author is aware of the difficulty in assigning persons to different strata.

[33] Some professed a desire to serve but felt there were factors that made it impossible. The reliability of this claim is open to question, of course.

[34] George C. Homans, *The Human Group* (New York: Harcourt Brace & World, Inc., 1950), p. 188.

[35] Felix Nigro, *Modern Public Administration* (New York: Harper & Row Publishers, 1965), p. 275.

[36] Interview No. 1.

Other Institutional Defenses 193

[37] Some might question this last item as a norm of our culture but it is a consistent theme in our history. Americans eschew a standing army but there has been a universal belief reinforced by the necessity of the frontier that every man should know something of the martial arts. Nor is there much hesitancy in using compulsion and enforcing discipline in the achievement of widely accepted goals such as are found in defense. Witness the unusual powers granted wartime presidents and the official and unofficial treatment of "slackers," "draft-dodgers," "aliens," and some types of conscientious objectors.

[38] His defense of an Ann Arbor board's reclassification of sit-in demonstraters to I-A in 1965 brought forth some mildly critical articles in such periodicals as the *New Republic* but they were tepid in comparison with some of the attacks on Hoover.

[39] Philip Selznick, *Leadership in Administration* (Evanston, Ill.: Row, Peterson, 1957), p. 5.

[40] *Ibid.*, p. 161.

[41] Marver H. Bernstein, *The Job of the Federal Executive* (Washington, D.C.: Brookings Institution, 1958); Philip S. Kronenberg, "The Interface Leader: the Politics of a Boundary Spanning Role," (unpublished paper, University of Pittsburgh, May 31, 1966).

[42] Selznick, *op. cit.*, pp. 62-64.

[43] *Ibid.*, p. 59.

[44] Interview No. 40.

[45] Interview No. 13.

[46] *Compensation Hearings, op. cit.*, p. 5.

[47] Interview No. 39.

[48] Derthick, "Citizen Soldier on Capitol Hill: The Political Life of the National Guard" (Ph.D. dissertation, Radcliffe College, 1962), p. 295.

[49] *Ibid.*

[50] Interview No. 40.

[51] William S. White, *Citadel* (New York: Harper and Bros., 1957), p. 11.

[52] Conversation with James Gearhardt of Rice University.

[53] *Compensation Hearings, op. cit.*, p. 5.

[54] 1940 Hearings on Burke-Wadsworth Bill.

[55] *Compensation Hearings, op. cit.*, p. 15.

[56] U.S. Congress, Senate, Subcommittee on Employment and Manpower, *Nation's Manpower Revolution*, National Commission on Automation and Technological Progress, Hearings, 88th Cong., 2nd Sess. (Washington, D.C.: U.S. Government Printing Office, July 1964), p. 2817.

[57] *Review, op. cit.*, p. 9667.

[58] Interview No. 40.

[59] Newsletter on Military Manpower of the American Veterans Committee, Feb. 2, 1967.

[60] The subject was brought up by Colonel Daniel C. Omer in a presentation at the National Conference on the Draft, sponsored by the American

Veterans Committee, Washington, D.C., Nov. 11, 12, 1966. System spokesmen had made this point before during the 1959 and 1963 extension hearings though no one paid much attention to it. Had the law ever expired and the system inducted students as their deferments ended with graduation it would have become painfully clear to one and all that student deferments had really become exemptions.

[61]Interview No. 39.

[62]*Review, op. cit.*, p. 9677.

[63]Keith R. Johnson, "Who Should Serve?" *Atlantic Monthly* (February, 1966), p. 66.

6

The Strain on Institutional Equilibrium

The Selective Service System achieved a remarkably long period of equilibrium in the years since World War II. The equilibrium rested upon recognition of the necessity of conscription in a world of power relationships, acceptance of the rationale for the Cold War and the Korean War, and upon satisfactorily meeting both the functional demands for military manpower when needed and the demands of political culture. The latter demands were met by adaptations of structure and processes to major values of political culture and the fact the wars undertaken were considered just. Finally the equilibrium was further buttressed by a variety of supplementary institutional defense mechanisms.

Despite the elaborate adaptations and defenses the System has come under unprecedented attack. Analysis of the capabilities of local boards suggest that it is more accurate to state that the attacks have come because of the adaptations and defenses rather than in spite of them. Adaptations have been made to certain elements of a political culture that have since changed and defenses that were acceptable in the Cold War era attract criticism during an unpopular "policy war" in Asia. The result has been a severe strain on institutional equilibrium.

The strain upon the equilibrium necessary for effective administration is not to be confused with the level of support for the policy in question. Support for conscription varies slightly with vicissitudes of foreign policy but always remains quite high.[1] It is not the policy that is under attack but the way it is administered. In August 1966 Louis Harris and Associates found support for drafting young men among 79 per cent of those polled but only 49 per cent thought the way the system worked was fair.[2] Four months later a Gallup poll showed the percentage who thought it fair had slipped to 43 per cent.[3]

This chapter will attempt to suggest some of the demographic facts, policy issues, and changes in political culture that have contributed to the strain on Selective Service's institutional equilibrium.

Viet Nam Buildup

Though the Vietnamese "situation" cannot qualify as a sole cause for the System's problems, it definitely is a major part of the strain upon it. By nearly all accounts the war is one of the most unpopular and divisive in our history. It is the severest test to date of the adaptability of Americans and their cultural values to the concept and techniques of unconventional warfare and/or limited war.[4]

The immediate threats of the earlier Cold War era have receded in memories. The Berlin Blockade, the fall of Czechoslovakia, the Korean War have become history for many. The 18 year-old draft-eligible of today was only a child during the Cuban Missile Crisis. Depending on one's views the Cold War has been "thawing" or taking on more subtle and sophisticated forms for years. America's heavy involvement in the Vietnamese War has therefore come as a rude shock.

Without a clearly definable enemy, goals, time limit for involvement or clear cut symbol of unwarranted assault, the war alone would generate sufficient controversy to make it rank as our most divisive to date. But obviously the use of conscripts in such a war, or even their use to release others so that they may fight it, inevitably brings about soul-searching that extends to a reexamination of the administrative system for conscripting.

Interviews in early 1966 and some of General Hershey's testimony before Congress suggest that Selective Service officials felt that Viet Nam, and the fact that it was a year for mid-term elections, were largely if not solely to blame for their difficulties:

Question: What do you think is causing all the "flap" at this time? What makes this situation different from others?
Respondent: [immediately] Viet Nam. One of our officers said it — shouldn't have — but he's right, "The people just aren't gung-ho for this war!"[5]

In fairness to the respondents it should be said that most of them went on to discuss other changes that were in the nature of variables of political culture. But men institutionalized to a system designed to stave off the "whether" question of conscription can be excused if they are slow to perceive environmental changes that bring their organizational style under attack so that the questions are over "how" conscription is administered.

While the judgment of the respondents in ranking the Viet Nam War as the most important change can be questioned, it remains unassailable that the war triggered the current crisis for the System. As the Special Commission said, the problem of who serves when not all serve is an enduring one, "but [it is] floodlighted today by the war in Vietnam."[6]

Surfeit of Manpower

One of the most significant of the non-cultural balance variables is a demographic one — the overabundance of men that are of draft age. The draft has always been a residual source of military manpower with heavy reliance on enlistments. The need for drafted manpower since World War II reached a high of 500,000 in 1953 but after that dropped to a rough average of 100,000 per year until the Viet Nam build-up in 1965.[7] While the number of conscripts needed had settled at a low level, the number of 18 year-olds entering the nation's manpower pool was continuing to increase sharply. Between 1955 and 1965 the number of 18 year-olds increased by 50 percent from 1,150,000 to 1,700,000. Selective Service said in June 1966 that 1,920,000 were reaching 18½ each year. The trend will continue into the 1970's and the Department of Defense admits that it expects the number of draft age men to reach more than 2,100,000 by 1974 — over 80 percent above the 1955 level.[8] (See Table 15)

The military manpower demands of Viet Nam have not really altered the overabundance of manpower. Even though some local boards have developed relative shortages of available I-A men under current policies and procedures this does not alter the issues

TABLE 15.   Men Reaching Age 18
(000's)

Year	Number	% Increase
1955	1,150	—
1960	1,330	16
1965	1,720	50
1970	1,930	68
1974	2,120	84

Source: *Review of the Administration and Operation of the Selective Service System,* Hearings before the Committee on Armed Services, House of Representatives, 89th Cong. 2nd Sess. (Washington, D. C.: Government Printing Office, 1966), p. 10003.

and questions of equity that arise from a surfeit of manpower. The issues grow out of the fact that with the overabundance, the number of men reaching age 26 who had served in the Armed Forces has dropped steadily and sharply. In 1958, 70 per cent of such men had served, but by 1966 the figure had dropped to 46 per cent. By 1974 it is projected that only 42 per cent will have served even if our force level stays as high as 3 million, or the number serving could fall as low as 34 per cent if a 2.7 million level is maintained. Even at the highest level of draft calls since 1953 the Armed Forces absorbed only 335,000 men through inductions in 1966. (See Table 16) There is no expectation that this rate of induction will increase appreciably even if more men are committed to Viet Nam.[9] Under such conditions the question of who serves when less and less serve becomes increasingly acute.

Compounding this increasingly contentious question is the fact that Selective Service had become extremely liberal in its deferment policies between the Korean War and the Vietnam build-up.[10] The Armed Forces also became increasingly selective in their procurement standards until 1966 when it lowered them somewhat.[11] The Universal Military Training and Service Act of 1951 prohibited higher minimum standards than had been applied during January 1945 but this was changed in 1958 to permit the President to modify requirements. While the Report of the Surgeon General of the Army insisted in 1966 that "only a few minor changes occurred in the medical requirement," it paradoxically admitted that mental standards were raised in 1958 which "somewhat more than doubled the percent of youths disqualified from accession to the military through *all* means (including and in addition to the draft).[12]

As a result of these increased deferments the sudden increase in draft calls for a highly controversial war created a traumatic effect

TABLE 16. Enlisted Personnel Entries by Major Source[1] FY 1948-1966 (000's)

	Total	Enlistees[2]	Draftees	Reserve Recalls	Percent Draftees
1948	281	281	—	—	—
1949	398	368	30	—	7.5%
1950	182	182	—	—	—
1951	1,826	630	587	609	32.1
1952	991	532	379	80	38.2
1953	961	397	564	—	58.7
1954	647	382	265	—	41.0
1955	695	480	215	—	30.9
1956	583	446	137	—	23.5
1957	576	396	180	—	31.3
1958	453	327	126	—	27.8
1959	451	340	111	—	24.6
1960	439	349	90	—	20.5
1961	446	386	60	—	13.5
1962	715	409	158	148	22.1
1963	447	373	74	—	16.6
1964	527	376	151	—	28.7
1965	454	351	103	—	22.7
1966[3]	933	598	335	—	35.9

[1]Excluding reenlistments.

[2]Includes male regular enlistments, other than prior service, and enlisted reservists voluntarily entering active duty tours of two years or more.

[3]Estimated.

Source: *Review of the Administration and Operation of the Selective Service System,* Hearings before the Committee on Armed Services, House of Representatives, 89th Cong. 2nd Sess. (Washington, D. C.: Government Printing Office, 1966), p. 9926.

on both the general public and the Selective Service System. Deferments that had been accepted in previous years seemed suddenly inequitable when men were being drafted for service in Viet Nam and particularly as battle casualties grew and no end seemed in sight. Deferments for athletes and screen actors that had created no interest before now became infamous and highlighted the questions of equity in terms that even the least politically sophisticated members of the public could comprehend and react to.

War Without Mobilization

Selective Service has always experienced fluctuations of supply and demand which it had to translate into slackening and tightening of deferments. The problems created were always mitigated by the fact that the need for military manpower became sufficiently urgent to result in development of acceptable formal or informal decision criteria for selection. Some difficulty was encountered in the Korean War which was our first modern limited war. Student deferments were begun and occasioned some controversy but mobilization was extensive enough to lessen the problems of equity.

The Vietnamese War is the first time Selective Service has had to operate under conditions that approach normalcy on the domestic scene, while hundreds of American soldiers (some of whom are draftees) die each week in a war that has grown greater in scope and military commitment than the Korean. Aside from some inflationary pressure on the economy, there has been little to alter the peacetime patterns of living for most Americans. The tightening of deferments was not uniform or thorough nor was it done under extensive and explicit policy guidance. The tightening that had taken place until late 1966 was largely as a result of informal processes. This made the "tightening-up" appear exaggeratedly capricious, irrational, and inequitable.

Reflecting American divisions over the war there has been great controversy over what deferments are acceptable. To some no *deferments* seemed acceptable in the face of mounting casualties; to others, no *inductions* seemed acceptable in light of the nature of the war. In the midst of these sharply divided reactions to its operations, Selective Service had to continue inexorably drafting *some* while *most* went about their normal business. A worse setting for acceptable operation of the System could scarcely be envisioned.

In a situation of near normalcy, which, if any, occupations and skills are critical? How can a largely urban population after years of hearing about farm surpluses feel agricultural deferments are important? The publicization of the shocking number of IV-F deferments by a presidential commission raised questions in the minds of a public for whom the low medical standards of the services have become folk humor.[13] The once highly acceptable deferments for the Reserves become controversial when they are not mobilized and there is no clear prospect of doing so.

The student deferment has been one of the most controversial and yet in many ways the most widely supported deferment. Perhaps this is because American values are in conflict in this area. Americans place an extremely high value on a college education that culminates in a baccalaureate. The value of graduate education is considerably less certain in American minds, yet it is widely perceived to be the most efficacious means of upward mobility. Louis Harris and Associates report 7 out of 10 people approve of deferments for college students. They also report "an undercurrent of uneasiness" in this overall support. Eighty-five per cent of the college educated (about 24 per cent of adult Americans) approve, but only 57 per cent of those with an eighth grade education (23 per cent of all adults) express approval.[14]

Part of the controversy arises from the fact that Americans also place a high value on equality (at least in outward manifestations) and the advantage the student deferment affords middle and upper class registrants has been painfully evident, even to the local board members. The rationale behind the student deferment arose from the need for scientists and technologists that had been made so evident by the Korean War defense build-up and by the shock of the Soviet Sputnik. In a book justifying and explaining the policy, M. H. Trytten in 1952 said:

> We are rebuilding our strength from the low point resulting from our precipitate demobilization of 1946 and 1947. This means that we are operating our research, development, and production facilities under extreme pressure for speed. Not only must we design and develop and produce a stockpile of weapons adequate to meet a possible military crisis, but we must also carry on activities essential to maintaining our civilization and its program.[15]

Perhaps some of today's discontent over the student deferment is explained by what Trytten said in 1952 in arguing for deferments based on examination scores.

> Over-all student deferment would make the fact of having the money to go to college the only criterion for classification as II-S. It would

surely appear to the general public to be class privilege. The only defense for student deferment is that the nation needs the special skills resulting from college training, and it cannot be argued in the face of competing demands for military manpower that the nation needs as many in college as care to go, or that it needs all who wish to go to college whether or not they show any promise of profiting from further education.[16]

Thus, with less than total mobilization, with an easing of the demands for scientists and technologists (or at least a recognition that there has been emphasis in this area to the detriment of the arts and humanities), and with the dropping of the college qualification test in 1963, all the conditions for controversy that Trytten had warned against thirteen years earlier have been created.

Selective Service has thus been forced to operate under conditions in which deferments of virtually every kind are criticized but efforts to tighten up on any deferments also create criticism. Small wonder then that Selective Service officials feel that somehow they were "left holding the sack" as more than one expressed it in interviews.

Sensitivity to Issues of Equity

Endeavoring to chart changes in political culture is only slightly more hazardous than attempting its general description at a point in time. There seem to be numerous factors that suggest a greater sensitivity to equity in American political culture. Increased education and growing political sophistication alone would account for much of this but there seems to be more than that at work.

This sensitization to issues of equity would seem to stem from a variety of sources. One of the primary ones worthy of being singled out is the so-called Negro Revolution. Harry Lazer, in his book *The American Political System in Transition,* points to the Negro Revolution and urbanization as the two fundamental forces of change moving American government from "a somewhat anachronistic device for maintaining the values of an outmoded society to an instrument for rational adjustment to the realities of the modern world."[17]

The Negro Revolution has been identified by many others as one of the most momentous changes in America. This is true because it is far more than a matter of desegregation, voting rights or open housing for Negroes. It is a social, political and economic revolution (hopefully of the non-violent, evolutionary American type). Many see it as the last major step yet to be taken toward fulfillment of the "American Dream" of political equality amidst abundance. President Johnson's praised and much-pilloried phrase "The Great Society" captures the sense of this. It is inseparable from forces and problems surrounding urbanization because the Negro belongs to the last great wave of unassimilated immigrants to move into the urban environment.

A host of writers have written on the role of the Negro and the South in American history. Gunnar Myrdal's *American Dilemma* and C. Vann Woodward's *The Burden of Southern History* are two outstanding examples that portray the moral dilemmas, the expedient warping of American politics, and the hypocrisy born of denying the American Negro the political and material rewards of the American Dream. According to supporters of the Revolution, these burdens and distortions of society and the political system are rapidly (albeit not rapidly enough for many) eroding under its pressures. Bayard Rustin expressed these broader dimensions of the Negro Revolution:

> The civil rights movement is evolving from a protest movement into a full-fledged social movement — an evolution calling its very name into question. It is now concerned not merely with removing the barriers to full opportunity but with achieving the fact of equality. From sit-ins and freedom rides we have gone into rent strikes, boycotts, community organization, and political action. As a consequence of this natural evolution, the Negro today finds himself stymied by obstacles of far greater magnitude than the legal barriers he was attacking before: automation, urban decay, *de facto* school segregation. These are problems which, while conditioned by Jim Crow, do not vanish upon its demise. They are more deeply rooted in our socio-economic order; they are the result of the total society's failure to meet not only the Negro's needs, but human needs generally.[18]

The heightened sensitivity that is posited here is a derivative of the fact that the problems of the Negro are the problems of our society. Rustin is explicit about the link between the Revolution and the growing sensitivity to equity in the larger society.

> The revolutionary character of the Negro's struggle is manifest in the fact that this struggle may have done more to democratize life for whites than for Negroes. Clearly, it was the sit-in movement of young Southern Negroes which, as it galvanized white students, banished the ugliest features of McCarthyism from the American campus and resurrected political debate. It was not until Negroes

assaulted *de facto* school segregation in the urban centers that the issue of quality education for all children stirred into motion. Finally, it seems reasonably clear that the civil rights movement, directly and through the resurgence of social conscience it kindled, did more to initiate the war on poverty than any other single force.[19]

If anything Rustin is modest in his claims for the far-reaching changes in concepts of equity the Revolution has fostered. Lazer goes further in stating that he feels the historic series of legislative reapportionment cases that culminated in *Baker* v. *Carr* are a direct outgrowth of the Negro Revolution.[20] He poses the question of why the Supreme Court chose to reverse itself on reapportionment and act as a leading precipitant of political change for the second time in a decade despite its high vulnerability as a non-elective institution of government.

> The Court acted partly because of the interlocking nature of the various elements within the political system's hierarchical structure. As we have seen, the breaking of one bond meant the loosening of the others; thus, the elimination of racial inequality cut the ground from under rural political control.[21]

Lazer feels that the civil rights problems sensitized the court to the harmful effects of obstruction in the legislative process and, fearing the fabric of society might not stand the strain of postponing urban problems, the court moved into the "political thicket" of apportionment.

It probably matters little how much credit for a heightened sense of equity should go directly to the Negro Revolution. One can subsume the Negro Revolution under a broader problem-focus of the status of the individual with regard to his government. Such a problem-focus is at once a symptom and a cause of a heightened sense of equity. Alan Westin points out that after 1938 the economic affairs of the country reached a plateau of contention with no radical departures and controversies since then. The major conflicts affecting our society domestically according to Westin have been matters of status, not property; the relationship of the individual to the power and the operation of government.

> The problems of Communism, loyalty, and internal security that reached their peak in McCarthyism involved the definition of political deviation and the limits of liberty. The revolution in race relations since the Second World War and in religious interrelations probes our concepts of equality. And it is in this arena, of status, that the great constitutional debate of our generation has been raging.[22]

Urbanization, of course, is interwoven with the great constitutional debate of which Westin speaks and therefore contributes to a greater concern for equity. Adrian and Press comment:

> Urbanization of society inevitably creates some new problems for individual freedom. Beyond the repressions attacked by the social service ideology are those created by a society of large scale organizations in which the individual is a relatively helpless unit.... Under such conditions, procedures for making decisions about individuals become crucial and are of importance to almost all.[23]

The effect of such a constitutional debate on an entire generation is a sensitivity to issues of equity — a major change in our political culture that has contributed to the strain upon Selective Service's equilibrium.

Selective Service was decidedly caught off balance when this increased sensitivity to equity was brought to bear upon it by the Viet Nam build-up. Note has been made previously of the immediate overloading of the formal appeal system and the pipeline jam that developed in 1965-66. The once elaborate mechanism for protecting the registrant's rights and facilitating his appeal had fallen into almost complete disuse. The Government Appeal Agents were still carried on paper by every board but during the six months of this study no instance of their use could be detected. Clerks admitted that they were never used as did state and national officials. In fact, any mention of them was in connection with World War II. It is interesting that General Hershey always spoke of the appeal agents as though they were operable.[24]

The explanation for their disuse was suggested by several of the clerks who indicated that the Government Appeal Agent introduced added contention and work that local boards did not want to tolerate.[25] The disuse of this mechanism was hit upon by the Special Commission repeatedly.[26] Not long after publication of the report local boards in California began providing the registrants with the names of appeal agents once again whether they were requested or not. It is not clear whether this was a nation-wide policy or not. It is unlikely that the appeal agent will ever be widely used. The position is allegedly supposed to represent both the registrant and the System. One appeal agent testified that "by the time the agent enters into the appeal, there is d—— little the Government appeal agent can do for the registrant."[27] And General Hershey's public claims that the agent is obliged to inform on his clients if they break the law is likely to discourage registrants from placing much confidence in them and lawyers from accepting the unpaid and thankless task.[28]

This study did not encompass a conscious effort to interview registrants and their knowledge of the appeal system. From the perspective of state and national headquarters there seemed to be a plentitude of people who knew and exercised their right of appeal. Nor could it be said that the System failed to inform the registrant of his rights of appeal or the proper procedures even though it usually did not provide him with the dubious benefit of the appeal agent.

The U. S. Youth Council undertook an unsystematic but extensive survey of its membership that indicated only 54.8 per cent of their interviewees "felt that they understood the appellate system by which they might change their status."[29] While this figure is extremely high for awareness of governmental procedures, it must be remembered that the survey is of students with high education and political efficacy and the matter in question is of crucial importance. (At times it is not melodramatic to say it is a matter of life and death.) In light of these considerations, 54.8 per cent is not an unusually high number who claim to understand the appeals procedure, though it is a high figure compared to most public awareness of governmental policy and procedures. Interestingly enough the same survey revealed that "only 27.2 per cent of those interviewed indicated that they would use it [the appellate system] even if they knew it."[30] According to many of the students "the system is unbeatable," and "an appeal would prejudice the board against me."[31]

This curious reaction is hard to explain. Lack of information and lack of familiarity with the System is the most feasible answer. The registrants evidently do not understand that an appeal is not taken until they have had an interview with their board. If the board keeps them in I-A after an interview there is nothing worse the board can do to them. They cannot induct them out of line with their birth date. Taking an appeal may not endear the registrant to the clerk or the board but there is really nothing to be lost by doing so, since the worst has been done.

Though Selective Service informs each registrant of his rights and how to appeal by information on the back of his Notice of Classification, it is true that the System understandably does little to encourage appeals. Clerks and board members would have to be something more than human to make work and trouble for themselves; and yet in view of the sharpened sensitivity to matters of equity, the institution unwittingly contributed to its difficulties and to challenges to its legitimacy by not facilitating and being more solicitous of desires to appeal.

The System was placed in a position of appearing to use the ignorance of the registrants to facilitate its operations. Selective Service consciously relies upon the individual to make his own appeal. This inattention to procedural rights of clientele is not uncharacteristic of large public agencies. But in most cases the agencies are dealing with groups and an individual client can always turn to a group which will represent his interests and bring pressure to bear. As indicated earlier, groups do bring pressure to bear on the System at upper levels but note has also been made of the way the System is carefully constructed to isolate the individual in his dealings with it by denying him the right to counsel. The fact that the System does react to group pressure at upper levels but also has several ways to defend against it at lower levels means that the registrants of upper strata, the politically articulate and influential, have a decided advantage in all approaches to the System from a simple request for an interview with a board (it must be in writing) to an informal appeal to a state director.

General Hershey described the way the responsibility is placed on the individual more than once throughout the 1966 hearings. He also admits to the wide use of informal appeals.

> So what I am getting at is what should be done? This pilot that was taken and put in I-A should appeal, because the appeal board was set up by the Congress, and was set up as the area in which you try to level out justice, the same as in the courts. Some judges, if I drive 65 miles an hour, will give me 3 months in jail, and the other fellow says "Don't do it again," and the appeal process is the place where we level out, and we have two level-out places. First of all, if the pilot was put in I-A he should appeal to the appeal board in Pennsylvania, if that is where he happens to be. If he wasn't satisfied with that, and there was one dissenting vote on the State appeal board he had an automatic appeal to the Presidential Board and if the appeal board was unanimous, he could go to the Director of Selective Service in Pennsylvania, and, if he wouldn't take an appeal to the President, our door is always open.[32]

The burden is upon the registrants, many of whom are not yet adults, to appeal their cases. As the General remarked at another point: "The registrant that is alert or the employer that is alert will immediately appeal."[33] The enormity of this burden becomes clearer if viewed against some of the evidence available on the sense of inefficacy citizens have with regard to dealing with government officials. Janowitz *et al.* conducted a study of how the public perceived administration in the city of Detroit in 1953-54. Respondents were asked:

> In general, if you had a problem to take up with a government bureau, would you do it yourself or do you think you would be better off if you got the help of some person or organization.

Only 16 per cent would approach such an agency without aid. Some 75 per cent felt they would need some kind of help. (See Table 17) As noted previously the System denies the registrant exactly the kind of help he needs.

Rather than compensating for the usual public unawareness, truculence and inattention, Selective Service consciously uses these characteristics of its clientele as tools of manpower procurement. The bitter remarks among board clerks were that "Anyone who wants to avoid induction can do so if he tries hard enough"; or "Why don't we just ask if there is anyone who would like to be drafted?" This latter procedure, they claimed, would be as effective as the present one for obtaining manpower.

Though appeal boards were used as a feedback and control mechanism (as were informal appeals to directors) they were used at a satisfice level — merely enough to protect the institution, not to protect every registrant. Actions coming before appeal boards gave upper echelons an idea of the problems so that they could take appropriate control measures, but there was no effort made to treat

TABLE 17. Attitudes Concerning Access to Government Agencies

	Number	Per cent
Would do it himself	123	16
Would try to do it himself; then get outside help	60	8
Would get help of an outsider	453	59
Depends	87	11
Not ascertained	41	5
	764	100

Source: Morris Janowitz, *et al.*, *Public Administration and the Public* (Ann Arbor, Mich. Bureau of Government, University of Michigan, 1958), p. 53.

the appeal system in anything but a way that was utilitarian for the System.

It should also be noted that despite the fact that General Hershey claims appeal boards "make things more uniform," Davis and Dolbeare and the Special Commission found them to be a source of variability and non-uniformity. In the case of the registrant working in an area and classified I-A by his local board that is geographically far-removed the appeal boards provide some means of representing area interests. But beyond this, appeal boards within a state vary widely and of course there is no uniformity interstate. Appeal boards are not provided with any special guidance or information that would give them a different basis than the boards for decisions. There is more thorough occupational and professional representation but their true rationale seems to have been distance from local situation which makes little sense when it is recalled that the local board has itself become quite remote in terms of knowledge of registrants.[34]

In Agudstria one of the state's two appeal boards was located in the same office as the seventeen Hill City boards. The members were of extremely advanced age and did not meet as a board but came in to review files individually and vote. Their production rate could scarcely have been high under such conditions or have done much to help unclog the pipeline. If many other appeal boards operated in similar ways the appellate procedures were in sore need of an overhaul. In any event, the System's appeal procedures not only failed to meet a more sophisticated sense of equity, they in fact further damaged the symbolic power of the System to legitimate.

A part of an increased awareness of the problems of equity must be attributed to the analysis of poverty in the midst of affluence by Potter, Galbraith, Harrington and others who have received so much popular attention and in turn generated many more books and articles as well as government policies and programs.[35] This is not to say that their analyses are unfailingly correct or the policies they imply are necessary, but that they have been widely accepted and the consciousness of the public does seem to have been reached. There seems to be a widespread awareness among the politically active and articulate that in the midst of mass plenty there is chronic poverty, and there is no better evidence of this awareness than the War on Poverty as a political slogan and set of programs. More important for the point to be made here is that among the politically articulate there has been developed a fairly sophisticated awareness of the limitations and handicaps imposed on the individual by poverty. Phrases such as "culturally disadvantaged" have entered the stream of informed political discussion. There has been considerable change in what Americans feel an individual can accomplish by his own efforts. All of this has set the stage for a probing analysis of an institution that had been uncritically accepted for nearly a quarter of a century.

Changed Concepts of Service and Conscientious Objection

Part of the discontent with the System and questioning of its equitableness seems to grow out of changed concepts of what constitutes service to one's country. Perhaps the two things for which President John F. Kennedy has been best remembered are the Peace Corps and his statement, "Ask not what your country can do for you; ask what you can do for your country." Both the statement and the Peace Corps struck a responsive chord in American youth. Other programs both private and public have tried to capture some of the success of the Peace Corps: Volunteers in Service to America, the Job Corps, Teacher Corps, Executive Corps, etc.

In May 1966 Secretary of Defense Robert McNamara made a speech proposing "a practical system of non-military alternatives to the draft" in which every young person in the United States would "give two years of service to his country whether in one of the military services, in the Peace Corps, or in some other volunteer development."[36] This speech was considered by many to be a "trial balloon." Several months later in August 1966, President Johnson also touched upon the subject.[37]

Within the space of a year the idea developed remarkable support and an extensive debate developed. Other prominent government figures like Secretary of Labor Willard Wirtz and Sargent Shriver of the Office of Economic Opportunity strongly advocated non-military national service. By the fall of 1966 as many as thirty-five congressmen and nine senators had made national service proposals.[38] A National Service Secretariat was established and began to operate as an interest group, holding a national conference and presenting its ideas to the Special Commission on the draft.

A surprisingly strong public support for alternative national service was indicated by the polls. The Gallup Poll in July of 1966 found the public favored national service by three and a half to one.³⁹ Louis Harris and Associates found similar sentiment in November 1966. Their polling indicated that people favored by nearly four to one the idea of a universal service program for all young men between 18 and 26 under which they could choose between a two year stint in the Armed Forces, the Peace Corps or in some other public service.⁴⁰

Persons supporting national service did so for a variety of reasons. Some saw it as a way to solve the problems they felt were inherent in Selective Service; some saw it as a modern version of universal military training which has generally come to be considered militarily obsolescent; others saw it as a way to cure some of the problems of poverty and cultural deprivation. Whatever the reasons for support, the changed concepts challenged Selective Service and made it appear to many as unsophisticated, and out of touch with modern attitudes and concepts.

When Selective Service began (again) in 1940 it was considered at the limits of propriety that an individual should be called upon to serve his country by helping to defend it. It is a measure of the changes in American attitudes toward government that national service was given serious consideration by the Special Commission.

There have also been changes in American conceptions of conscientious objection. Whereas before this claim for deferment was looked upon as almost solely the province of accepted and established "pacifist churches" it is beginning to be seen as legitimate when advanced by persons outside these narrowly defined groups. Whether recent Supreme Court decisions like *U. S.* v. *Seeger* mirrored this change or stimulated it is hard to say. In the case of Daniel Seeger the court developed the parallel belief doctrine.

> We believe that under this construction, the test of belief "in a relation to a Supreme Being" is whether a given belief that is sincere and meaningful occupies in the life of its possessor a place parallel to that filled by the orthodox belief in God of one who clearly qualifies for the exemption. Where such beliefs have parallel positions in the lives of their respective holders we cannot say that one is "in a relation to a Supreme Being" and the other is not. We have concluded that the beliefs of the objectors in these cases meet these criteria . . .⁴¹

It seems likely that this demand for a broader basis for conscientious objection is something more than mere rationalization of distaste for Viet Nam, that it is symptomatic of the general secular trend in society. General Hershey, the System and its allies have vigorously sought to reverse this trend rather than adapt to it.

Decline of Localism and Traditionalism

Localism

It matters little whether one wants to claim that Selective Service was designed for conditions of 1866 or conditions of 1917. In either case American society was much more localistic, a nation of small towns and farms. In both years rural population exceeded urban. Of course the rural and small town norms and outlook dominated American society long beyond those years. It has probably been only since the advent of the 1960's that the urban majority has begun to make its prominence felt. But there is no denying the fact that America is an urban society today. In 1960 over 70 per cent of the population lived in areas designated as urban by the U.S. Bureau of Census and 64 per cent lived in a metropolitan area having a central city of at least 50,000 people. Approximately one-fourth of the total lived in the twelve largest metropolitan areas. At present one can be sure that all of these figures have increased substantially.[42] The complex, anonymity of urban life is now more characteristic of America than the small town and farm. As Morton and Lucia White wrote:

> The wilderness, the isolated farm, the plantation, the self-contained New England town, the detached neighborhood are things of the American past. All the world's a city now and there is no escaping urbanization, not even in outer space.[43]

Daniel Bell has echoed this theme.

> It is only within the past few decades that the United States has become a truly National Society in which economic or political or social action in one section immediately affects every other.[44]

We have developed a National Society within the lifetime of Selective Service. An institution designed to relate to the political culture of a "folk" society with localistic perspectives is attempting to operate in a radically changed environment.

The typical American today might best be portrayed as spending childhood in a suburban home, and nuclear family; passing through an extended adolescence and prolonged education; passing into an adult world where associations are with nationally organized professional, vocational, institutional or corporate groups; and a world that is highly mobile with his occupation or profession requiring changes of residence on the average of every four to five year.[45]

The examples of inequities that are brought up in virtually all discussions of Selective Service are those that emphasize the lack of apparent reasons or consistency in board decisions; of men working in the same positions in the same corporation or government agency, who were classified in opposite ways by their respective boards; of adjacent boards one of which drafted married men while the other did not.[46] These are complaints of persons whose lives revolve around institutions and associations *not* local communities; and whose associations, be they political, social or economic, know no boundaries. Every discussion of American government and politics treats a decline in localism as a variable of fundamental importance.

> One of the most noticeable features of our population is its mobility. Increasingly, Americans are leaving their home towns and even their home states. The effect is to destroy local attachments, loyalty to states, and interest in local and state government, bringing a decline of sectional cleavages and increasing the sense of national unity and the interest in national solutions for American problems.[47]

About 40 per cent of all native "white" Americans move from one state to another by the time they reach adulthood; and southern Negroes have been part of the greatest migration for a single decade of American history (1.5 million left the South between 1950 and 1960).[48] Thirty-six million, or more than one-fifth of all Americans change their addresses every year with 11 million of them moving to different counties and 5.5 million to different states.[49] As a consequence, "the government" has generally come to mean the one in Washington.

The incredible mobility of Americans has dissolved local attachments. No more anachronistic feature of Selective Service can be found than the regulations that subject a registrant to the jurisdiction of his original board of registration regardless of how often he changes residence.[50]

The institutional philosophy expressed by General Hershey stands in sharp contrast to the decline of localism:

> Well, I still think that if each community does its share, they ought to be allowed to do it in a way they want to do it, because I think people will fight longer when they participate in the decisions than they will when somebody furnishes them ready made.[51]

Or, on another occasion:

> I believe government ought to be as close to a citizen as possible. Washington is a long way off — a mysterious place. So when a fella says, "Who decided that?" You can say "Why they did over at the capitol." And if he says "Where's that?" Someone is gonna say,

"Why over at Topeka, the capital, you fool. Where in h——do you think the capitol is anyway?" In other words, he knows where Topeka is, how to get there, or call on the phone and make himself felt.[52]

Early in this study the change in American attitudes toward the states and the concept of federalism was noted. The National Society of which Bell speaks may be a new development, but the *idea* that the United States of America is a union created not by the states but by the national community is an old one. This of course was the argument of the Federalists. They were opposed by the Jeffersonians who contended that it was a compact of states, each with its own sovereignty. The historical survey of conscription in America reflected the fact that the union concept of the Constitution came to prevail. Samuel Beer refers to the union concept of the Constitution as the National Idea and points out that this view of the Constitution has blended with traditions of democratic reform to create what is today called Liberalism.

This of course is much the same idea Lazer expresses when he says the whole political system has changed and now rests upon liberal assumptions. More important for the present discussion is Beer's point.

> The National Idea is not only a view of American federalism, but also a principle of public policy. As a principle of public policy, it is a doctrine of what today is commonly called "nation-building." Its imperative is to use the power of the nation as a whole not only to promote social improvement and individual excellence, but also to make the nation more solidary, more cohesive, more independent in its growing diversity: in short to make the nation more of a nation.[53]

The structure and processes of Selective Service, which were once supposedly attuned to American political culture now run directly counter to it as the National Idea and the National Society have come to full development in the last few decades. The System's ties with the state now seem quaint, anachronistic, and fragmented.

The state headquarters are a major source of variability and are thus of questionable utility. The lack of meaningful participation by the state governments also adds another bit of obvious discrepancy between institutional myth and reality and is objectionable. On the other hand, a meaningful tie to state governments might do more harm than good. The significance of state govern-

The Strain on Institutional Equilibrium

ments in the political attitudes of citizens is not known. Students of state and local government like York Willbern contend that states have lost their sense of community and seemingly any effective basis for organizing important aspects of human activity.[54] And Under Secretary for Housing and Urban Development Robert Wood claims that, "They command less attention, less loyalty, and less respect from the public and therefore seem without a general purpose.[55]

General Hershey's concept of America is localistic and small town. It is not unfair to say that he conceives of America as a reification of his home town of Angola, Indiana. Nor is this unnatural; since there must be at least one board per county, there are far more local boards in the System "representing" small towns than there are urban. The fact that this does not reflect the registrant population does not apparently assume importance in his, or the institution's, collective consciousness. His contacts are with the traditional small town elements of America and the states — local boards, state headquarters, congressmen, senators, the American Legion, the V.F.W., National Guard, Governors' Conferences, the Boy Scouts, etc.

The General and the institution's perceptions of its environment are shaped by the System's structure and processes. During an interview General Hershey discussed the cohesion of his small town: "Why, I was back in Angola last year in the 'five-and-dime' and people still recognized me and knew me. That's the sort of relationships government ought to be based on, I think."[56] The truth of the matter is that the General's picture has been on every television screen and wire-photo service in America. He would probably be recognized in any dime store in America.

General Hershey still invokes the symbols of small-town, grass roots democracy, and speaks of Vermont maples and Louisiana king syrup. The responses from Congress are still reassuring for the most part as the following exchange with Mendel Rivers indicates.

General Hershey: I have to live with each of these States — and each of these States is the best State I am in the day I am in it. Make no mistake about that.
The Chairman: That is the best way I know to protect your longevity.
General Hershey: When I go to Charleston [the Chairman's home town], I don't even talk about upstate South Carolina.
The Chairman: General Hershey, you are doing very well. Go ahead.[57]

Hershey's defense of the institution from 1965 to 1967 while it was under severe attack, has to be counted as a brilliant tactical victory. But the decision to defend the institution against all change (for this is virtually what he did) may have been a strategic blunder.[58] Selznick distinguishes between "routine" and "critical" decisions for institutions. The latter are decisions which affect institutional survival. The decision to fight off all changes may have been such a critical decision, and in view of the long run, inexorable trends of political culture, the General may have made the wrong choice.[59]

Localism is still a potent symbol especially for congressmen but its appeal has limits, and changed circumstances seem to have brought Selective Service up against those limits. Even among congressmen not all were persuaded. Representative Chet Holifield of California may have expressed the doubt that many Americans have apparently begun to feel over the localism of Selective Service when he said:

> The theory is that one's neighbors and friends are better able to judge what is fair for a particular community. I do not necessarily question that theory any more than I do the basic system itself, but I am beginning to wonder whether the principle is being overly taxed to the point of being self-defeating.[60]

Perhaps many Americans no longer have any doubts. They may feel like Congressman Schweiker.

> This is just the type of thing [some states allegedly slowing processing to reduce men available] that a national pool would do away with. You wouldn't get the argument of New Jersey versus New York or Pennsylvania. We have been the United States of America for some time and this is the only department I know that doesn't recognize it.[61]

Traditionalism

Traditionalism according to Max Weber is an authority which emphasizes "the arbitrary power of the master and the limitation of that power by sacred tradition."[62]

> The master is entitled to make arbitrary and unilateral demands whenever it suits his whims or interests, because the traditional limits upon such demands are ill defined. The master obviously has a major interest in keeping these limits vague, even where he seeks to observe them, for once he adopts a formal regulation he may be forced to observe his own rules...[63]

This description of traditional authority is of course over-drawn to suit the purposes of Weber's ideal-type.[64] Quite obviously however, it is an uncomfortable approximation of the local board's authority as originally intended. Certainly the authority of the local board is closer to traditional than legal-rational. General Hershey still portrays the board in traditionalistic terms, expects registrants to relate to it on such terms and to accept such authority as legitimate. He speaks of the local boards in terms not unlike some stern but benign collective patriarch of the registrant.

A question from a student at Carnegie Tech produced this exchange:

> *Student:* What if a student loses rank and credits in transferring from one school to another?
> *Hershey:* I think you should share with your draft board every item in your favor, and maybe some of the unfavorable ones. After all, the man you're talking with on the board may not have done well in college himself. Maybe you'll stir something in his heart.[65]

Or:

> I am not saying they are policies, because we have 4,000 draft boards. They are individuals who have been around a long time. They have lived many years in the operation of this System, and I think their judgment is pretty good, and their compassion, I believe, is much greater than a lot of people think.[66]

No elaborate discussion is necessary to establish that legitimate authority of 1866 and/or 1917 was more traditionalistic than today. One of the most notable changes in government is the development of bureaucracy, particularly since 1930. Bureaucracy is antithetical with traditional authority. The development of the National Society, National Idea, and urbanism all have intensified this trend toward the weakening of traditional authority since the birth of Selective Service.

Hauser has described the influence of urbanism in enhancing rationality and weakening traditionalism.

> In the new urban matrix of social interaction, a new human nature has been bred which is still in process of social evolution. The "city mentality," characterized by its sophistication, objectivity, utilitarianism and rationalism, is on the one hand a product of the urban environment, and on the other a major force producing and influencing changes in our social heritage, in our economic, social and political institutions and in the urban environment itself.[67]

Conclusion

More than the institution's philosophy is out of harmony with political culture. The structure and processes derived from that philosophy are naturally in discord as well. Specifically the local boards and quotas which the institution's leadership maintained were the chief structural component of institutional equilibrium are now a major factor of imbalance.[68]

The local boards and quotas are political symbols intended to legitimate decisions. In a more localistic and traditionalistic society it was more important that the processes of the draft be adapted to individual and community circumstances. It is, of course, still important, but if the volume of criticisms against the System has any meaning at all it is that the *national political community* demands uniformity and consistency *before* adaptations to the idiosyncratic. This can be also be seen in the response of board members to the following question of the Special Commission. "Do you think that local boards should be consistent in their judgment even if it occasionally means that a registrant with a borderline claim to deferment must be denied?" Of those questioned, 85.5 per cent agreed; 59.4 per cent agreed strongly and 26.1 per cent somewhat agreed.[69] With the particular trends in American political culture suggested above, a structure with processes which contribute to disuniformity, inconsistency and inequality is in danger of destroying its symbolic power to legitimate decisions.

No effort will be made to elaborate further on the lack of uniformity and the inconsistency of the Selective Service System, since this has been admirably documented by the Special Commission.[70] Nor does it matter so much where the variability arises, because more of it arises from other sources than from the boards themselves. The board members are remarkably homogeneous in their views and attitudes considering the fact that one is dealing with roughly 15,000 men. Davis and Dolbeare found attitudes remarkably uniform among veterans and non-veterans; church members and non-members; rural and urban; college and non-college graduates.[71]

Unfortunately, however, boards are a source of more variability than can be tolerated under today's conditions and they stand out as symbols of variability at a time when the demand is for national uniformity and consistency. They also receive the blame for variation that arises from other sources. Those sources of variability are: lack of adequate national policy guidance; variance in guidance from state headquarters; the impact of quotas on board manpower pools; and the impact on strata within a board's jurisdiction stemming from national deferment policies.

If the reader will recall the analysis of Selective Service's adaptations to political culture, he will note that in many instances the adaptations were serving purposes other than originally intended. For example:

(1) Both formal and informal appeals were not only a means to assure the registrant of equity but a control mechanism for upper echelons so that board decisions could be kept at a satisfice level of uniformity and equity.

(2) The institutional myth of decentralization was not merely a philosophy of "grass-roots" decisions but was (a) used to disperse targets for interest groups and decrease the visibility of accommodations with them; (b) a defensive mechanism to obscure responsibility; (c) a means to secure support for valuable allies such as Congress and the National Guard.

(3) Ties to the states do not truly involve them in operations but serve the functions cited above under decentralization and as a source of recruitment for the paramilitary cadre.

Such changes in the original purpose of ties to key values of political culture are both a symptom and cause of the strain on institutional equilibrium. Changes in the original purposes of ideology or structures and processes is a continual hazard for an institution. It must be acutely sensitive to its environment. However, in attempting to find equilibrium with the environment it runs the hazard of developing rigidity that can cause it to lose its sensitivity to environmental change. It develops patterns of support, communications and operation that can be at considerable variance from original purposes but appear to provide stability. Equilibrium easily becomes stability, which in turn can become rigidity. Selznick describes the process thus:

> But when an enterprise begins to be more profoundly aware of dependence on outside forces, its very conception of itself may change, with consequences for recruitment, policy, and administrative organization at many levels. As a business, a college, or a government agency develops a distinctive clientele, the enterprise gains the stability that comes with a secure source of support, an easy channel of communication. At the same time, it loses flexibility. The process of institutionalization has set in.[72]

It is testimony to the staying power of the institution and the quality of its alliances that nothing was changed in the 1967 renewal that the leadership of Selective Service was not either favorable or indifferent toward. As mentioned earlier, it remains to be seen whether this was a short-run tactical victory or a long-run, strategic blunder. Given the extreme institutionalization of Selective Service due to its chronic insecurity, given the heavy burden of values it carries and the inflexibility they have created, perhaps it is not correct to speak of the decision to completely defend the status quo as right or wrong. Perhaps it was merely inevitable. Only so much can be done by creative leadership, for beyond a certain point, the environment will determine an institution's fate.

Notes

[1]June A. Willenz, ed., *Dialogue on the Draft,* Nov. 11-12, 1966, American Veterans Committee, Washington, D.C., p. 64.

[2]*Ibid.*

[3]*Life,* December 9, 1966.

[4]For a discussion of this question see an article with virtually the above sentence for a title, Robin M. Williams, Jr. in *The Annals* (May 1962), pp. 82-92.

[5]Interview No. 37.

[6]National Advisory Commission on Selective Service, "In Pursuit of Equity: Who Serves When Not All Serve?" (Washington, D.C.: Government Printing Office, February, 1967), p. 3. Hereafter cited as *Commission Report.*

[7]A low of 60,000 was recorded in 1961.

[8]See Statement of Thomas D. Morris, Assistant Secretary of Defense for Manpower, *Review of the Administration and Operation of the Selective Service System,* Hearings before the Committee on Armed Services, House of Representatives, 89th Congress, 2nd sess. (Washington, D.C.: Government Printing Office, 1966), pp. 9923-26 and 10003. Hereafter cited as *Review.*

[9]*Dialogue on the Draft, op. cit.,* p. 117.

[10]This is admitted by everyone and there seems little need to thoroughly document it. See Morris's statement reproduced in *Dialogue, op. cit.,* p. 117 or General Hershey in *Review, op. cit.,* p. 9624. It was also reflected in the System's communications which spoke of "current liberal deferment policies."

[11]See Statement of Morris, *Dialogue on the Draft, op. cit.,* pp. 20-21.

[12]See U.S. Office of the Surgeon General, United States Army, *Supplement to the Health of the Army,* Washington, D.C. (July, 1966), pp. 6, 41, and note 2 on that page.

[13]The report, *One-Third of A Nation,* was requested by President Kennedy who was reportedly shocked by rejection figures. U.S., President's Task Force on Manpower Conservation, *One-Third of a Nation: A Report on Young Men Found Unqualified for Military Service* (Washington, D.C.: U.S. Government Printing Office, 1964). See also Col. George Walton, *The Wasted Generation* (New York: Chilton Book Company, 1965). Rejection rates for draftees averaged 36.1 per cent from 1950 to 1961, 53 per cent in 1964, 44 per cent in 1965. See *Supplement to the Health of the Army, 1966, op. cit.,* p. 10.

[14]*Dialogue on the Draft, op. cit.,* p. 64.

¹⁵M. H. Trytten, *Student Deferment in Selective Service* (Minneapolis: University of Minnesota Press, 1952), p. 26.

¹⁶*Ibid.*, p. 31.

¹⁷Harry Lazer, *The American Political System in Transition* (New York: Thomas Y. Crowell Company, 1966), p. 83.

¹⁸Bayard Rustin, "From Protest to Politics: The Future of the Civil Rights Movement" in Fred Krinsky and Gerald Rigby, *Theory and Practice of American Democracy* (Belmont, California: Dickenson Pub. Co., Inc., 1967), p. 515.

¹⁹*Ibid.*, p. 411.

²⁰The reversal was of *Colegrove v. Green*, 328 U.S. 549.553-554, 556 (1946). The cases were: *Baker v. Carr*, 369 U.S. 186 (1962); *Gray v. Sanders*, 372 U.S. 368 (1963); *Wesberry v. Sanders*, 376 U.S. (1964); *Reynolds v. Sims* 377 U.S. 533 (1964). *Baker v. Carr* is usually considered the historic breakthrough with the others more or less anticlimactic.

²¹Lazer, *op. cit.*, pp. 230-231. Lazer points to *Gomillon v. Lightfoot* as the case linking civil rights with reapportionment. This case concerned the constitutionality of the Alabama legislature redrawing the boundary lines of Tuskegee so as to dissolve the growing political power of highly literate Negroes associated with Tuskegee Institute.

²²Alan Westin, "Liberty, Justice and Law" in Emmette S. Redford and David B. Truman, *Politics and Government in the United States* (New York: Harcourt, Brace & World Inc., 1965), p. 515.

²³Charles R. Adrian and Charles Press, *The American Political Process* (New York: McGraw-Hill Book Company, 1965), p. 576.

²⁴See *Review, op. cit.*, p. 9695 and *passim.*

²⁵Davis and Dolbeare found the same atrophy in Wisconsin. See "Who Gets Drafted," Institute for Research on Poverty, Madison, University of Wisconsin, 1967, p. 33.

²⁶For example, see p. 6 of recommendations, *Commission Report, op. cit.*

²⁷*New York Times*, May 16, 1968, p. 6c.

²⁸*Ibid.*

²⁹Reed Martin, "Survey on Youth Opinion on the Selective Service System," United States Youth Council, p. 9.

³⁰*Ibid.*

³¹*Ibid.*, p. 10.

³²*Review, op. cit.*, p. 9634. See also pp. 9663, 9655.

³³*Ibid.*, p. 9653.

³⁴See Davis and Dolbeare, "Who Gets Drafted," *op. cit.* pp. 34-36 and *Commission Report, op. cit.*, pp. 107-28.

³⁵David Potter, *People of Plenty: Economic Abundance and the American Character* (Chicago: University of Chicago Press, 1959); John Kenneth Galbraith, *The Affluent Society* (Boston: Houghton Mifflin Company, 1958); Michael Harrington, *The Other American: Poverty in the United States* (New York: The Macmillan Company, 1962).

³⁶Address to the American Society of Newspaper Editors, Montreal, Canada, May 18, 1966.

The Strain on Institutional Equilibrium   223

³⁷ Quoted in *Commission Report, op. cit.*, p. 61.

³⁸Terrence Cullinan, "National Service: The Future Solution" (unpublished paper presented to the Special Commission), pp. 16 and 19. For an annotated bibliography on the profusion of articles, speeches and books on National Service, see Donald J. Eberly, ed., *A Profile on National Service* (New York: Overseas Educational Service, 1966).

³⁹Cited in "National Service Newsletter" published by National Service Secretariat, New York, November 1966.

⁴⁰*Ibid.*

⁴¹*United States* v. *Seeger,* 380 U.S. 163 (1965).

⁴²Adrian and Press, *op cit.,* pp. 50-53.

⁴³Morton and Lucia White, *The Intellectual Versus the City* (Cambridge: Harvard University Press and M. I. T. Press, 1962), p. 239.

⁴⁴Daniel Bell, "Toward a Communal Society," *Life,* May 12, 1967, p. 113.

⁴⁵For an excellent description of this new "typical" American, see Solon T. Kimball and James E. McClellan, *Education and the New America* (New York: Random House, Inc., 1962), *passim.* See also Philip M. Hauser, "On the Impact of Urbanism on Social Organization, Human Nature and the Political Order" in Philip B. Coulter, ed., *Politics of Metropolitan Areas* (New York: Thomas Y. Crowell Co., 1967), p. 5.

⁴⁶See for example, letters from constituents placed in hearing record. *Review, op. cit.,* pp. 9729-32.

⁴⁷Emmette S. Redford and David B. Truman, *op. cit.,* p. 36.

⁴⁸Angus Campbell, *et al., The American Voter* (New York: John Wiley & Sons, Inc., 1960), p. 442.

⁴⁹Marian Irish and James Prothro, *The Politics of American Democracy,* (3rd ed.; Englewood Cliffs, New Jersey: Prentice-Hall Inc., 1965) p. 31.

⁵⁰Davis and Dolbeare noted that the work of the Appeal Boards consisted in large part of appeals by men who no longer lived in their boards' areas but who had been classified by them. See "Little Groups of Neighbors," *op. cit.* See also *Commission Report* which recommended abolishing the rule.

⁵¹*Review, op. cit.,* p. 9698.

⁵²Interview No. 39.

⁵³Samuel H. Beer, "Liberalism and the National Idea," in *Public Interest,* No. 5 (Fall, 1966), 71.

⁵⁴York Willbern, "The States as Components in an Areal Division of Power," in Arthur Maass, ed., *Area and Power* (Glencoe: The Free Press of Glencoe, 1959).

⁵⁵Robert Wood, "The States and Communities" in Redford and Truman, *op. cit.,* p. 888.

⁵⁶Interview No. 39.

⁵⁷*Review, op. cit.,* p. 9690.

⁵⁸*Ibid.,* pp. 9662 and 9706.

⁵⁹General Hershey indicated at several points that he wanted no changes in the law. See pp. 9662 and 9706 of *Review, op. cit.* There were in fact no changes which did not have his approval.

⁶⁰*Ibid.*, p. 9762.

⁶¹*Ibid.*, p. 9771.

⁶²Reinhard Bendix, *Max Weber: An Intellectual Portrait* (New York: Doubleday & Company Inc., 1962), p. 331.

⁶³*Ibid.*, p. 332.

⁶⁴Weber described the ideal-type as "like a utopia which has been arrived at by the analytical accentuation of reality." Max Weber, *The Methodology of the Social Sciences,* translated and edited by Edward A. Shils and Henry A. Finch (Glencoe: The Free Press of Glencoe, 1949), p. 90.

⁶⁵*Review, op. cit.,* p. 9735, quoting from the *Pittsburgh Post-Gazette.*

⁶⁶*Ibid.*, p. 9649.

⁶⁷Hauser, *op. cit.,* p. 8.

⁶⁸Reference was made earlier to Davis and Dolbeare's findings in rural Wisconsin.

⁶⁹*Commission Report,* p. 185.

⁷⁰*Ibid.,* pp. 73-128, and Davis and Dolbeare, "Who Gets Drafted," *op. cit.*

⁷¹"Little Groups of Neighbors," *op. cit.,* pp. 31-35. They did find urban members more sympathetic to conscientious objectors and lower income boards more prone to believe the draft bears heavier on lower classes.

⁷²Philip Selznick, *Leadership in Administration* (Evanston, Ill.: Row, Peterson, 1957), p. 7.

7

The Draft War of 1967: Strategic Victory or Delaying Action?

The details of the 1967 "draft war" are revealing on two points: the entrenched position of the institution and the strength of its alliances; and the sharply divergent perceptions of "draft war" participants as to what ails the System.

The worst crisis in the System's history began to take shape during the 1963 hearings on renewal of the Universal Military Training and Service Act. During those hearings Department of Defense spokesmen had argued (as they had in 1959) that all those registrants qualified and "available" in I-A were being inducted. But the growing manpower surplus and an awareness that liberal deferments could only partially cope with it made Pentagon officials feel that their arguments for the status quo would soon become untenable. They were further disturbed by President Kennedy's concerned inquiries into military manpower. These had been inspired by the report of a Presidential Task Force on Manpower Conservation titled *One Third of a Nation,* and the vociferous negative reactions that arose when he tried to cope with the manpower surplus by placing childless married men lower in the order of call-up, thus giving them a protected position. As a result of these stimuli, the Department of Defense decided upon a study of Selective Service and military manpower needs in September 1963. The study was not begun until February of 1964.

In April 1964 President Lyndon Johnson issued a public order that the Department of Defense undertake a study of the Selective Service System and military manpower needs. This ex post facto order was probably designed to spike rising congressional criticisms and calls for a commission to undertake a study, but may also have been designed to dampen a potential issue in the upcoming Presidential campaign. If this was the intention of the order it succeeded. The draft did not become a major issue.

But criticism was only slightly abated and as the American commitment in Viet Nam increased and draft calls rose, criticism again began to intensify. By early 1966, the results of the Pentagon study began to "leak" to the press. The leaks indicated that the study group had concluded that in the long run some alternative system had to be found.[1] In May of 1966, impetus was given to the mounting criticism when Secretary of Defense McNamara made a speech, generally regarded as a trial balloon, which admitted the draft system contained inequities and proposed one or two years service to the nation by every American.[2]

In Congress, pressure mounted on L. Mendel Rivers, Chairman of the House Armed Services Committee, to conduct an investigation into the operations of Selective Service. Rivers and his committee are old institutional allies of the System. He agreed to a full-scale review only with reluctance and throughout the hearings seemed to use his powers as chairman to protect the System as much as possible.[3]

Proposal, Counter-Proposal, Stalemate

The lengthy and contentious hearings seemed to leave too many questions unanswered. They showed clearly that all was not well with the System and rather than dampening criticism, seemed to intensify it. With the deadline for 1967 renewal coming into view, President Johnson appointed a National Advisory Commission on Selective Service, chaired by Burke Marshall.[4]

But Congress has always taken seriously its constitutional prerogative to "provide for the common defense" and it did not view this presidential initiative altogether favorably. Chairman Rivers has shown himself to be an apt student of his predecessor "Uncle Carl" Vinson who was once reported as saying that he had no desire to be Secretary of Defense, that he preferred to run the Pentagon from Capitol Hill. Therefore, Rivers announced the formation of a Special Civilian Advisory Panel to be chaired by retired

General Mark Clark, charged with investigating the draft question fully and recommending changes to the committee.

The result of these moves and counter moves was that three sets of policy recommendations appeared in rapid and confusing succession. The Marshall Commission was due to release its report in January 1967 but sought a delay. Meanwhile the Clark panel released its report in February. The Marshall Commission finally made its study public on March 4th. Two days later the President sent Congress a special message on the draft.

The Clark panel's recommendations seem to have been developed on the implicit assumption that they were supposed to reassure Congress that only minor adjustments in the System were necessary. It recommended:

(1) The order of call be changed to the youngest registrants and those with expiring deferments. Maximum vulnerability should be at age 19-20. If the registrant was not inducted during that period he would be placed in a lower priority in each successive year.
(2) No lottery be used and the same selection process continued. (Though recommendation No. 1 above is a form of limited lottery for call-up.)
(3) The power of local boards be undiminished and efforts at great uniformity; tenure of members limited to 10 years; and the boards be given more understandable criteria in conscientious objector cases.
(4) The House Armed Services Committees of Congress monitor decisions for uniformity.
(5) Undergraduate student deferments be granted automatically and terminated when they get their undergraduate degree or reach age 24. Graduate student deferments be ended except in critical occupations identified by the National Security Council on recommendation of a "national manpower resources board" that would be established.
(6) Retention of state and local quotas.
(7) Miscellaneous recommendations that reflected perfectly the positions of General Hershey and Chairman Rivers were:
    a. Justice Department prosecution and handling of conscientious objectors, draft card burners and draft evaders should be accelerated.
    b. Physical and moral standards of acceptance be lowered.
    c. Rejection of lottery, Volunteer Army proposals, and the

use of electronic data processing equipment by Selective Service.[5]

In sharp contrast, the National Commission's recommendations were a wholesale assault on the institution of Selective Service. General Hershey's view of the Commission expressed later in the renewal hearings left no doubt that he perceived it in such terms.

> *The Chairman:* That is why I don't agree with the Burke Marshall majority report about changing the whole business and bring everything to Washington, and having the local boards be just a perfunctory sort of a thing. I don't believe, if I read you, that you agree with all of this.
> *General Hershey:* There should be a reorganization of the Burke Marshall Commission. I only need one word to tell you about how I agree with it.
> *The Chairman:* Go ahead and tell me.
> *General Hershey:* I don't.

The recommendation so distasteful to the General called for the following changes:

(1) The order of induction be changed so that younger registrants would be inducted first.
(2) The order of induction be determined by lottery from a single national pool with one year of maximum vulnerability after which the registrant could only be liable for emergencies.
(3) Virtually all student deferments be ended with presently enrolled undergraduates being permitted to complete their education.
(4) All occupational and agricultural deferments be ended but hardship deferments continued.
(5) Consolidation of the System under a single, national headquarters which would have the power to set binding national standards for eight regional offices which would coordinate and monitor the policies and service eight appeal boards.
(6) The establishment of area offices on a population basis (at least one for each state, 300 to 500 total). These offices would register, classify and see to it that registration coincided with residence by means of modern data-handling techniques.
(7) "Local boards" at the area-office level would function in a "first appeal" rather than a decision-making capacity. The appeal system would be overhauled with opinions in writing, activation of appeal agents, with a longer period to appeal but more rapid handling.

(8) Local boards in their new "first appeal" capacity would be changed to represent all elements of the public they serve; permit a maximum of five years tenure by members; provide for a maximum retirement age; permit presidential appointment without limitation to nominees of governors; permit women to serve on boards.[6]

The dichotomous nature of the proposals would have indicated to even a politically imprudent President that proposals for wholesale revision of the System would find little sympathy in Congress. No one has accused President Johnson of a lack of political prudence therefore it should have come as no surprise when he chose to include few of the recommendations of the Commission. None of those included in his proposals would have fundamentally altered the System. The message recommended:

(1) Changing the order of induction to the youngest first.
(2) That by January 1969 a limited lottery (Fair and Impartial Random System, FAIR) replace consideration for selection by order of call within the I-A classification.
(3) Graduate student deferments be eliminated in most areas. (Recommendation on undergraduate deferments was delayed.)
(4) Insuring draft boards represent communities but that their status or roles not be changed pending recommendations of the National Commission.

The Outcome: The Act of 1967

There was one major and a few minor points on which all the proposals before Congress agreed. Even where there was agreement there was no resultant action in some instances. There was agreement that graduate student deferments must be ended. Despite outcries from institutions of higher education there was no mass support for the continuation of graduate deferments and they were ended. All proposals called for changing the order of call to place the youngest first but perhaps because this became entangled with the fight over a "lottery" system and perhaps because the heavy quotas for Viet Nam had pushed the age for induction about as low as it could go, there was no action on this point. Finally, the most significant agreement was in the need for some form of "lottery" system. But perhaps because of confusion over the complexity of the proposed lotteries and perhaps because of the emotional burden the term bears, Congress prohibited its implementation without further Congressional review.

There was some shifting in the position of General Hershey and the System from the total, unyielding defense of 1966. The major change was on the "lottery." Hershey seemed to recognize or admit for the first time that all the surplus manpower pool could never be absorbed by liberal deferments. Recognition of this fact led him away from his 1966 position of heaping ridicule on the concept and claiming it had been tried before.[7] In general, however, the President's proposed changes were so few and minor that Hershey had no problem supporting them though he did so with a clear lack of enthusiasm that delighted the House Armed Services Committee.[8] His unenthusiastic "I am a team-player" support may have been instrumental in killing a lottery with the committee which had become accustomed to reading between the lines of Hershey's testimony.

There is now admission that something is wrong with the System but from the melange of proposals emerge two distinctly different views of what it is that is wrong. The System and its allies, the Clark panel and Congress (if we take the negligible changes in the law as evidence) hold the view that the structure and processes of Selective Service are basically sound — an unconscious assumption perhaps that they are in consonance with American political culture. Apparently they feel there are some minor adjustments that can be made, like limiting the age and tenure of members, but the bulwark of the System, the local boards and decentralization are fundamentally sound. If one views local boards and variability as a positive good, as does General Hershey, then complaints of lack of uniformity make no sense at all. The biggest problems facing the System in this view are the unpopularity of the Viet Nam War with restless youth and the surplus of manpower.[9] The first problem, according to this view, can best be handled by more resolute and expeditious prosecution of evasion and the latter by a "lottery" system if absolutely necessary. (Congress may not be convinced that the public is ready for a "lottery.")

The other view of what is wrong with the System is reflected in the Marshall Commission's report. The assumption manifested there is that the bulwark of the System (local boards and decentralization), have become its greatest liability — that the problems of the System are not caused by the reaction of youth to Viet Nam or by the surfeit of manpower though they are aggravated by them; what is wrong with the System is the lack of uniformity and inequity that can only be cured by changing local boards and decentralization — perhaps an implicit assumption that these values are more dominant in our political culture than localism and traditionalism thus putting the System's structure and processes in dissonance with American political culture.

The Armed Services Committee and the majority of congressmen seemed incapable of understanding how an institution that reflected so many values they themselves cherish could have anything fundamentally wrong with it. To most of them only the Clark panel's proposals made sense while the Marshall Commission's proposals were totally alien. This feeling seemed to have deeper reasons behind it than the mere fact that the Clark panel was a congressional agent while the National Commission represented presidential prerogative and initiative. During General Clark's testimony in May of 1967, one member of the House Armed Services Committee verbalized this deeper reason for congressional affinity with Clark's proposals.

Mr. Ichord: Mr. Chairman, I also want to commend the General for the overall philosophy expressed in the panel's report. For the last few days, I have been quite upset by some of the testimony because there has been philosophy which is entirely foreign to my philosophy, but the philosophy expressed in this report I can well understand.[10]

Mr. Lennon, another member, expressed what seems to have been on the minds of many members who are ever-aware of the extensive "grass-roots" nature of the System: "I would commend you and your panel on attempting to preserve the existing organizations of the local boards."
General Hershey's view of the Clark panel is also revealing.

Mr. Lennon: So I would assume that as between the Marshall Commission's recommendations and the Clark panel's recommendations, that you find yourself generally more in agreement with the recommendations of the Clark panel here.
General Hershey: Oh completely. There are a lot of good reasons for that.[11]

In the struggle between these two views that of Selective Service and its allies prevailed, sweepingly and totally. The law finally passed by Congress in 1967 had a new title, the Military Selective Service Act of 1967. It required:

(1) The President to establish national criteria for the draft and to the extent "consistent with national interest" require that the criteria be administered uniformly by local boards.

(2) Limitation of service on local boards to 25 years or to retirement at age 75.
(3) Acceptance of women as local board members.
(4) That draft cases be given scheduling preference in federal court dockets.

It also prohibited:

(1) The induction of undergraduate students until they completed their baccalaureate degrees, reached age 24, or lost good standing; unless the President found the needs of the Armed Forces required induction.
(2) Changing the order of call presently used i.e. prohibited a "lottery."[12]

The extent to which the new law rejected the National Commission and embraced the Clark proposals was evident in the angry and dismayed remark of Burke Marshall that the law was "worse than it was before." The Commission urged selection for consideration by random means, Congress responded by prohibiting it without further congressional review; the Commission recommended elimination of undergraduate deferments, Congress guaranteed them; the Commission called for limiting enlistment in Reserves and National Guard, Congress assured the opportunity to enlist even after induction orders had been issued; Congress chose to strike out at the Supreme Court by restricting the results of its decisions, speeding prosecution of conscientious objectors and preventing court inquiry into the propriety of classifications; and finally the Commission urged a complete restructuring of Selective Service so as to eliminate the problems of local boards and local quotas; Congress refused to tamper with these in any way.

The only official consideration given the problems of Selective Service within government circles that continued after 1967 was undertaken by a special Task Force appointed by President Johnson. It consisted of the Secretary of Defense and the Directors of Selective Service and the Bureau of the Budget, and its assigned task was to study the findings of the National Commission. The Task Force eventually called for rejection of most of the structural proposals advanced by the Commission and its report is a repetitious reaffirmation of all of Selective Service's values and perception. General Hershey was "very favorably impressed" with the findings of the Task Force.[13]

Thus all the circumstances which brought on the 1967 "draft war" remain — the crisis for the System is not yet over. The manpower surplus continues to swell in spite of Viet Nam and should the war end the surplus will be staggering. The continuation of undergraduate deferments will perpetuate the inequity, and socioeconomic discrimination involved in that policy. The economically advantaged and politically efficacious will still be able to use the Reserves and National Guard as refuges from active service or combat and they will still be able to use the System's formal and informal appeals procedure to their advantage. The power relationships of the System and its less articulate and powerful registrants remain heavily weighted in the System's favor. The preservation of local boards will mean that inequity and disuniformity will continue unabated. It is highly unlikely that anything will come of the 1967 law's exhortation to the President to establish national criteria and to the extent "consistent with national interest" require that it be uniformly administered. The rather minor changes in the tenure and recruitment of local board members assures that they will continue to make a mockery of institutional myths about them. With the possible exception of a lottery, no foreseeable changes in the System or its environment seem likely to avoid a further crisis. The end of the fighting in Viet Nam may alleviate the life and death nature of the System's inadequacies, but it will heap even greater pressure upon it in the form of a manpower glut.

Future Changes: Grand Alternatives?

What is the likely future for the System? During 1968 the System and General Hershey became campaign issues in a way that was totally unprecedented. Nelson Rockefeller, Eugene McCarthy, Robert Kennedy, and Hubert Humphrey all attacked the System and made it clear that Hershey's customarily *pro forma* resignation would be accepted were they to become President; Richard Nixon took a somewhat tentative position in favor of a volunteer army; and one of the most prominent "non-candidates" for President, Senator Edward Kennedy, has made changing the System something akin to his personal mission in life. General Hershey in one of his most serious malapropisms left the impression that he supported George Wallace for President — a blunder that did nothing to decrease the controversy centering upon him and the System.[14] In view of the unchanged nature of the conditions which put a strain on the institution's equilibrium and the fact that it and the Director have become political issues, it seems safe to predict the System will change. The manner of change is not as easy to predict.

It seems unlikely that the grand "alternatives" to conscription like a volunteer army and universal national service will replace some form of Selective Service.[15] There are two principal reasons why grand alternatives will be rejected, neither of them unfamiliar to students of American foreign policy and public administration. First, the dominant image of the realities of international relations extant among scholars, practitioners, opinion-makers and attentive public is one that calls for a conscription system.[16] Second, politico-administrative decisions involving such far-reaching changes as these are almost always made incrementally and gradually.

The "image of reality" of international relations might be summed in the following way:

> Soviet (and now presumably Chinese) imperialism grows not only out of ideology but historic and geo-political drives that can be blunted, shaped and redirected through the application of diplomacy and military power. They can be contained, as George Kennan said over twenty years ago. If they are, their behavior will change to less aggressive forms. Currently, Soviet and Chinese imperialism, in an effort to avoid thermonuclear confrontation, has chosen the vehicle of subverting, supporting and capturing control of revolutionary movements or "wars of national liberation."

From this image of reality there has followed logically a need for a large strategic military force to deter nuclear attack and a large standing army with high mobility that can counter "brush fire wars" and fomented insurgency.

It seems unlikely that those responsible for formulating and executing American defense policy (or those relevant groups among intellectuals and the informed public) will conceive of the possibility of supporting such a force structure without, at the very least, a standby conscription system. The "grand alternatives" like a volunteer army or universal national service either do not seem congruent with the dominant image of reality or involve too many problematic or possible unintended consequences to win acceptance. The force structure presently felt to be necessary — requires a high level of manpower and the capacity to expand even further in the face of crisis. Few persons are confident that this can be done without conscription. The second reason that radical departures from Selective Service are unlikely is that politico-administrative decision-makers eschew "total" solutions or major shifts in policy and procedures. They prefer bearing familiar costs of considerable proportion to the confrontation of costs of unknown magnitude. The political costs of conscription are becoming increasingly apparent but they remain preferable to the unknown costs of an all-volunteer force. The likelihood of gradual change lies not only in the nature of the politico-administrator's role but in the nature of democracy itself. As Charles Lindblom notes, administrators who used anything but an incremental approach would be largely irrelevant in a democracy.[17]

Conscription provides flexibility to those who are most likely to have influence upon and responsibility for defense policy within a framework of known political costs. This does not mean it will provide the immediate physical capacity to respond to a given crisis because of the lag between induction and the production of soldiers. However, conscription does provide the political capacity to respond to crisis and it is in this sense that it is so important to decision-makers, opinion-makers and their attentive public. They want the capacity to begin expansion of the armed forces in response to a perceived crisis without instigating a national debate. Critics have put this concern in negative form. Milton Friedman, a strident supporter of the volunteer army, declares:

> The flexibility provided by conscription has another side. It means that, at least for a time, the administration and the military services can proceed fairly arbitrarily in committing U.S. forces.[18]

A more positive way of viewing this need for flexibility is to point out that the complexity of foreign policy, the increasing obscurity of national interest, and growing public sophistication, make for unparalleled restrictions on the actions of decision-makers. The complexity and obscurity is matched, however, by greater rather than lesser threats of national security. Rightly or wrongly, politico-administrative decision-makers feel that they can only make so many trips to the well — that they can go through the arduous task of marshalling opinion only a limited number of times without exhausting their political capital (of good will, support, leverage, political I.O.U.'s, etc.). They husband their political resources and are loathe to squander them; any time they can make a move in foreign and defense policy without going to a public debate they are likely to do so. Until an alternative is offered that is indisputably as flexible in meeting manpower needs as conscription, or until its acceptance costs become too great, decision-makers are likely to favor changing it only incrementally if at all.

The cogent argument of Milton Friedman that conscription's flexibility is overvalued because "emergencies must be met by forces in being however they are recruited," is unlikely to alter the favorable disposition of decision-makers toward conscription.[19] This is so because decision-makers (and opinion-makers and attentive publics as well) tend to pose only policy alternatives that are familiar to them from past controversies.[20] Or put another way, decision-makers' preference for conscription may represent part of what Samuel Huntington calls the cultural lag between structural and strategic policy, i.e. conscription may not in fact be the "structural policy" that can best provide the flexibility required by today's strategy but the cultural lag prevents serious consideration of major alternatives.[21]

Finally, incremental changes in conscription seem more likely than its abandonment not only because human and organizational frailty prefers the convenience of flexibility but for the more edifying reason of genuine concern on the part of those responsible for national security. Will the level of public understanding be sufficient to permit action when it is crucially needed? Will there be time to go to Congress and obtain the necessary information? Will the structures of secrecy permit the full disclosure vital to a complete public debate? These are very real and as yet unanswered questions that confront those responsible for foreign and defense policy.[22] The grand alternatives to conscription are unlikely to seriously threaten Selective Service.

Tinkering With the System

Many incremental changes in the System are possible without seeking Congressional approval. In fact all the changes made or contemplated with the exception of a lottery are within the purview of the President. Any Chief Executive who makes changes by executive orders, however, must be sure that if they affect decentralization and local boards he is prepared to pay the political costs of such a move. Congress has a variety of ways of subtly obtaining revenge upon a President who acts in ways it considers unwise though constitutionally correct.[23]

The significant question is not whether the President can make incremental changes without congressional approval, but rather which incremental changes will ease the strain upon the System's equilibrium.[24] Inducting the youngest men first and the cessation of graduate student deferments are two changes that have been urged by critics and which might be expected to ease some of the strain between the System and its environment. But the heavy calls of the last few years have pushed the induction age about as low as is possible, thus obviating the need for a formal change at this time and graduate student deferments were ended in February 1968. Theoretically taking the youngest first would ease disruption of lives for registrants, cut down pressure for such a wide range of deferments (the reasons for them multiply with age), decrease the pressure of interest groups and generally decrease criticism. But neither of these changes has had any notable effect.[25]

The effect of instituting a lottery is unclear. Some observers feel that the future of the System after the Viet Nam war depends on whether or not it accepts a lottery, for one of the greatest sources of strain on the System's equilibrium is the excess of manpower. This condition preceded the Viet Nam war and it will post-date it. It led to the jerry-built system of "channeling" and liberal deferments which have done so much to attract hostility and criticism. It is the factor which presses local boards into induction-deferment decisions of increasingly dubious criteria, and calls into question the institutional myths of local board autonomy, individual consideration of each case, and local boards of friends and neighbors. To be sure the changes in political culture are the setting for the challenge to the institutional myths but it is the pressure of excess manpower and the resulting decisions of boards that bring forth the challenge.

It is still unclear how far Hershey and the institution's cadre have gone toward accepting the idea of a lottery. It may be that they are uncertain as to the effect upon the institution. It can be argued that a lottery would merely cut the number of registrants processed by the System thus decreasing the friction with its environment, while leaving intact its key structural component — the local boards and the central myth of decentralization. But argument can also be made that the decrease in registrants processed would lead to the atrophy of local boards for lack of interesting work to engage the volunteer membership.[26] Observations made in the Hill City study would lead to the conclusion that such would not be the case — that the advanced age of most members coupled with the difficulty, trouble and time involved in meetings militates against any great wave of dismay among local board members if the number of meetings were drastically reduced. Nor would there be any obvious need to eliminate local boards because of the needless expense since the bulk of System members are volunteers and since the clerks are among the lowest paid workers in federal service.

The degree to which it would alleviate the strain on the System depends on how much Americans have been sensitized to issues of equity, how much localism has lost its appeal, to what degree broader concepts of national service have taken root, and the extent to which traditionalistic forms of authority, like local boards, have lost legitimating power. In other words alleviation of strain by a lottery depends on the extent to which American political culture has changed and to what degree the discrepancies between it and the System's structure and processes are kept visible to the politically attentive segment of the public. There is no clear answer on these matters.

Though it cannot be clearly ascertained whether a lottery would ease the strain on the System's equilibrium, the logic stemming from the analysis of this study is that a drastic (but incremental, in the sense used throughout this discussion) revision of its structural and ideological base can bring the System back into congruence with its political culture. Such changes as those constituting the core of the Marshall Commission's report would bring about such results. These were: consolidation under a single national headquarters which would set binding standards for eight regional offices and appeal boards; area offices based on population registering and classifying those truly resident in the area, with "local boards" attached to act in a "first appeal" rather than a decision-making capacity.

It is true that these changes would constitute virtually a new System but with the same name and some of the same outwardly visible characteristics. But such drastic change within traditional forms is not inconsistent with the Anglo-American method of political change. Whether such drastic incremental changes will be dictated by circumstances is not perhaps a foregone conclusion but they are at least a strong likelihood. Only time can ultimately provide the answers as to how the System will be changed and the strain upon it eased. Regardless of how it is done those involved in formulating and executing foreign and defense policy will undoubtedly make changes to ease the strain a matter of some priority.

A conscription system must have some equilibrium between demands of its function and the demands of political culture if it is to survive or serve any useful function. It must, in other words, be able to perform its task and to have that task accepted as legitimate by the public. At stake is nothing less than the security of the nation. Given the "image of reality" of international relations held by the present generation of decision-makers, opinion-makers and attentive publics, a conscription system that can efficiently deliver manpower for a large multi-functional force structure is a matter of urgent necessity. The clash of American political culture with the realities of counterinsurgency warfare has added a new and painful dimension to this necessity as has the clash of political culture with the institution of Selective Service. Either foreign policy or Selective Service or perhaps both are going to have to be altered before things return to some state of normalcy.

Conclusion

This study set out to show why a nation with strong antimilitarist, anti-conscription and pro-militia traditions came to accept conscription and to do so for a long period of time. It has been submitted that much of the answer lies in the development of a system with structure and processes that were closely related to prominent values extant in American political culture. Throughout the entire study, the theme of institutional balance between demands of function and political culture has emerged and re-emerged and been helpful in understanding the relationship of Selective Service and conscription to a changing America.

Much of this study has been devoted to a detailed exploration of the historic events which had a direct bearing upon the way Selective Service planners developed the System in 1917. The historic events are direct and relevant contributors to the structure and ideology — the ethos of the institution.

Considerable attention was also given to detailed analysis of the institution's adaptations to American political culture. Part of the purpose of this analysis was to provide a "case study" of the importance of environment for an administrative system and to demonstrate Zald's contention that organizations have "collective identities and systemic properties." Selective Service amply illustrates the claims of such students of organizations as Zald and White that the environments of organizations and their exchange with them are of crucial importance in determining structures, modes of operation, and as White said "the whole orientation of a system to itself." Given a negative task in what it perceived to be a hostile environment, Selective Service developed a structure and processes that identified with key values of political culture as a means of gaining acceptance and deflecting hostility.

At the vital core of these institutional adaptations are decentralization and local boards. They were felt to be crucial by those who designed the System and they have not diminished in their importance in affecting its entire operation. The analysis of local boards and their operation was designed not only to elaborate upon the most important of institutional adaptations but also to seek to answer the question of why the System has encountered such unprecedented criticism after decades of stability. If the analysis made has validity, the local boards and decentralized operations have ceased to be the mainstay of institutional defenses and have become the weakest of the links with political culture. Assuming they ever had the symbolic legitimating power ascribed to them, they have now become visible symbols of incongruity between the System and changing American political culture, and are major contributors to the strain upon institutional equilibrium.

But it is of course too simplistic to say that local boards are the major contributors to strain upon the System's equilibrium. For this is only meaningful against the backdrop of changes in political culture and circumstances like Viet Nam as outlined in Chapter 6, "The Strain on Institutional Equilibrium." The local boards did not change, but the environment in which they must operate as symbols of legitimacy *has* changed and it is in this sense that they contribute to strain on equilibrium. This point is subtle but important and much of the criticism of the System stemming from the New Left clearly fails to understand it. Much of that literature has tried to base criticism upon the domination of local boards by members of community elites or "the establishment." But this is not the heart of the problem nor is it very accurate.[27]

A third major question posed at the outset of this study is why the unprecedented criticism and contention of 1967 did not result in any significant changes. The answer was suggested in Chapter 5, "Other Institutional Defenses," which discussed defenses not related to political culture such as institutional allies and certain favorable circumstances that have served to protect the institution, like the differential impact on strata. The most prominent of these defenses were the alliance the System has developed with Congress which still responds positively to the values to which Selective Service was designed to relate; and the leadership skill of General Hershey.

Another factor that helps explain the lack of change is the institutional rigidities within Selective Service. Hopefully the analysis of the System offers some good examples of how organizational commitment becomes institutional rigidity. Perhaps there is a direct relationship between perceived hostility in an environment, the strength of institutional ideology and commitment, strength of ties to institutional allies, and general loss of adaptability to changes in the environment. A general inability to perceive environmental changes may be the outcome of extreme institutionalization such as is found in Selective Service.

In addition to the three questions posed about conscription in America this study has been concerned with three interests of the author: organization theory (the consequences of this concern for the study have been discussed above), civil-military relations, and national security policy. It is hoped that this study has suggested some questions for further study in civil-military relations. Selective Service is a para-military institution serving as a juncture between the civil society and the military. The System is illustrative of the particular ways such an institution staffs itself so that it can operate in both realms and how it self-consciously structures itself so as to identify with civil society and thus mitigate compulsion. Chapter 3 explored the functionality of a para-military cadre in forming the System, in maintaining a closed personnel system, restricting partisan political influences, in contributing to a "mobilization crisis" ethos that motivates the thousands of volunteer workers, and in eliminating dissension over the purposes for which men are conscripted which might hamper effectiveness.

Finally, it is hoped that this study has contributed to an understanding of the importance of the politics of administration and particularly, though not exclusively, in the realm of national security policy. Politics is inseparable from administration; administration of policy is but a continuation of the political process. If this study of Selective Service shows nothing else, it shows that the politics of administration (or organizations or institutions) is one of the chief determinants of policy formulation, execution, outcome and feedback. In the politics of administration lies the explanation for Selective Service's successes, difficulties, impregnable defense against any significant changes, and possibly the predictions of the outcome of future attempts to change the policy and means of administering it.

Ultimately one is led back to the matter of national security policy. The future of Selective Service and national security policy (foreign and defense) are inseparable. What happens to Selective Service in the future depends in large part upon the shape of American politics and the resulting attitudes on foreign and defense policy after the Viet Nam war ends. The war has become a nightmare for Americans. Just as the unthinkable horrors of thermonuclear war created a small band of conscious nuclear pacifists and a larger uncounted number unconsciously of the same belief, so it appears have the horrors of Viet Nam created counter insurgency pacifists. Wars of proxy for limited policy aims create painful problems of understanding; they do not conform to historical experience or familiar patterns of thinking about war. As Harlan Cleveland points out, "there are no satisfying answers to those comfortable old questions: 'When did the war start?'; 'Who started it?' and, especially, 'How are we doing?' "[28] It is hard to believe America will ever look at limited war in the same way again.

American foreign policy has surely reached some sort of fateful turning point. Cleveland describes America's mood thus:

> The consequent collision of violence and restraint in American foreign policy has produced — quite naturally — a mood of frustration and uncertainty among us. Each international crisis is maddeningly unclear — too violent to be called peace, too constrained to be declared as war. Victory, superiority, and surrender are words in history books, not concepts for contemporary analysis. We have come to think of all-out nuclear war as almost unthinkable, conventional aggression as almost impossible, and guerilla war as almost unwinnable. A people that has always known whether it was at war or at peace is at odds with itself instead.[29]

The agonizing reappraisal of national security policy that is just surfacing is exacerbated if not stimulated by the crisis within America's borders. The problems of the Negro Revolution and urban living have coalesced to confront Americans with their greatest domestic crisis since the Civil War. Neither the future of the Selective Service nor national security policy can be isolated from the implications of events. The Constitution, as Samuel Huntington reminds us, defines six purposes of government: the achievement of unity, tranquility, welfare, justice, and liberty within American society and to provide for the common defense. The American government has generally discharged the last function satisfactorily. Now the other functions cry out for attention as well, and priorities will be reordered under the cross pressures at work. Virtually every major political figure counts upon utilizing the vast sums now spent upon the war to attack America's domestic problems. If, as some economists are suggesting, present foreign policy will not permit a reduction in defense spending even if the war ends, it is not unlikely that the present policy will come under severe scrutiny and attack.

Paul Lauter and Florence Howe also feel that the future of the draft or Selective Service is intertwined with the future of American foreign policy. They conclude their review of books on draft resistance with a comment suitable for ending this study.

> In the changing climate of opinion, the continuation of the draft in the face of increased evasion and resistance may intensify doubts about the cause for which armies are being conscripted. Thus the long-term question about the draft is not what system of conscription will be followed but what it will be used for. And the prospect is that today's opposition to the draft will become part of a continuing struggle to alter America's relationships to the rest of the world, and to change American society at home.[30]

Notes

[1] *New York Times,* May 30, 1966, p. 1. The report was finally released in June of 1966 during the first round of hearings on the draft. It said very little about Selective Service operations in a direct way. It urged continuation of current deferment policies and drafting younger men first. The alleged leaks and the fact that a study was felt necessary did more to stir up criticism of Selective Service than the report itself.

[2] *San Diego Union,* July 15, 1966, p. A-34.

[3] Throughout the hearings, Rivers manifested more than customary cordiality and by imposing a ten minute limit on questions of Committee members, he managed to cut off questioning each time it began to get difficult for Hershey.

[4] Its formal title: Civilian Advisory Panel on Military Manpower Procurement. See Civilian Advisory Panel on Military Procurement, Report to the Committee on Armed Services, House of Representatives, 90th Cong., 1st Sess. (Washington, D.C.: Government Printing Office, 1967).

[5] Extension of the Universal Military Training and Service Act, Hearings before the Committee on Armed Services, House of Representatives, 90th Cong. 1st Sess. (Washington, D.C.: Government Printing Office, 1967), p. 2591. Hereafter referred to as *Extension of U.M.T. and S., 1967.*

[6] National Advisory Commission on Selective Service, "In Pursuit of Equity: Who Serves When Not All Serve?" (Washington, D.C.: Government Printing Office, February, 1967).

[7] *Review,* op. cit., pp. 9627, 9638. The fishbowl lotteries of World Wars I and II were to determine *when* a person would be called up for examination at a time when nearly everyone sooner or later would be so called. The lotteries now proposed are to determine *which persons* will be liable to consideration for induction from a vast pool, the bulk of which will never be considered. Thus the lotteries of the past and those proposed today are vastly different. Among those who have studied the System there are some who feel that Hershey has not really changed his mind on a lottery in any way. Kenneth Dolbeare has taken this position in conversations with the author.

[8] *Extension of the UMT & S Act, 1967,* pp. 2612-77.

[9] See *Report of the Task Force on the Structure of Selective Service System* (Washington, D.C.: U.S. Government Printing Office, Oct. 16, 1967), p. 1-4.

[10] *Extension of the UMT & S Act, 1967, op. cit.,* p. 2591.

[11] *Ibid.,* p. 2642.

[12] See Public Law 90-40 (90th Cong. June 1967), reported in *U.S. Law Week,* June 17, 1967, Vol. XXXV, No. 50.

[13] See UPI dispatch of April 29, 1968. The Task Force Report is also briefly described in the *New York Times,* April 30, 1968, p. 2. Originally reported as not available for distribution, it is now being distributed upon request. See *Report of the Task Force, op. cit.*

[14] It is highly unlikely that anything will come of the 1967 law's exhortation to the President to establish national criteria and to the extent "consistent with national interest" require that it be uniformly administered.

[15] The literature on these "alternatives" is now extensive. The literature pertaining to national service is cited in Chapter 6. For a discussion of a volunteer army, see Walter Oi, "The Dubious Need for the Draft," and "The Costs and Implications of an All-Volunteer Force," as well as Milton Friedman, "Why Not a Voluntary Army?" Both are reprinted in the hearings *Extension of the U.M.T. and S. Act, op. cit.,* pp. 2105-48.

[16] For a discussion of the relationship of public opinion to foreign policy and the stratification of the public, see James N. Rosenau, *Public Opinion and Foreign Policy* (New York: Random House, Inc., 1961), especially ch. 4.

[17] See his classic description of incremental decision-making, "The Science of Muddling Through," *Public Administration Review,* Vol. XIX, Spring, 1959.

[18] *Extension of the U.M.T. and S. Act,* 1967, *op. cit.,* p. 2102.

[19] *Ibid.,* p. 2124.

[20] See Lindblom, *op. cit.*

[21] See Huntington's *The Common Defense* (New York: Columbia University Press, 1961), p. 432 ff. This lag between structure and strategy is one of the major points made by James Gerhardt concerning the postwar fights over Universal Military Training. See James M. Gerhardt, "Military Manpower Procurement Policies, 1945-1967 (unpublished Ph.D. dissertation, Harvard University, 1967), chs. I-II, *passim.* Harry Howe Ransom makes a similar point calling it a "problem of organizational lead-time." See his *Can American Democracy Survive Cold War* (New York: Doubleday & Company, Inc., 1964), introduction and *passim.*

[22] For a discussion of the administration's concern for flexibility see *Extension of the U.M.T. and S. Act, 1967, op. cit.,* p. 2102.

[23] Students of politics and government are familiar with these and would point to retaliatory action in the form of appropriations cuts, refusals to consent to personnel appointments, or delaying other crucial or related legislation. See Joseph P. Harris, *Congressional Control of Administration* (New York: Doubleday & Company, Inc., 1964), *passim.*

[24] It should be noted that incremental changes are not synonymous with small changes. Incremental refers to changes in the existing System as opposed, for example, to "grand alternatives."

[25] The end of graduate deferments drew negative responses from graduate schools and educators but any termination of deferments draws fire and the System and its allies would prefer it came from graduate schools, which may be a source of articulate criticism but are vulnerable as elitist, "egg-head," and as a haven from the draft. For a discussion of support for ending graduate deferments and the immediate reasons behind the move see Paul Lauter and Florence Howe, "The Draft and Its Opposition," *New York Times Review of Books,* June 20, 1968, p. 25.

[26] Kenneth Dolbeare has argued thusly in conversations with the author.

[27] See for one example assorted monographs and pamphlets of the Wisconsin Draft Resistance Union, Madison, Wisconsin.

[28] Harlan Cleveland, "Pax Ballistica, The Uncertain Peace," *Saturday Review*, June 29, 1968, p. 11.

[29] *Ibid.*

[30] Paul Lauter and Florence Howe, *op. cit.*, p. 31.

Bibliography

Books

Baum, Bernard H., *Decentralization of Authority in Bureaucracy,* Englewood Cliffs, N.J., Prentice-Hall, Inc., 1961.

Beer, Samuel H. and Adam B. Ulam, *Patterns of Government,* New York, Random House, Inc., second edition, 1965.

Bell, Wendell, et. al., *Public Leadership,* San Francisco, Chandler Publishing Company, 1961.

Bendix, Reinhard, *Max Weber: An Intellectual Portrait,* New York, Doubleday Anchor Book, 1962.

Bernardo, Joseph C. and Eugene H. Bacon, *American Military Policy: Its Development Since 1775,* Harrisburg, Pa., Military Service Publishing Co., 1955.

Carper, Jean, *Bitter Greetings: The Scandal of the Military Draft,* New York, Grossman Publishers, 1967.

Chapman, Bruce, *Wrong Man in Uniform,* New York, Trident Press, 1967.

Coates, Charles H. and Roland J. Pellegrin, *Military Sociology,* University Park, Md., Social Science Press, 1965.

Coffman, Edward M., *The Hilt of the Sword,* Madison, University of Wisconsin Press, 1966.

Crowder, Major General Enoch H., *The Spirit of Selective Service*, New York.

Davis, James W. and Kenneth M. Dolbeare, *Little Groups of Neighbors*, Chicago, Markham Publishing Co., 1968.

———, "Selective Service and Military Manpower Procurement: Induction and Deferment Policies in the 1960s," in Austin Ranney (ed.) *Political Science and Public Policy*, Chicago, Markham Publishing Company, 1968.

Derthick, Martha, *The National Guard in Politics*, Cambridge, Mass., Harvard University Press, 1965.

Dupuy, Ernest, *The Compact History of the U.S. Army*, New York, Hawthorn, revised edition, 1961.

Eberly, Donald J. (ed.), *A Profile on National Service*, New York, Overseas Educational Service, 1966

Ekirch, Arthur A., Jr., *The Civil and the Military: A History of the American Anti-Militarist Tradition*, New York, Oxford University Press, 1956.

Evers, Alf, *Selective Service: A Guide to the Draft*, Philadelphia, J. B. Lippincott Co., 1957.

Fesler, James W., *Area and Administration*, Birmingham, University of Alabama Press, 1964.

———, "The Politics of Field Administration," in Ferrel Heady and Sybil Stokes, *Papers in Comparative Public Administration*, Ann Arbor, University of Michigan Press, 1962.

Fitzpatrick, Edward A., *Conscription and America*, Milwaukee, Wis., Richards Publishing Co., 1940.

Foot, M. R. D., *Men in Uniform*, London, Weidenfeld and Nicolson, 1961.

Huntington, Samuel P., *The Common Defense*, New York, Columbia University Press, 1961.

———, *The Soldier and the State*, Cambridge, Harvard University Press, 1957.

Jacobs, Clyde E. and John F. Gallagher, *The Selective Service Act: A Case Study of the Governmental Process*, New York, Dodd, Mead & Co., 1967.

Janowitz, Morris, *et al.*, *Public Administration and the Public*, Bureau of Government, Ann Arbor, Mich., University of Michigan, 1958.

——— (ed.), *The New Military*, New York, Russell Sage Foundation, 1964.

———, *The Professional Soldier*, New York, The Free Press, 1960.

Lazer, Harry, *The American Political System in Transition,* New York, Thomas Y. Crowell Company, 1966.

Leach, Jack, *Conscription in the United States: Historical Background,* Rutland Vt., Charles E. Tuttle Publishing Co., Inc., 1952.

Little, Roger (ed.), *Selective Service and American Society,* New York, Russell Sage Foundation, forthcoming.

Millis, Walter, *Arms and Men: A Study in American Military History,* New York, New American Library of World Literature, Inc., 1958.

──────, *Individual Freedom and the Common Defense,* New York, The Fund for the Republic, 1957.

Selznick, Philip, *TVA and the Grassroots,* Berkeley, University of California Press, 1949.

──────, *Leadership in Administration,* Evanston, Ill., Row Peterson, 1957.

Simon, Herbert, *Administrative Behavior,* New York, The Macmillan Company, second edition, 1957.

────── and James G. March, *Organizations,* New York, John Wiley & Sons, Inc., 1958.

Stafford, Robert T., et al., *How to End the Draft,* Washington, D.C., The National Press Inc., 1967.

Tax, Sol (ed.), *The Draft,* Chicago, University of Chicago Press, 1968.

Tompkins, Frank, *Chasing Villa,* Harrisburg, Pa., Military Service Publishing Company, 1934.

Truman, David B., *Administrative Decentralization,* Chicago, University of Chicago Press, 1940.

──────, *The Governmental Process,* New York, Alfred A. Knopf, Inc., 1958.

Trytten, M. H., *Student Deferment in Selective Service,* Minneapolis, University of Minnesota Press, 1952.

Upton, Emory, *The Military Policy of the United States,* War document No. 290, Washington, D.C., 1917.

Vagts, Alfred, *A History of Militarism,* New York, W. W. Norton & Company, Inc., 1937.

Walton, Col. George, *The Wasted Generation,* New York, Chilton Book Company, 1965.

──────, *Let's End the Draft Mess,* New York, David McKay Co., Inc., 1967.

White, Morton and Lucia, *The Intellectual Versus the City,* Cambridge, Mass., Harvard University Press and M. I. T. Press, 1962.

White, William S., *Citadel,* New York, Harper & Bros., 1957.

———, *Home Place: The Story of the U.S. House of Representatives,* Boston, Houghton Mifflin Company, 1965.

Willbern, York, "The States as Components in an Areal Division of Power," in Arthur Maass (ed.), *Area and Power,* Glencoe, Free Press of Glencoe, 1959.

Wood, Leonard, *The Military Obligation of Citizenship,* Princeton, 1915.

Public Documents

Administrative Procedures Act, U.S. Codes, 60 Stat. 237.

Annual Report of the Director of Selective Service, Washington, D.C., Government Printing Office, 1966. Annual from 1948 to 1967, semi-annual thereafter.

Background of the Military Policy of the U.S., Air University, H.Q. AFROTC, 1958.

Backgrounds of Selective Service, Special Monograph No. 1, Vol. II, part 1, Washington, D.C., Government Printing Office, 1947.

Bureau of the Budget, *The U.S. at War: Development and Administration of the War Program by the Federal Government,* Washington, D.C., Government Printing Office.

Civilian Advisory Panel on Military Procurement, *Report to the Committee on Armed Services,* House of Representatives, 90th Congress, 1st sess., Washington, D.C., Government Printing Office, 1967.

The Classification Process, Special Monograph No. 5, Vol. I, Selective Service System, Washington, D.C., Government Printing Office, 1950.

Compensation for Selective Service System Employees, Hearing, House of Representatives, 89th Congress, 2nd sess. on H.R. 14357, Washington, D.C., Government Printing Office, April 18, 1966.

Congressional Record, 79th Congress, 1st sess., part 6.

Congressional Record, 80th Congress, 2nd sess., part 3.

Extension of the Universal Military Training and Services Act, *Hearings before the Committee on Armed Services,* House of Representatives, 90th Congress, 1st sess., Washington, D.C., Government Printing Office, 1967.

Hearings before a Subcommittee of the Committee on Appropriations, House of Representatives, 89th Congress, 2nd sess., February 1, 1966.

House Committee on Armed Service Report 1881, Washington, D.C., Government Printing Office, May 7, 1948.

Legal Aspects of Selective Service, revised Jan. 1, 1963, Lt. Gen. Hershey, Washington, D.C., Government Printing Office, 1963.

Manpower Implications of Selective Service, Hearings before the Subcommittee on Employment, Manpower and Poverty of the Committee on Labor and Public Welfare, United States Senate, 90th Congress, 1st sess., March, 1967.

Military Selective Service Act of 1967, 50 App. U.S.C. 454 (g).

National Advisory Commission on Selective Service, "In Pursuit of Equity: Who Serves When Not All Serve?" Washington, D.C., Government Printing Office, February, 1967.

Nation's Manpower Revolution, Hearings Before the Subcommittee on Employment and Manpower of the Committee on Labor and Public Welfare, United States Senate, 88th Congress, 1st sess., November and December, 1963, Washington, D.C., Government Printing Office, 1964.

One-Third of a Nation: A Report on Young Men Found Unqualified for Military Service, Washington, D.C., Government Printing Office, 1964.

Organizaton and Administration of the System, Special Monograph No. 3, Vol. 1, Washington, D.C., Government Printing Office, 1951.

Problems of Selective Service, Special Monograph No. 16, Vol. I, Text, Washington, D.C., Government Printing Office, 1952.

Provost Marshal General, *Second Report to December 20, 1918,* Washington, D.C., Government Printing Office.

Public Law, 12, 65th Congress, 1st sess., May 18, 1917.

Report of the Director, Office of Selective Service Records, 1947-48, Washington, D.C., Government Printing Office, 1950.

Report of the Task Force on the Structure of Selective Service System, Washington, D.C., Government Printing Office, October 16, 1967.

Review of the Administration and Operation of the Selective Service System, Hearings before the Committee on Armed Services, House of Representatives, 89th Congress, 2nd sess., Washington, D.C., Government Printing Office, 1966.

Selective Service in Peacetime, Monograph No. 1, Washington, D.C., Government Printing Office, 1946.

Selective Service Regulations, Form 999-A, "The Selective Service," Vol. III, sec. 22, second edition, Washington, 1918.

Selective Training and Service Act of 1940, P. L. 783, 76th Congress, 3rd sess., Ch. 720, sec. 3(a).

Supplement to the Health of the Army, Office of the Surgeon General, U.S. Army, Washington, D.C., July, 1966, issued annually.

29 State 167 (June 3, 1916), sec. 5; Stat. 76z (June 4, 1920), sec. 5

The U. S. Constitution

Universal Military Training and Service Act of 1951, Sec. 10, para. 4(b), subpara. 4.

U.S. Provost-Marshal-General's Bureau, *Final Report Made to the Secretary of War by the Provost Marshal General of the United States from the Commencement of the Business of the Bureau March 17, 1863 to March 17, 1866,* Washington, D.C., Government Printing Office, I, 143, 1866.

Selective Service System Documents and Papers

Local Board Advice No. B-7-9, from State, 17 June 1966.

Local Board Advice No. B-7-2 from State, 28 Nov. 1966.

"Manual of Observance, A Tribute to General James Oakes," National Headquarters of Selective Service System, Washington, March 17, 1966.

Memo to Local Boards from State, 3 May 1966.

Memoranda to All State Directors, Sept. 30, 1940 to Oct. 15, 1943, Washington, D.C., Government Printing Office.

Operations Bulletin No. 18 amended 1955, and Operations Bulletin No. 228.

Operations Bulletins Nos. 257 and 287.

Operations Bulletin No. 296, March 31, 1966.

"Selective Service," Office of Legislative Liaison and Public Information, March 1, 1965, National Headquarters, Selective Service System.

State Director Advices Nos. 539 and 726.

State Director Advice No. 567, 13 February, 1962.

The 50th Anniversary of the 1917 Selective Service Law 1917-1967, Observance Manual, National Headquarters, Selective Service System, Washington, February 22, 1967.

U. S. Supreme Court Cases

Arver v. *United States,* 245 U. S. 366.

Ayers v. *United States,* 9 Cir., 240 F. 2d 802, cert. denied, 352 U. S. 1016, 77 S, Crt. 563 (1957).

United States v. *Seeger,* 380 U. S. 163 (1965).

Supreme Court Reporter, 245-247 U. S. Vol. 38, 1917, New York, West Publishing Co., 1918.

Articles and Periodicals

Bell, Daniel, "Toward a Communal Society," *Life,* May 12, 1967.

Beer, Samuel H., "Liberalism and the National Idea," in *Public Interest,* No. 5 (Fall, 1966).

Burns, C. Deslisle, "Militarism," *Encyclopedia of the Social Sciences,* X, New York, Macmillan Company, 1933.

Clark, Burton, "Organizational Adaptation and Precarious Values: A Case Study," *American Sociological Review,* XXI (1956).

Dahl, Robert A., "Business and Politics: A Critical Appraisal of Political Science," *American Political Science Review,* LIII (1959).

Dornbush, Sanford M., "The Military Academy as an Assimilating Institution," *Social Forces,* XXXIII (1955).

Friedman, Milton, "An All-Volunteer Army," in the *New York Times Magazine,* May 14, 1967.

Hodge, Robert, et al., "Occupational Prestige in the United States," *American Journal of Sociology,* LXX (November 1964).

Johnson, Keith R., "Who Should Serve?" *Atlantic Monthly,* February 1966.

Lader, Lawrence, "New York's Bloodiest Week," *American Heritage,* X (June 1959).

Lockmiller, David A., "Enoch H. Crowder: Soldier, Lawyer, Statesman, 1859-1932," The University of Missouri Studies, Vol. 27 (1955).

Lovell, John P., "The Professional Socialization of the West Point Cadet," in *The New Military,* Morris Janowitz (ed.), New York, Russell Sage Foundation, 1964.

Martin, Reed, "Survey on Youth Opinion on the Selective Service System," United States Youth Council.

Mayer, Albert J. and Thomas Ford Hoult, "Social Stratification and Combat Survival," *Social Forces,* XXXIV (December 1955).

"National Service Newsletter" published by National Service Secretariat, New York, November 1966.

Newsletter on Military Manpower of the American Veterans Committee, February 2, 1967.

Perrow, Charles, "Organizational Prestige: Some Functions and Dysfunctions," *American Journal of Sociology,* LXVI (1961).

———, "The Analyses of Goals in Complex Organizations," *American Sociological Review,* XXVI (1961).

———, "A Framework for the Comparative Analyses of Organizations," *American Sociological Review,* XXXII (1967).

Selznick, Philip, "Foundations of the Theory of Organizations," *American Sociological Review,* XIII (1948).

White, Leonard D., "Decentralization," *Encyclopedia of Social Science,* V, New York, Macmillan Company, 1931.

Wilson, Charles H., "The Selective Service System: An Administrative Obstacle Course," *California Law Review,* 54 (1966).

Unpublished Dissertations and Manuscripts

Altman, Stuart and Alan E. Fechter, "The Supply of Military Personnel," paper presented at the Meetings of the American Economic Association, December, 1966.

Cullinan, Terrence, "National Service: The Future Solution," unpublished paper presented to the Special Commission.

Davis, James W. and Kenneth M. Dolbeare, "Little Groups of Neighbors," unpublished paper, University of Wisconsin, 1967.

———, "Who Gets Drafted," Institute for Research on Poverty, Madison, University of Wisconsin, 1967.

Duggan, J. C., "The Legislative and Statutory Development of the Federal Concept of Conscription for Military Service," unpublished Ph.D. dissertation, The Catholic University of America, 1946.

Gerhardt, James, "Military Manpower Procurement Policies 1945-1967," Ph.D. dissertation, Harvard University, 1967.

Hansen, W. Lee, and Burton A. Weisbrod, "Economics of the Military Draft," unpublished paper.

Heaphey, James, "Spatial Aspects of Development Administration," unpublished paper delivered at Seminar of A. S. P. A., Comparative Administration Group, July 1965.

——— and Philip S. Kronenberg, "Toward Theory-Building in National Comparative Public Administration," unpublished paper, University of Pittsburgh, January 1966, published as a CAG paper by the American Society for Public Administration.

Oi, Walter, "The Costs and Implications of An All-Volunteer Force," unpublished paper.

Philipps, Denis Sinclair, "American People and Compulsory Military Service, unpublished Ph.D. dissertation, New York University, 1955.

Riggs, Fred, "Structure and Function in Development: A Dialectical Approach," a paper delivered at the Chicago Convention of the American Political Science Association, Sept. 9, 1967.

Spencer, Samuel Reid, Jr., "A History of the Selective Training and Service Act of 1940 from Inception to Enactment," unpublished Senior Thesis, Harvard University, 1951.

Stewart, Donald Dean, "Local Board, A Study of the Place of Volunteer Participation in the Bureaucratic Organization," unpublished Ph.D. dissertation, Columbia University, 1950.

Wamsley, G. L., "Aviation Cadet Pre-Flight Training School: A System for Subculture Inculcation-Assimilation," unpublished paper, University of Pittsburgh, 1964.

White, Orion F., Jr., "Notes for a Model of Political Administration," unpublished manuscript, University of Texas, 1966.

Zald, Mayer, "The Political Economy of the Y. M. C. A.: Structure and Change," unpublished manuscript, Vanderbilt University, 1967.

Reports and Monographs

Klassen, Albert D., "Military Service in American Life Since World War II: An Overview," National Opinion Research Center, University of Chicago, September 1966.

Lang, Kurt, *Military Sociology: A Trend Report and Bibliography*, London, Basil Blackwell and Mott, Ltd., 1965.

Oppenheim, Karen, "Attitudes of Younger American Men Toward Selective Service," Military Manpower Survey, Working Paper No. 5, National Opinion Research Center, University of Chicago, March 1966.

Willenz, June A., ed., *Dialogue on the Draft,* Nov. 11-12, 1966, American Veterans Committee, Washington, D. C.

Index

Adjutant Generals, 75, 169, 185
Administrative Procedure Act
  of 1946, 165-6
Air Force Association, 185
Almond, Gabriel, 16
American Legion, 72, 118, 128,
  185, 218
Annual Report of the Director,
  70, 103, 168
Anti-militarism, 17, 95, 239
Appeal Boards, 90, 208, 209
Appeals by the Directors, 60-3, 65
Appeals to the Directors, 60,
  63, 65
Armed Forces Examination and
  Induction Stations, 167, 168
Armed Services Committee,
  House of Representatives, 91,
  226, 231
Arver v. *U.S.*, 22
Association of the U.S. Army,
  185
Auditors, 57
Automatic data processing, 152

Baker v. *Carr*, 204
Baker, Newton, 30
Beer, Samuel, 214
Bell, Daniel, 212, 214
Black Muslims, 146
Boards of Instructions, 32, 35
Bounties, 29
Burke-Wadsworth Bill of 1940,
  38

Channeling, 105, 107, 237
Civil-Military junctures, 6
Civil-Military relations, 5,
  240, 241
Civil Service Commission, 138
Civil War, 25, 242
Clark, Grenville, 38
Cleveland, Harlan, 241
Closed personnel systems, 55,
  82, 241
Coates, Charles H., 17
Conscientious objectors, 146, 211
Constitution, 20, 22, 25
Containment, 5

255

Critical skills list, 66, 149
Crowder, Enoch, 30, 36, 51, 103

Davis, James, 85, 113, 114, 115, 116, 119, 146, 156, 172, 173, 175, 176, 209, 218
Decentralization:
  historical context, 14, 36
  its appeal to political culture, 52-3, 95, 156-7, 239
  other functions, 65-72
    interest groups, 65-69
    Congress, 70-72
  relation to reforms, 237
  shield against partisanship, 89
  support by control mechanisms, 54-64
Department of Defense, 111, 185, 225
  draft study, 226
Derthick, Martha, 75, 78
Deserters, 27
Dick Act of 1903, 31
Differential impact on strata, 170 ff., 240
District Appeal Boards, 34
Dolbeare, Kenneth, 85, 113, 114, 115, 116, 119, 146, 156, 172, 173, 175, 176, 209, 218
Draft riots, 28, 51
Dupuy, Ernest R., 36
Dykstra, Clarence, 39

Enrollment officers, 27, 29
Evaders, 27
Evers, Alf, 73, 74

Field Division Representatives (national), 167-9
Field Representatives (state), 57-8
Fitzpatrick, Edward, 23, 31, 104
Foreign policy, 4, 240-2
Friedman, Milton, 235
Friends and neighbors, 104, 110, 113, 131

Gallagher, John F., 117

Gallup polls, 1, 38, 196, 210
Giles bill, 24
Government Appeal Agents, 32, 35, 165-6, 205
Governors, 27
Graduate student deferments, 148

Hamilton, Alexander, 21
Hardship-dependency, 145
Harris polls, 2, 42, 196, 201, 211
Hartford Convention, 24
Hauser, Philip, 217
Heaphey, James, 54
Hershey, Lt. General Lewis B., 74, 151
  appeal agents "informing", 166, 205
  Clark Panel, 227
  clerks' salaries, 137
  conscientious objection, 211
  draft's impact, 171
  informal appeals, 207, 209
  leadership as a defense, 181-90, 240
  localism of local boards, 213
  lottery, 230, 237
  1968 campaign issues, 233
  relation to Field Representatives and State Directors, 169
  Task Force on the Structure of Selective Service, 232
  traditionalism of local boards, 217
Holifield, Congressman Chet, 139, 216
Homans, George, 181
Hoover, J. Edgar, 183
Hoult, Thomas Ford, 170, 171
Howe, Florence, 242
Huntington, Samuel, 6, 14, 236, 242

Induction, stay of, 92
Informal appeal channels, 62, 90
Institutional elan, 82

Index

Institutional equilibrium, 15, 95, 158
  strains on, 195-219, 238-40
Institutional leader, 183, 184
Institutional myth, 96, 150, 219, 237
Institutional rigidity, 219
Interest groups, 65, 185
Irish, Marion, 70

Jacobs, Clyde E., 117
Janowitz, Morris, 6, 208
Jehovah's Witnesses, 146
Johnson, General Hugh, 51
Johnson, President Lyndon B., 210, 226, 229
Joint Army and Navy Selective Service Committee, 37, 76
Justice Department, 90, 91, 147

Kennan, George F., 5, 234
Kennedy, Senator Edward, 233
Key, V.O., 90
Knox, General Henry, 20, 22
Korean War, 41, 171, 185
Kramer, Colonel Harry C., 37
Kronenberg, Philip S., 183

Lang, Kurt, 5
Lauter, Paul, 242
Lazer, Harry, 202, 204
Leach, Jack, 22, 23
Legal Advisory Board, 32
Legal-rationalism, 53
Legionnaire outlook, 128, 129
Liberal deferments, 105, 237
Lincoln, Abraham, 25, 26, 28
Lindblom, Charles, 235
Local Boards:
  advices, 59, 62
  anomie over function, 104
  autonomy, 54, 64
  bulletins, 59, 60
  clerks, 58, 136-45
  jurisdictional lines, 112
  lack of information, 129-136
  memoranda, 59, 60
  occupations of, 122-4
  politics, 83
  problematic decisions, 145
  recruitment and tenure, 116-21
  socio-economic changes in jurisdictions, 121
  status as veterans, 126-8
  traditionalism of, 216-8
  volume of classifications, 143
  weighted power relations, 165
  World War I, 33
Localism, 83
  decline of, 212-16
Lottery, 39, 229, 237

McNamara, Secretary of Defense Robert, 189, 210, 226
Madison, James, 23
Manpower Divisions, 65, 67, 69, 153
Manpower river, 151-3
Manpower surfeit, 197-200
March, James, 8
Marshall, Burke, 226, 232
Mayer, Alfred E., 170-1
Medical Advisory Board, 32, 35
Memoranda for State Directors, 59
Mexican Mobilization of 1916, 31
Mexican War, 24
Middle class values of boards, 122
Military academies, 6
Military Selective Service Act of 1967, 229-232
Militia, 17-19, 24, 26
Militia Act of 1792, 23
Militia Act of 1862, 25
Millis, Walter, 21, 31, 41
Minuteman Myth, 17, 19
Monroe, James, 23
Myrdal, Gunnar, 203

National Advisory Commission on Selective Service, findings on:

anomie of boards over
  function, 135
anonymity of board members,
  113, 114
basic problems of Selective
  Service, 230-1, 238
draft impact on Negroes, 171
general findings, 228-9
influence of clerks, 139, 142
tenure of board members, 119
National Aeronautics and Space
  Administration, 111
National Appeals Board, 62, 63
National Guard, 1, 31
  haven for higher strata, 172,
    232-3
  institutional ally for System,
    185, 215, 219
  para-military cadre, 75-80
  role in establishing Selective
    Service, 36-7
  staying induction for
    enlistment in, 157
  quotas credited for enlistment
    in, 151-2
National Guard Association, 72
National Headquarters, 72
National health, safety and
  interest, 106, 110, 111, 130, 131
National Idea, 214, 217
National manpower policy, 115-6
National Security Agency, 11
National Security Council, 148-9
National Service Secretariat, 210
National Society, 212, 214, 217
Negativism toward politics, 95
Negro revolution, 202, 204, 242
Neo-Hamiltonians, 31, 37, 38,
  43, 77, 81, 82
Nigro, Felix, 52, 181
Nixon, Richard, 233
Non-classified civil service, 137
Non-rational decisions, 130

Oakes, General James, 13, 14,
  29, 52

Oakes' Report, 29, 30, 32
Occupational deferments, 65,
  107, 126, 149
Office of Selective Service
  Records, 40
Office of War Mobilization, 70
Operations Bulletins, 59
Oppenheim, Karen, 177-9
Organization theory, 7

Para-military cadre, 76, 79-80,
  82, 157, 169, 241
Pellegrin, Roland J., 17
Permanency of System, 188-9
Personal knowledge of
  registrants, 112, 131
Pipeline, 89, 91
Political culture, 6
  anti-militarism and
    anti-conscription, 42
  clash with Civil War draft, 26,
    28, 51
  consonance with World War I
    & II draft, 36, 38, 51
  contemporary changes, 144,
    156-8, 212-219
  decentralization, 53
  institutional adaptations to,
    103, 150, 165
  institutional equilibrium, 15,
    41, 95, 237-40
  localism, 67
Political impermeability, 82
Polk, President James K., 24
Presidential Task Force on
  Manpower Conservation, 225
Problematic classifications,
  145-50
Proceduralism, 89, 182
Prothro, James, 70
Provost Marshal General, 26-8,
  30, 32, 35-7
Provost Marshal General James
  Frye, 29

Quotas, 27-29, 151-154, 157

Index

Redford, Emmette S., 31, 71, 82, 89
Regular Army, 24-5, 36
Regulations, 56
Reserve deferments, 174
Reserve Officers Association, 185
Reservists, 37 *(see also* National Guard)
Rivers, L. Mendel, 215, 226-7
Root, Elihu, 38
Rustin, Bayard, 203-4

Schweiker, Congressman Richard, 216
Selective Service Act of 1940, 39
Selective Service Newsletter, 55, 177
Selective Service Reserve, 77, 79, 168
Selznick, Philip, 55, 183-4, 216, 219
Shays' Rebellion, 20
Shriver, Sargent, 210
Simon, Herbert, 8
Spanish-American War, 30
Special Civilian Advisory Panel, 64, 84-6, 226-7, 230-1
State Adjutant Generals, 37
State Director Advices, 81
State Quotas, 153
State Scientific Advisory Board, 111
Stewart, Donald, 93, 117, 129, 153
Structural-functional analysis, 4
Student deferments, 107, 147-9, 172, 201
Surgeon General of the Army, 198

Task Force on the Structure of Selective Service, 232
Tenure *(see* Local Boards)
Traditionalism of Local Boards, 216-8
Truman, David, 31, 65, 71
Truman, President Harry S., 40

Trytten, M.H., 201
Universal Military Training, 41
Universal Military Training and Service Act of 1951, 42, 137, 165, 186, 198, 225
Universal National Service, 233
U.S. Youth Council, 206
U.S. v. Seeger, 147, 211

Value integration, 60
Verba, Sydney, 16
Veterans of Foreign Wars, 72, 185, 215
Viet Nam War, 2, 4, 5, 145, 171-2, 196-7, 200, 237, 241
Vinson, Congressman Carl, 226
Volume of Classifications, 143
Voluntarism, 92, 95
Volunteer Army, 4, 233

Wallace, Governor George, 233
War Manpower Commission, 70, 104
War of 1812, 23, 24
War on Poverty, 168, 184, 209
Washington, General George, 18, 19
Weber, Max, 216, 217
Weighted power relationships, 165
Westin, Alan, 204-5
White, Chief Justice Edward, 22
White, Morton and Lucia, 8, 93, 212
White, Orion, 239
White, William S., 70, 186
Willbern, York, 215
Wilson, President Woodrow, 31
Wirtz, Secretary of Labor Willard, 210
Wood, Robert, 215
Woodward, C. Vann, 203
Word-of-mouth policy guidance, 56

Zald, Mayer, 7, 239